X-23

FAMILY ALBUM

WRITER **MARIKO TAMAKI**

ISSUES #1-5

ARTISTS **JUANN CABAL** WITH **MARCIO FIORITO** (#5)
COLOR ARTIST **NOLAN WOODARD**
COVER ART **MIKE CHOI** & **JESUS ABURTOV**

ISSUE #6

ARTIST **GEORGES DUARTE**
COLOR ARTIST **CHRIS O'HALLORAN**
COVER ART **ASHLEY WITTER**

LETTERER **VC'S CORY PETIT**

ASSISTANT EDITOR **ANNALISE BISSA**
EDITOR **CHRISTINA HARRINGTON**
X-MEN GROUP EDITOR **JORDAN D. WHITE**

SPECIAL THANKS TO **MIKE O'SULLIVAN**

COLLECTION EDITOR **JENNIFER GRÜNWALD** ▪ ASSISTANT EDITOR **CAITLIN O'CONNELL**
ASSOCIATE MANAGING EDITOR **KATERI WOODY** ▪ EDITOR, SPECIAL PROJECTS **MARK D. BEAZLEY**
VP PRODUCTION & SPECIAL PROJECTS **JEFF YOUNGQUIST** ▪ SVP PRINT, SALES & MARKETING **DAVID GABRIEL**
BOOK DESIGNER **JAY BOWEN**

EDITOR IN CHIEF **C.B. CEBULSKI** ▪ CHIEF CREATIVE OFFICER **JOE QUESADA**
PRESIDENT **DAN BUCKLEY** ▪ EXECUTIVE PRODUCER **ALAN FINE**

X-23 VOL. 1: FAMILY ALBUM. Contains material originally published in magazine form as X-23 #1-6. First printing 2018. ISBN 978-1-302-91308-3. Published by MARVEL WORLDWIDE, INC., a subsidiary of MARVEL ENTERTAINMENT, LLC. OFFICE OF PUBLICATION: 135 West 50th Street, New York, NY 10020. **Printed in Canada.** DAN BUCKLEY, President, Marvel Entertainment; JOHN NEE, Publisher; JOE QUESADA, Chief Creative Officer; TOM BREVOORT, SVP of Publishing; DAVID BOGART, SVP of Business Affairs & Operations, Publishing & Partnership; DAVID GABRIEL, SVP of Sales & Marketing, Publishing; JEFF YOUNGQUIST, VP of Production & Special Projects; DAN CARR, Executive Director of Publishing Technology; ALEX MORALES, Director of Publishing Operations; DAN EDINGTON, Managing Editor; SUSAN CRESPI, Production Manager; STAN LEE, Chairman Emeritus. For information regarding advertising in Marvel Comics or on Marvel.com, please contact Vit DeBellis, Custom Solutions & Integrated Advertising Manager, at vdebellis@marvel.com. For Marvel subscription inquiries, please call 888-511-5480. **Manufactured between 11/16/2018 and 12/11/2018 by SOLISCO PRINTERS, SCOTT, QC, CANADA.**

10 9 8 7 6 5 4 3 2 1

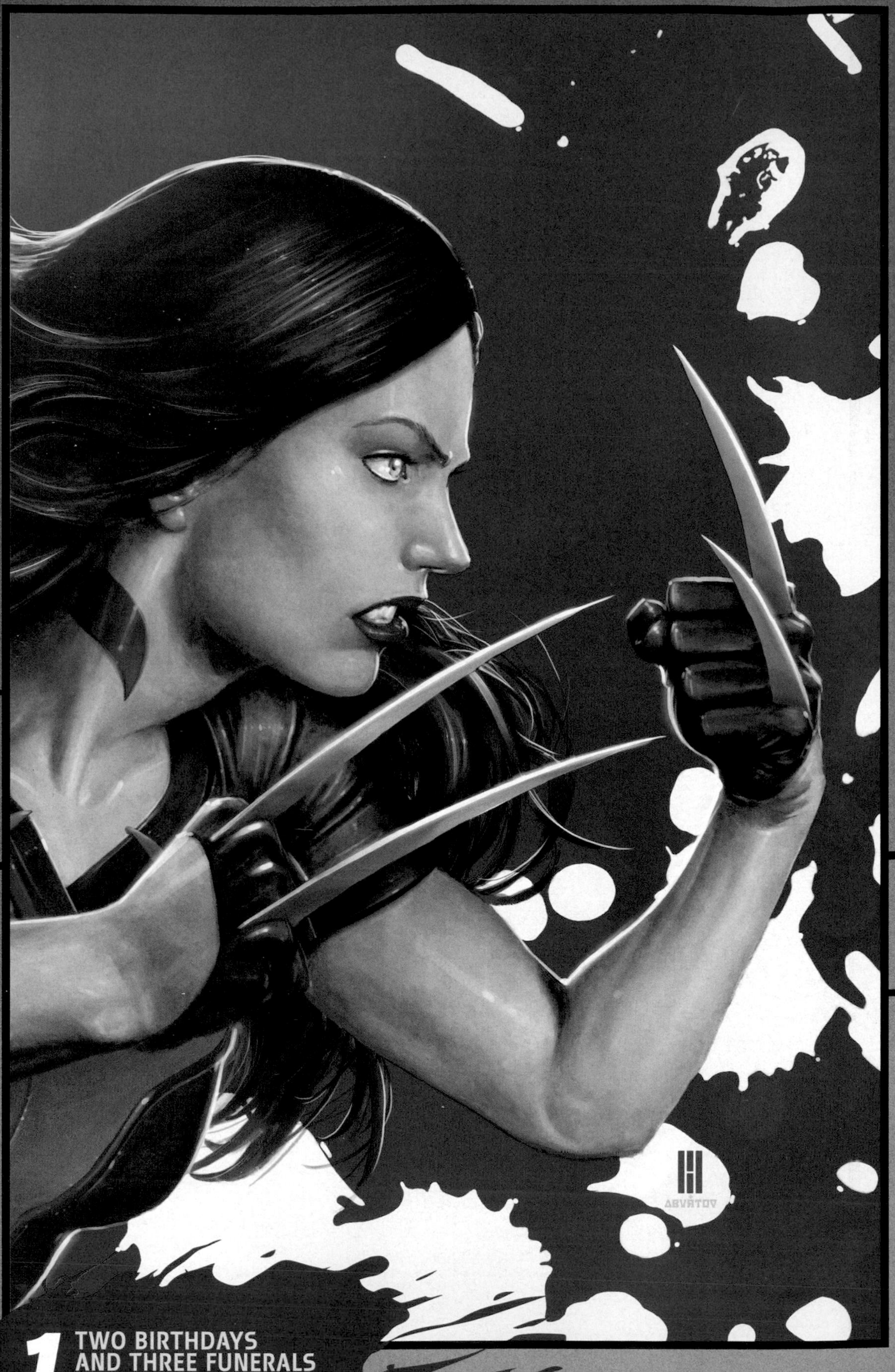

1 TWO BIRTHDAYS AND THREE FUNERALS
PART 1

WEAPON X
MY MUTANT FAMILY ALBUM.
MY MOM...
Master of DNA
Sarah Kinney
...RENOWNED GENETICIST...
...AND KEY FIGURE IN THE TOP-SECRET PROGRAM TO CREATE...
...ME.
AND THAT IS THE LEAST COMPLICATED PART OF THAT STORY.
MY CHILDHOOD BEDROOM.
X-23
MY DNA, WHICH ALCHEMAX USED TO MAKE CLONES OF ME.
ALCHEMAX genetics
S: X-23
LOT NO.586
EXP
X-23
"SISTERS."
SOME OF WHOM LATER TRIED TO KILL ME.
MOST OF WHOM ARE NOW DEAD.
WE ARE HERE BECAUSE MUTANTS MAKE GOOD WEAPONS.
AND, YES, I'M TRYING TO CHANGE THAT.
NOT EASY WHEN YOU'RE ONLY EVER A MEMORY AWAY FROM WHERE YOU CAME FROM.

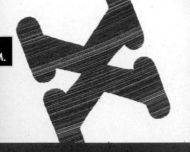

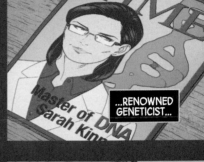

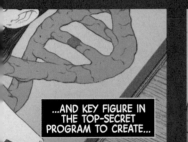

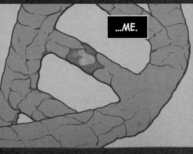

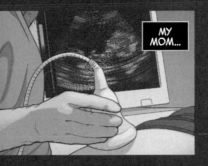

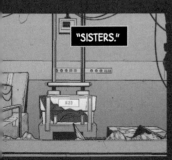

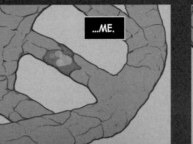

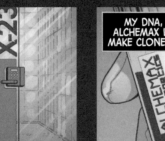

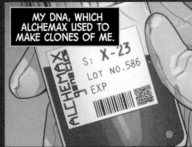

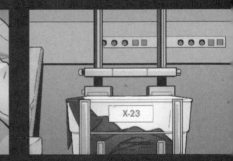

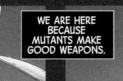

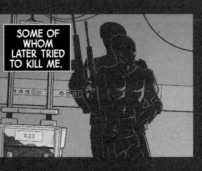

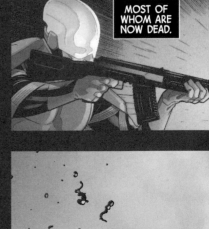

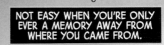

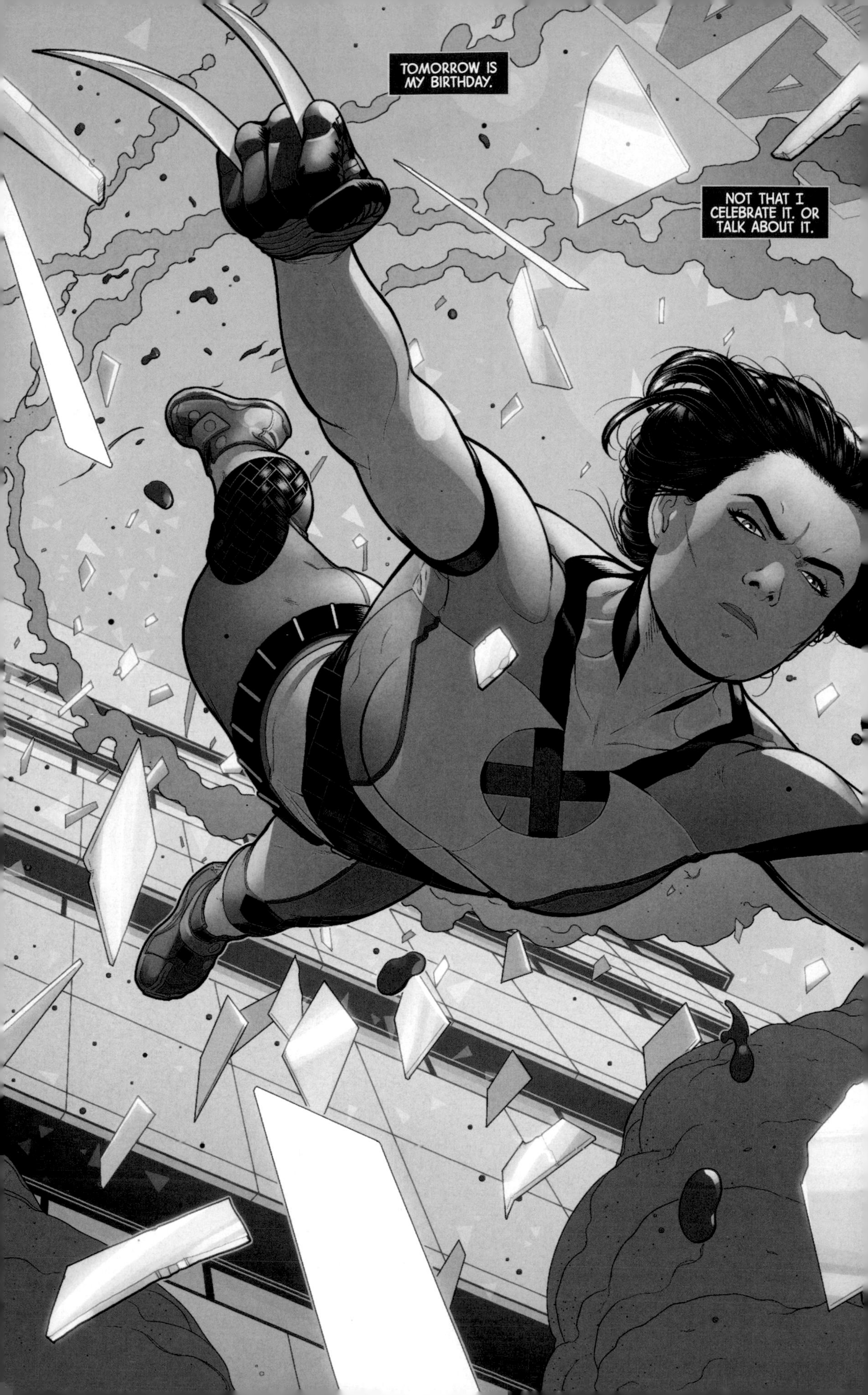
TOMORROW IS MY BIRTHDAY.
NOT THAT I CELEBRATE IT. OR TALK ABOUT IT.

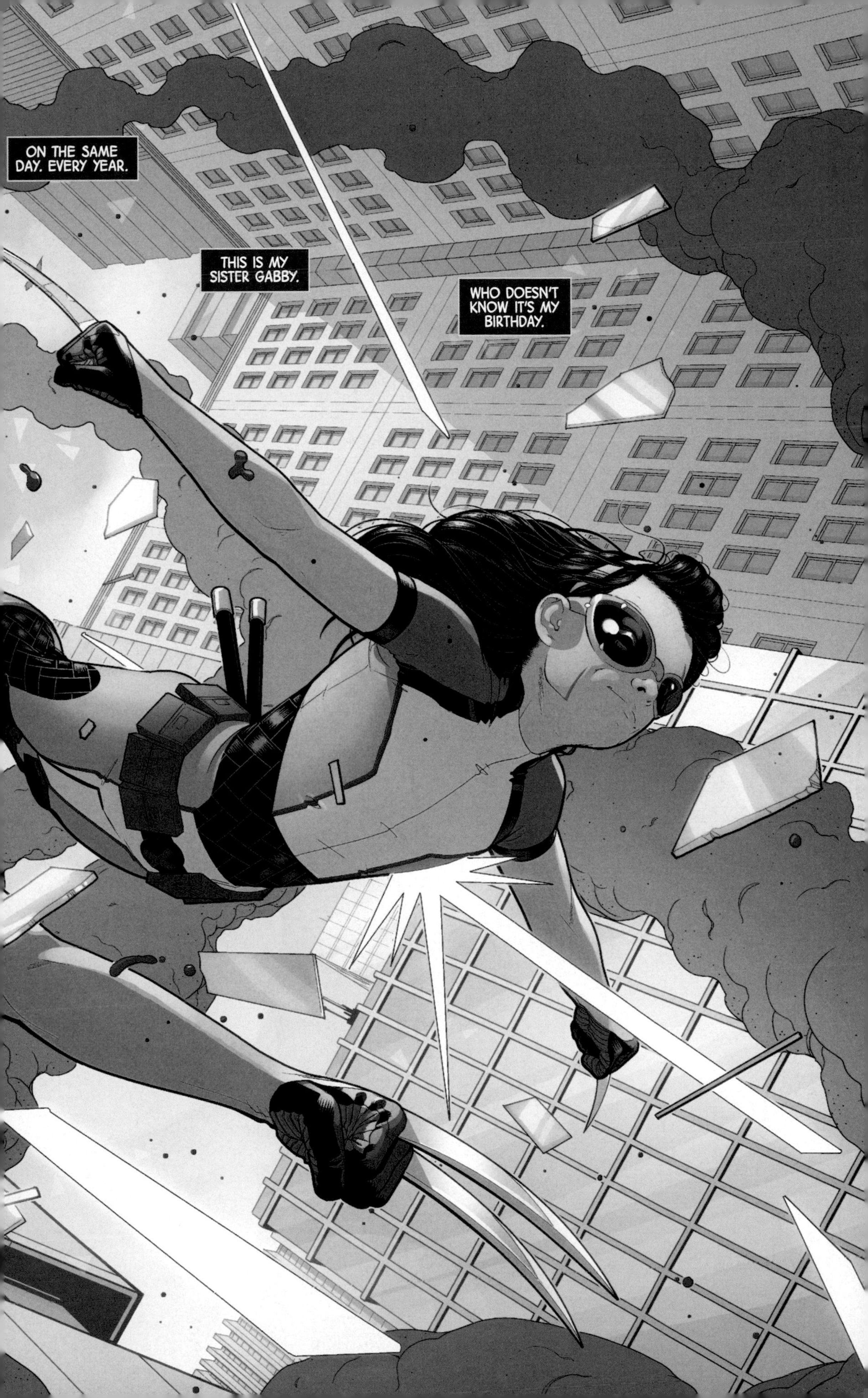
ON THE SAME DAY. EVERY YEAR.
THIS IS MY SISTER GABBY.
WHO DOESN'T KNOW IT'S MY BIRTHDAY.

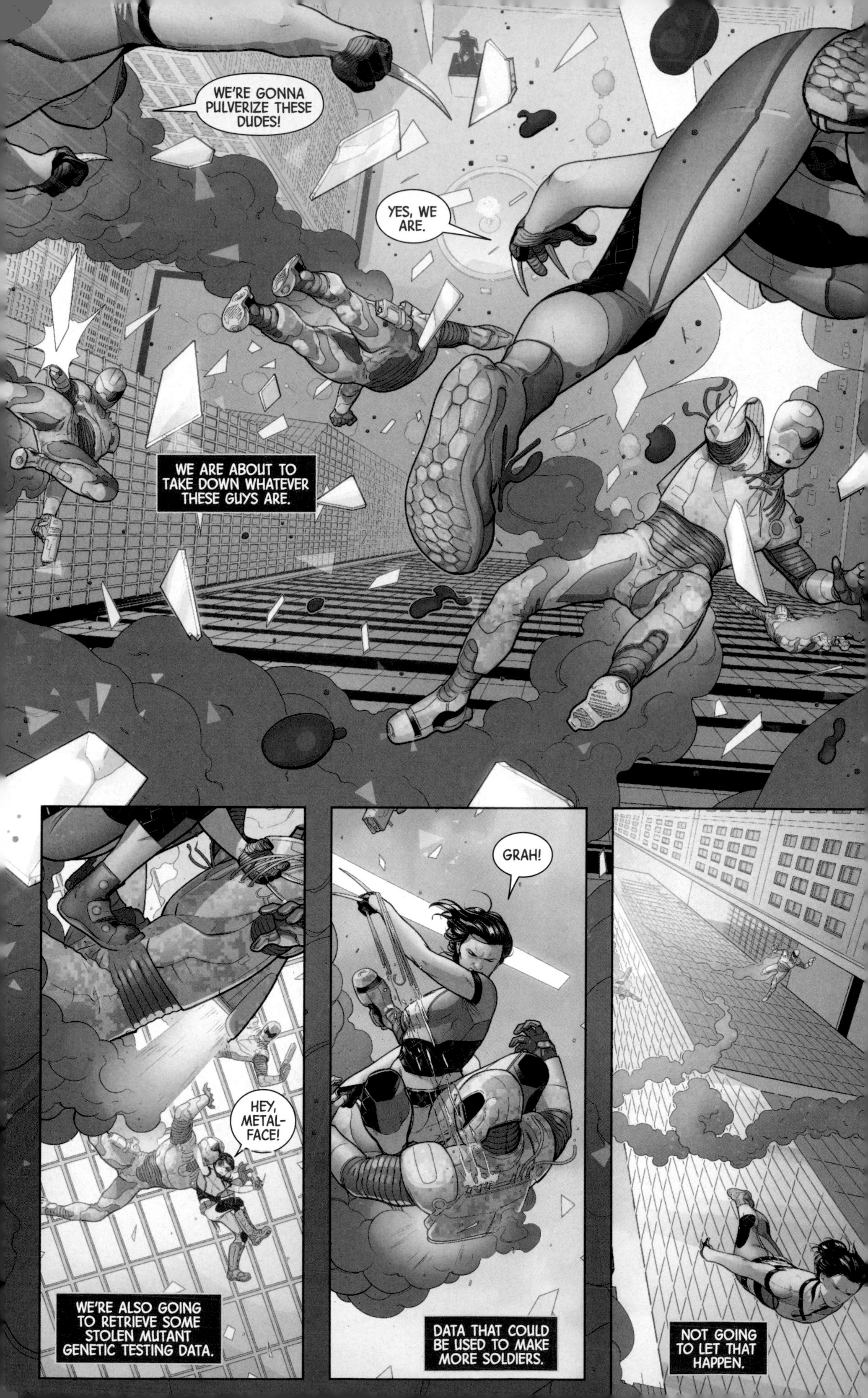
WE'RE GONNA PULVERIZE THESE DUDES!
YES, WE ARE.
WE ARE ABOUT TO TAKE DOWN WHATEVER THESE GUYS ARE.
HEY, METAL-FACE!
WE'RE ALSO GOING TO RETRIEVE SOME STOLEN MUTANT GENETIC TESTING DATA.
GRAH!
DATA THAT COULD BE USED TO MAKE MORE SOLDIERS.
NOT GOING TO LET THAT HAPPEN.

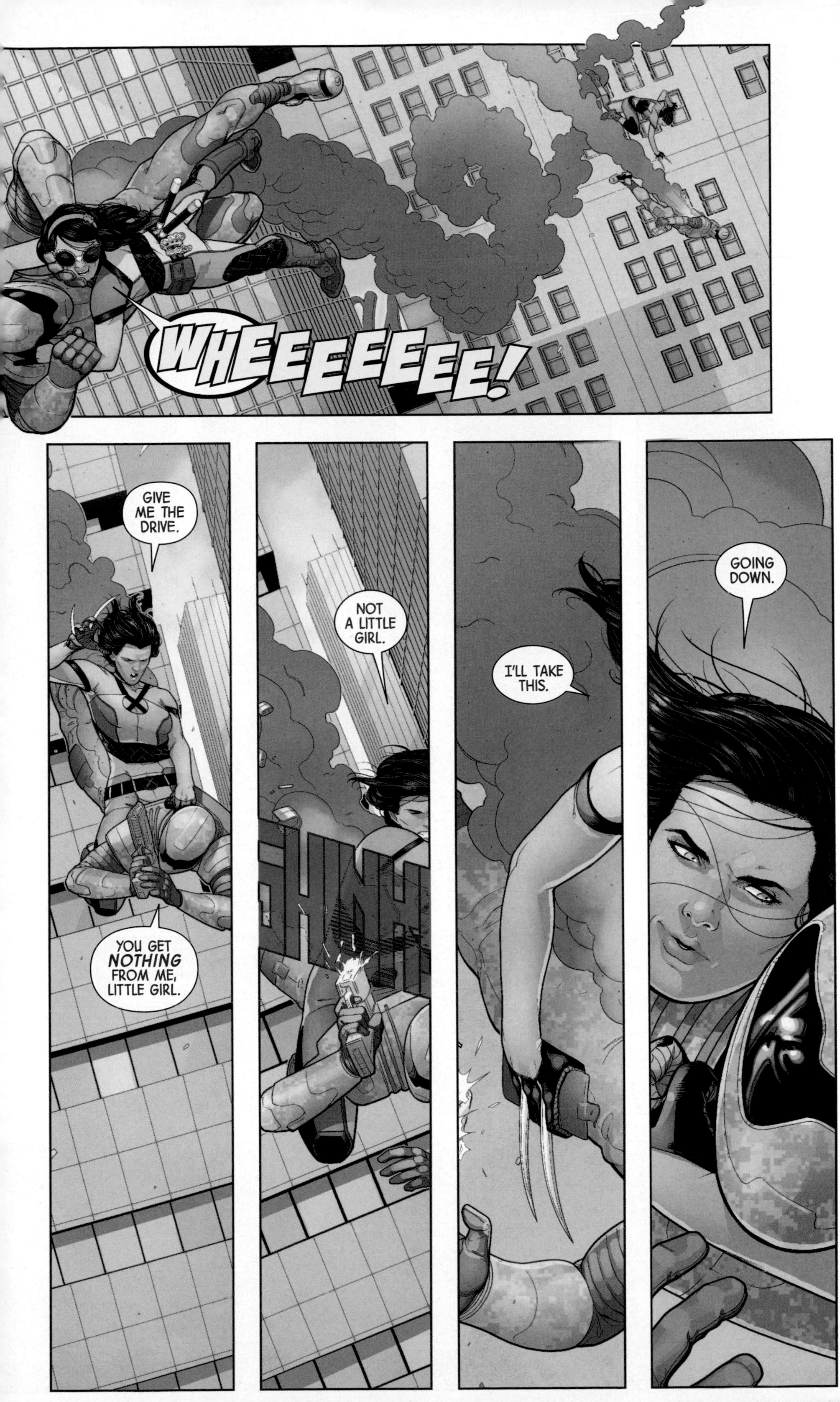
WHEEEEEEEE!
GIVE ME THE DRIVE.
YOU GET NOTHING FROM ME, LITTLE GIRL.
NOT A LITTLE GIRL.
I'LL TAKE THIS.
GOING DOWN.

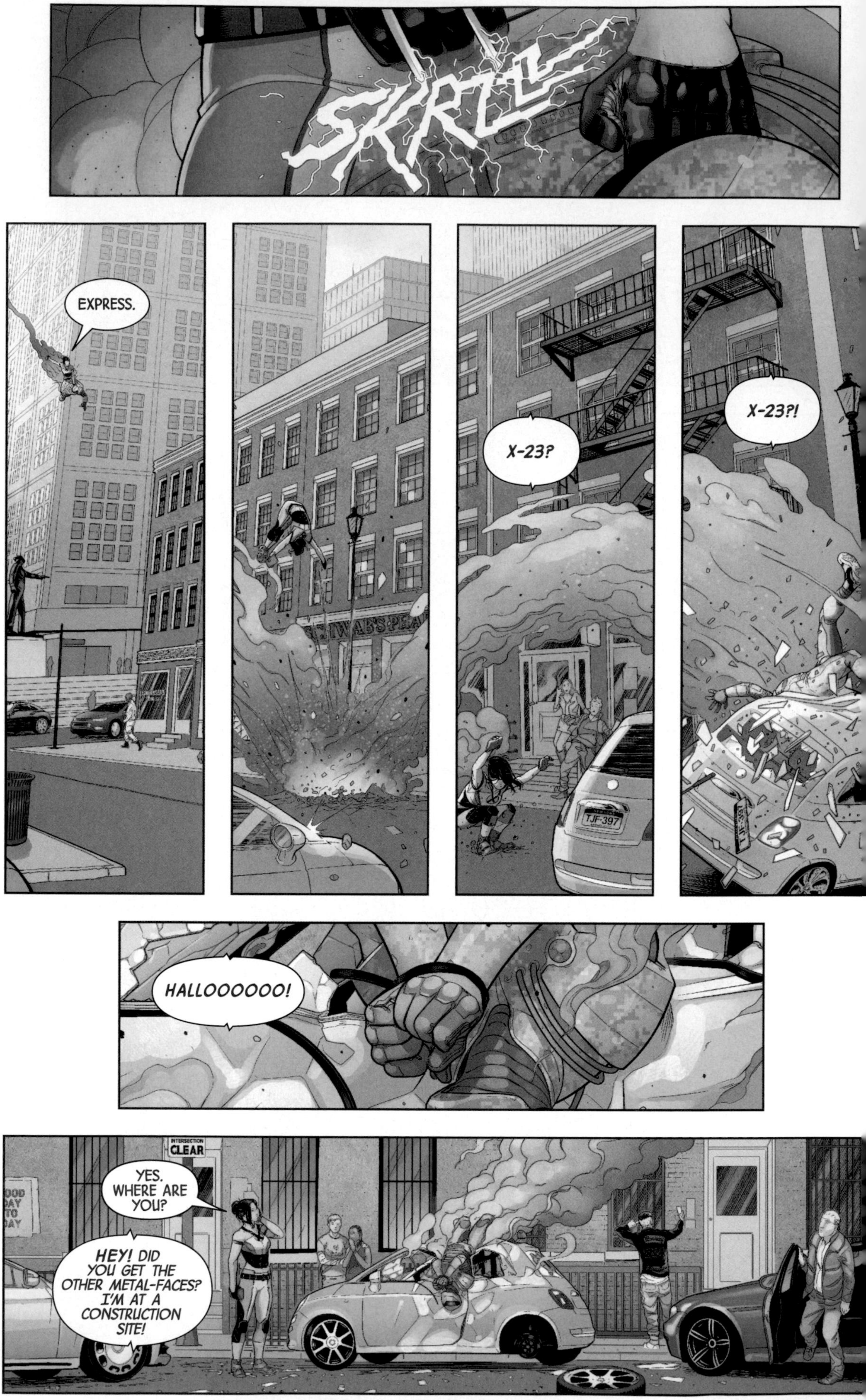
SKRZZZ
EXPRESS.
X-23?
X-23?!
HALLOOOOOO!
INTERSECTION CLEAR
YES. WHERE ARE YOU?
HEY! DID YOU GET THE OTHER METAL-FACES? I'M AT A CONSTRUCTION SITE!

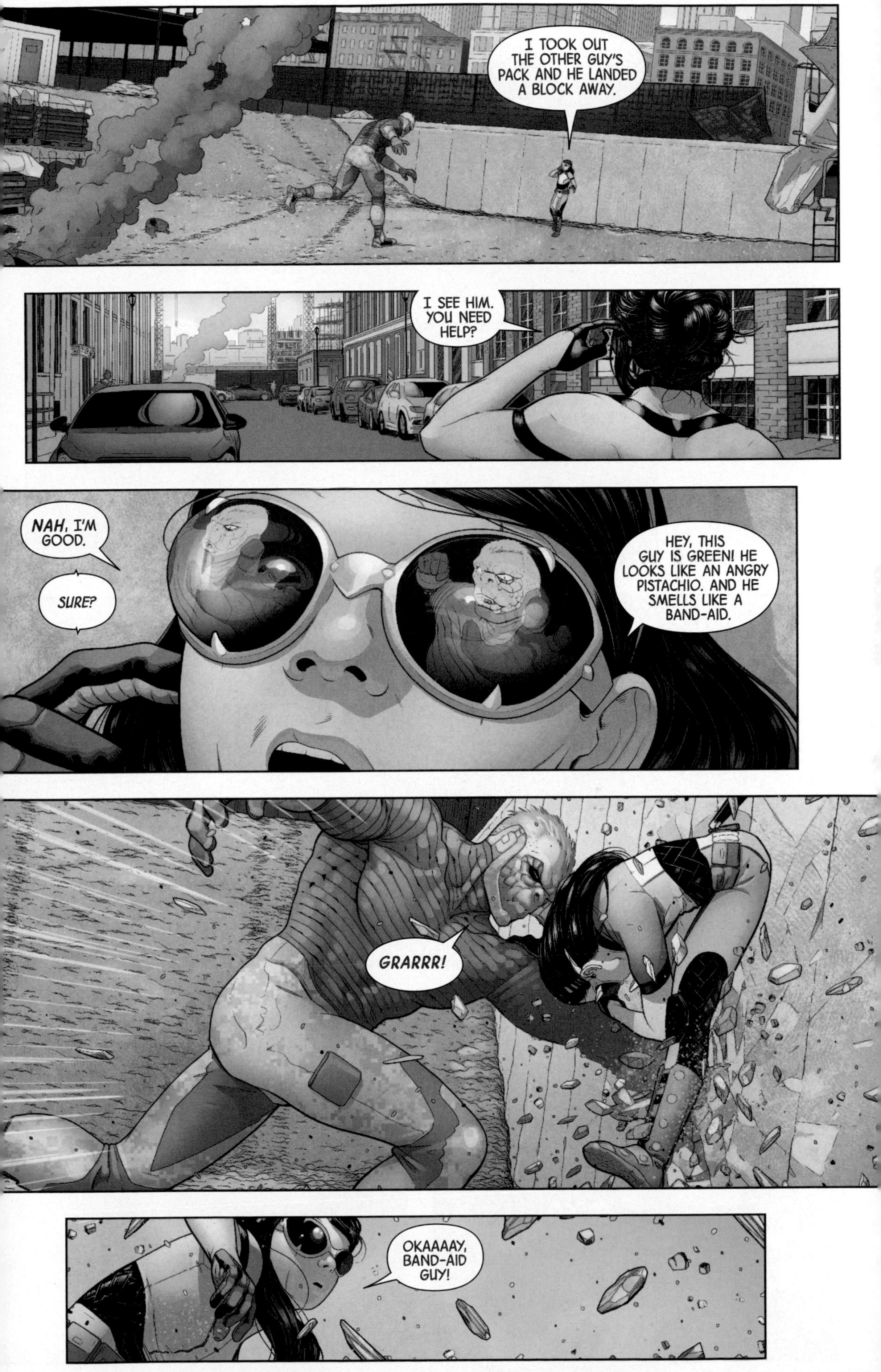
I TOOK OUT THE OTHER GUY'S PACK AND HE LANDED A BLOCK AWAY.
I SEE HIM. YOU NEED HELP?
NAH, I'M GOOD.
SURE?
HEY, THIS GUY IS GREEN! HE LOOKS LIKE AN ANGRY PISTACHIO. AND HE SMELLS LIKE A BAND-AID.
GRARRR!
OKAAAAY, BAND-AID GUY!

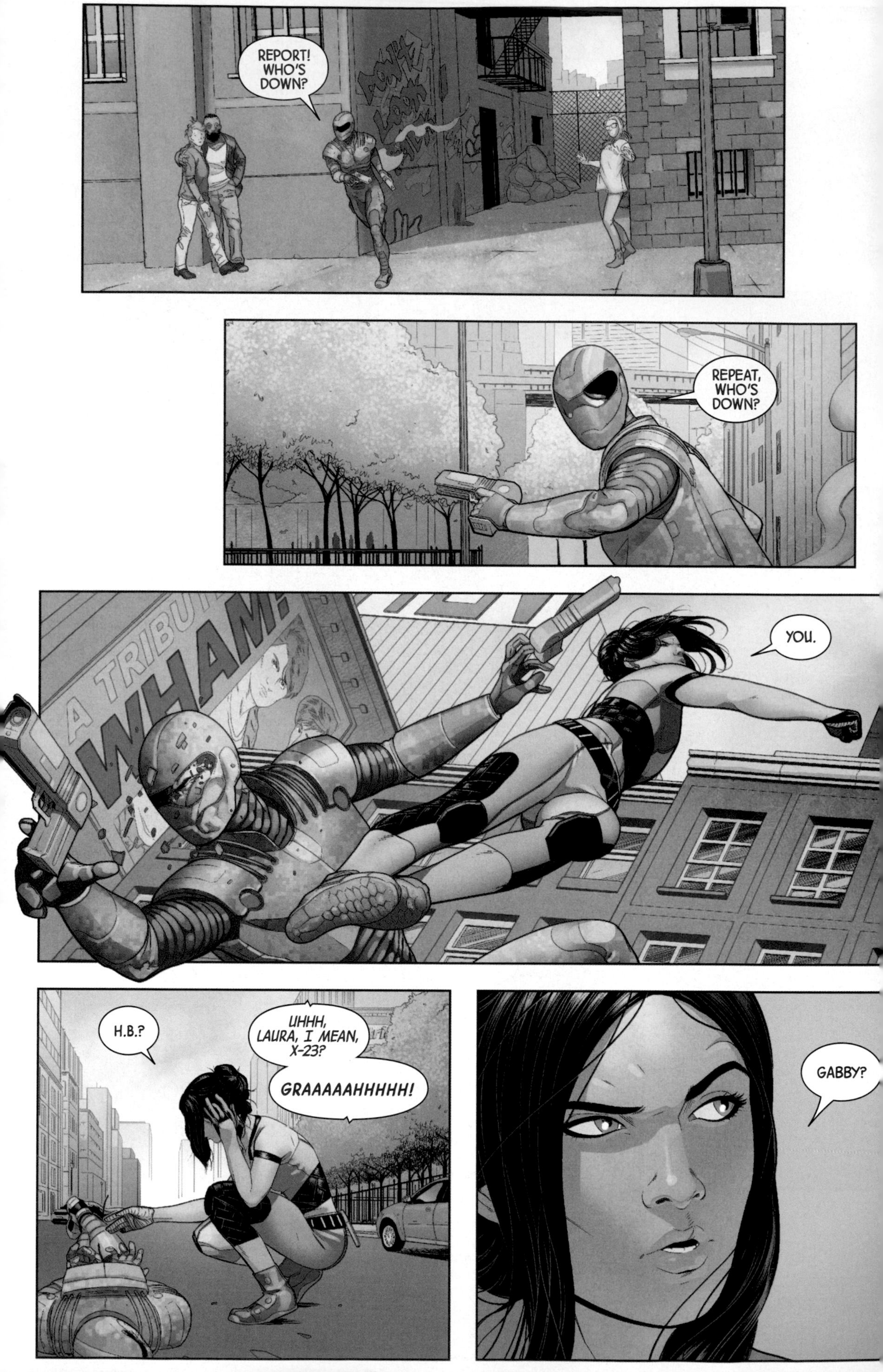
REPORT! WHO'S DOWN?
REPEAT, WHO'S DOWN?
YOU.
H.B.?
UHHH, LAURA, I MEAN, X-23?
GRAAAAAHHHHH!
GABBY?

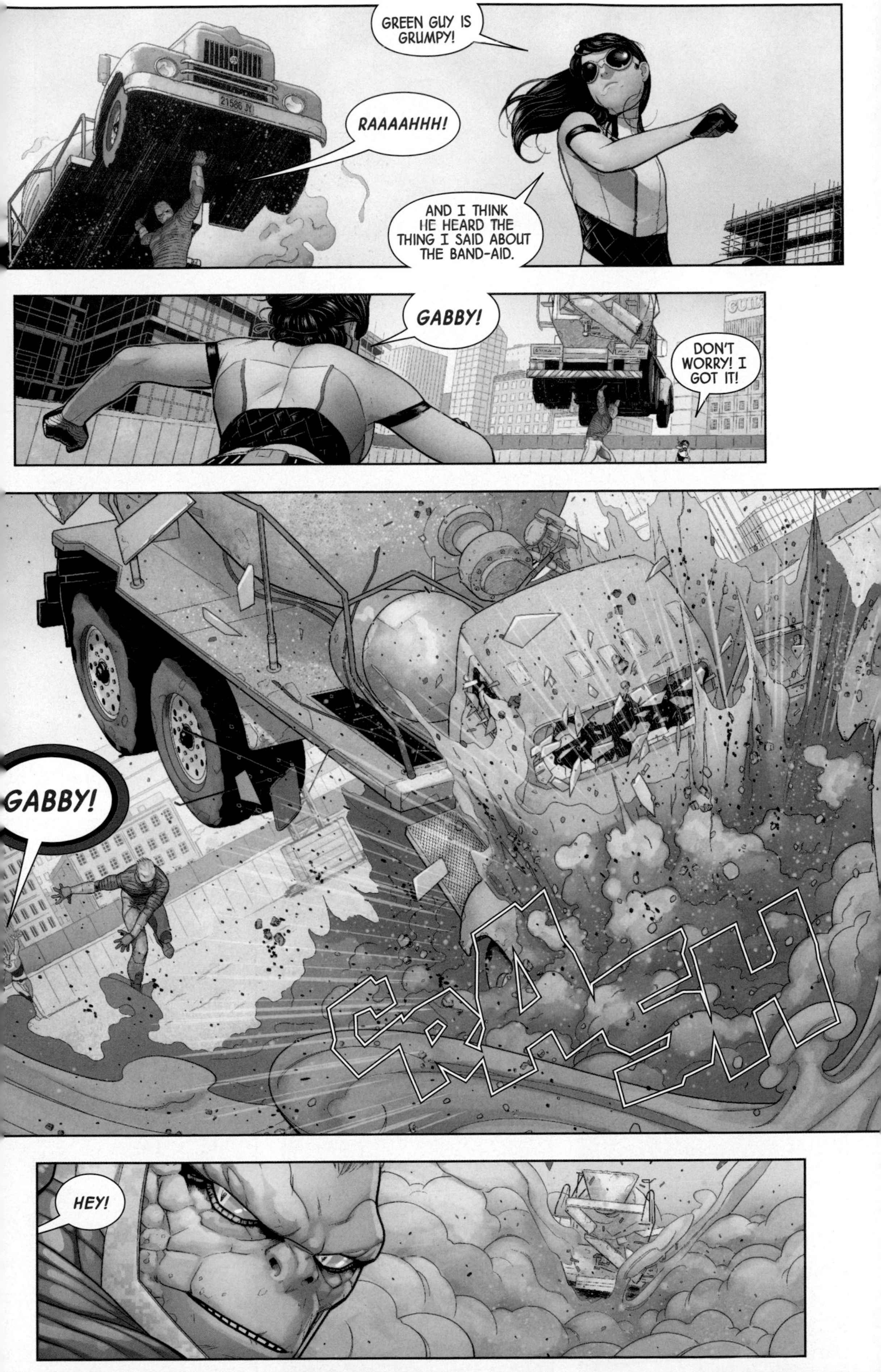
GREEN GUY IS GRUMPY!
RAAAAHHH!
AND I THINK HE HEARD THE THING I SAID ABOUT THE BAND-AID.
GABBY!
DON'T WORRY! I GOT IT!
GABBY!
CRAASH
HEY!

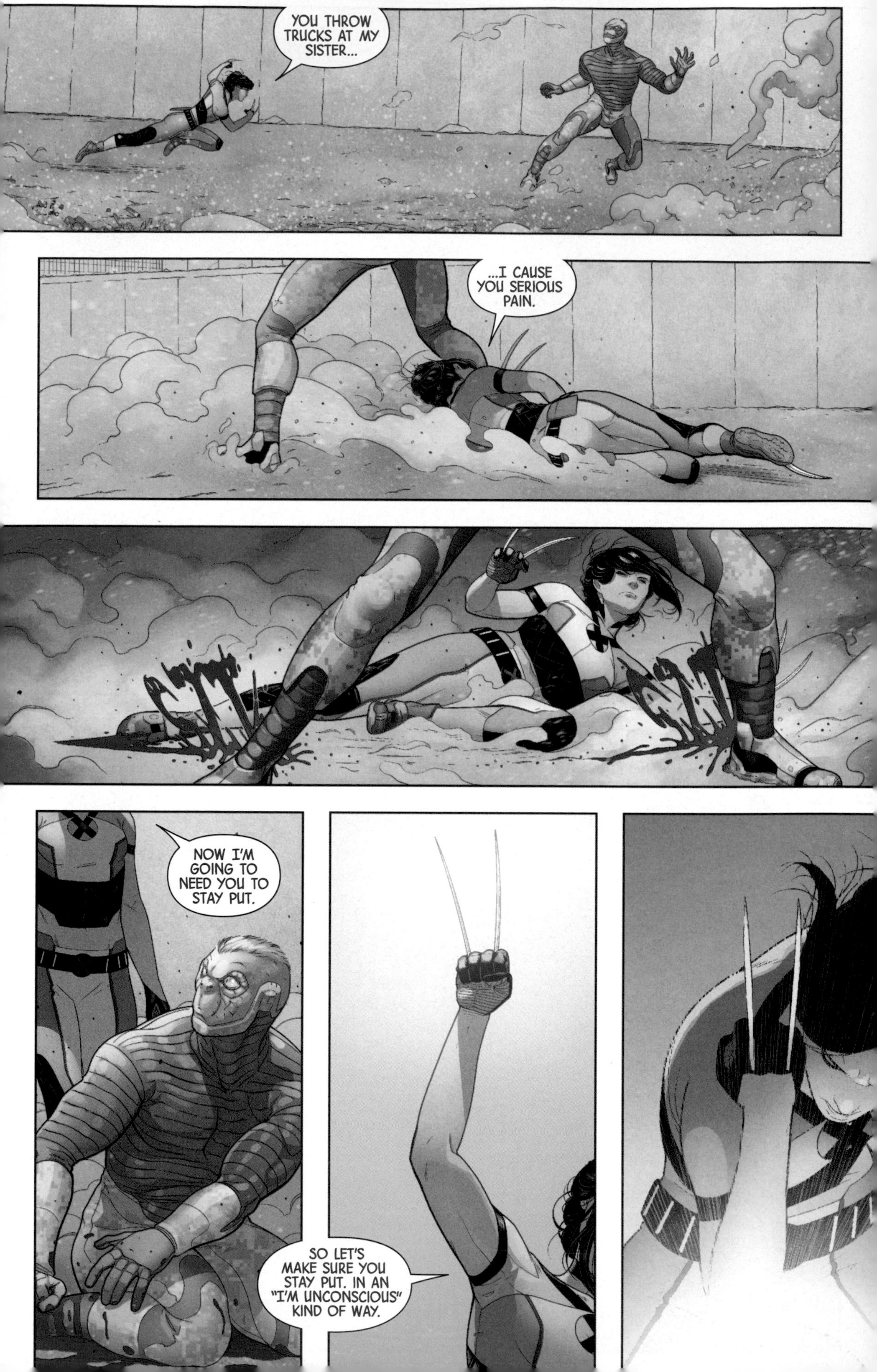
YOU THROW TRUCKS AT MY SISTER...
...I CAUSE YOU SERIOUS PAIN.
NOW I'M GOING TO NEED YOU TO STAY PUT.
SO LET'S MAKE SURE YOU STAY PUT. IN AN "I'M UNCONSCIOUS" KIND OF WAY.

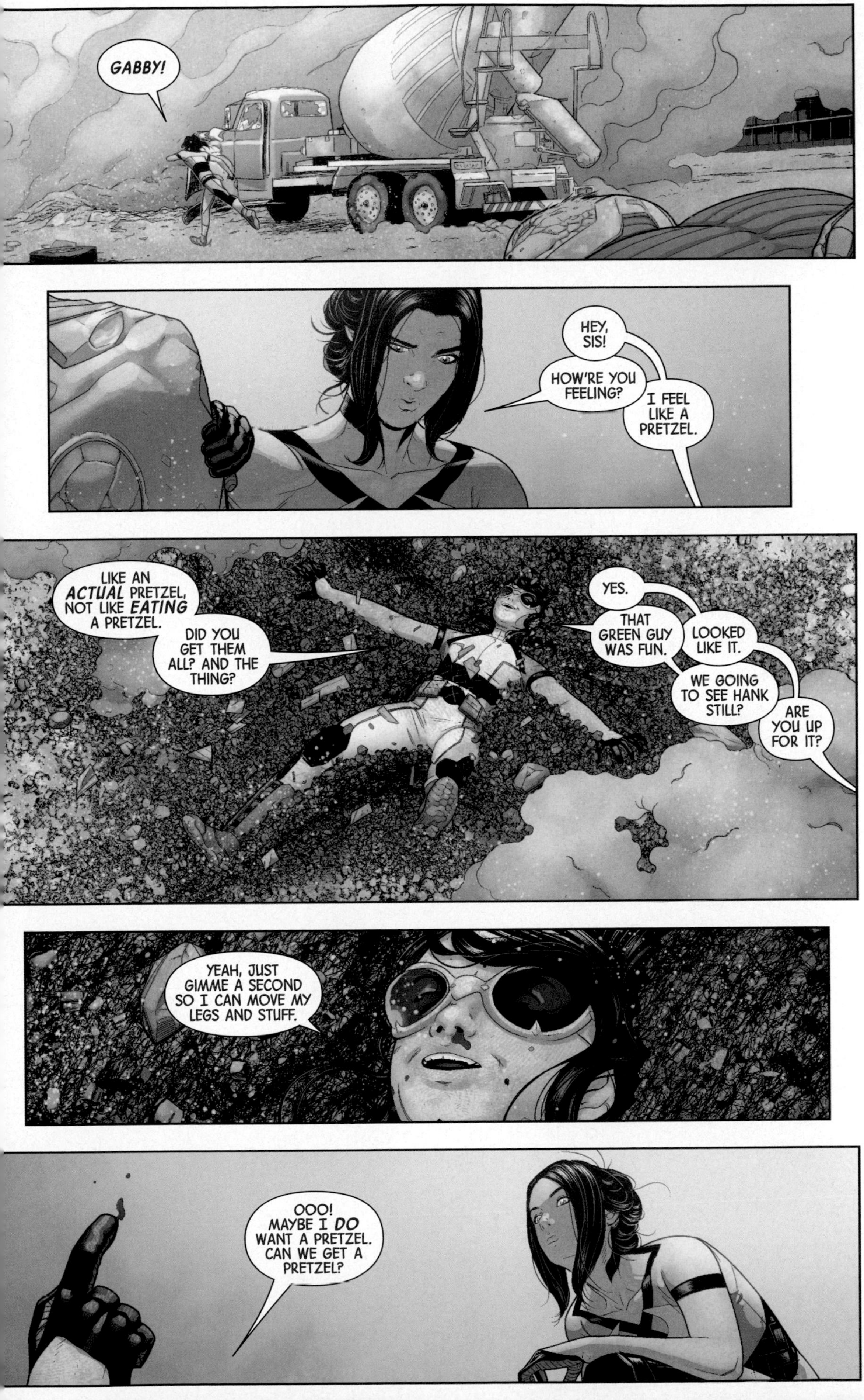
GABBY!
HEY, SIS!
HOW'RE YOU FEELING?
I FEEL LIKE A PRETZEL.
LIKE AN ACTUAL PRETZEL, NOT LIKE EATING A PRETZEL.
DID YOU GET THEM ALL? AND THE THING?
YES.
THAT GREEN GUY WAS FUN.
LOOKED LIKE IT.
WE GOING TO SEE HANK STILL?
ARE YOU UP FOR IT?
YEAH, JUST GIMME A SECOND SO I CAN MOVE MY LEGS AND STUFF.
OOO! MAYBE I DO WANT A PRETZEL. CAN WE GET A PRETZEL?

THEY WERE FERRYING BLACK-MARKET GENETIC MAPPING DATA.

MARKET SEEMS TO BE EXPANDING AT AN INCREASING RATE.

XAVIER INSTITUTE
FOR MUTANT EDUCATION AND OUTREACH

MORE AND MORE WELL-FUNDED ORGANIZATIONS, MAKING SUPER-SOLDIERS WITH WOLVERINE DNA.

BUT WE GOT THIS ONE.

AND NOW?

NOW I'LL DESTROY IT

IT WON'T BE THE LAST.

I KNOW. THIS IS WHAT I'M DOING NOW. THIS IS WHAT I DO. FOR NOW.

YES.

YOUR MESSAGE SAID YOU HAD SOMETHING FOR ME.

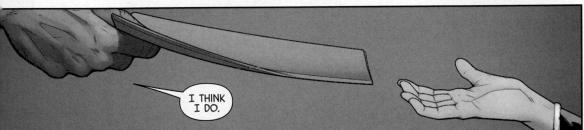

I THINK I DO.

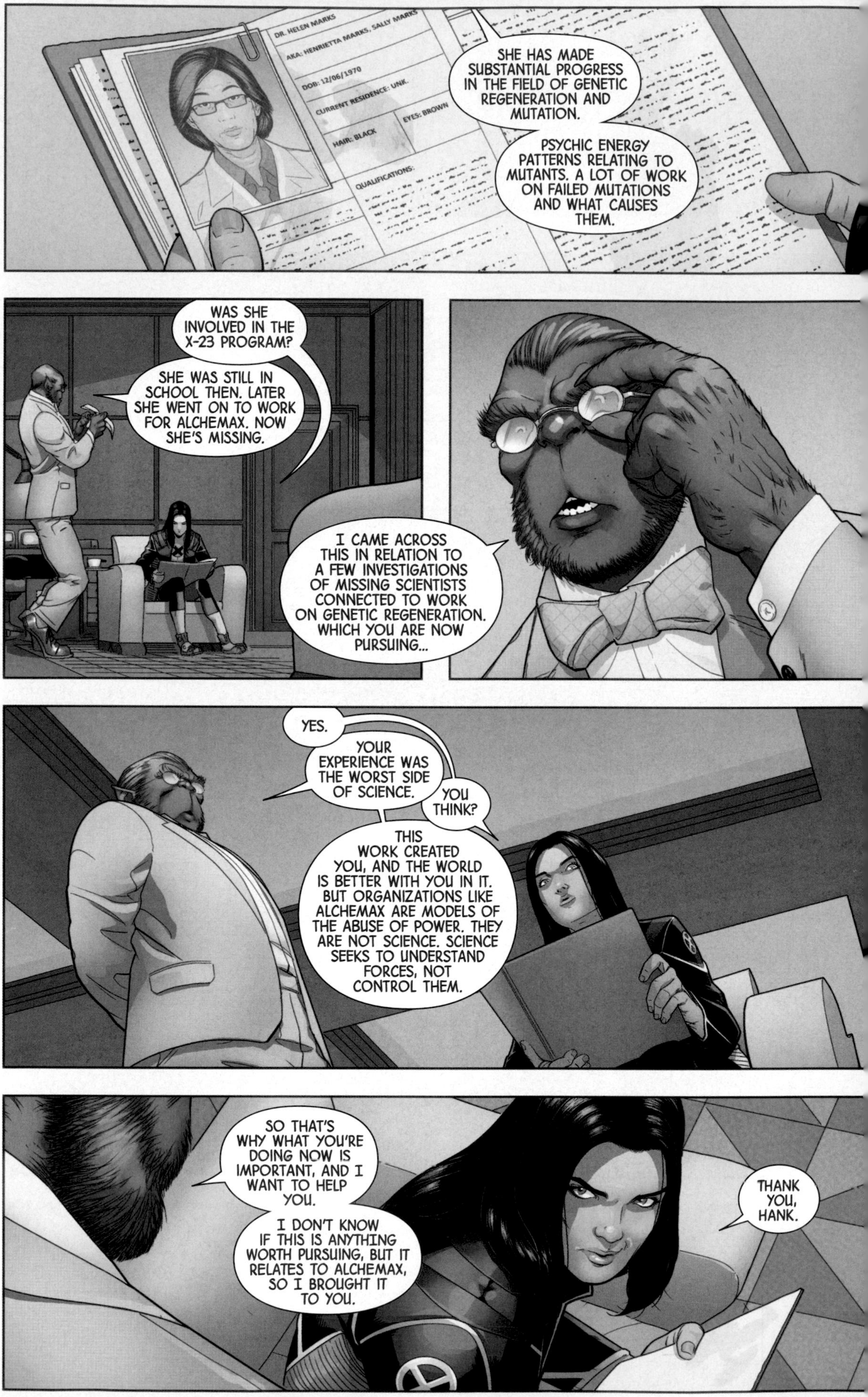
DR. HELEN MARKS
AKA: HENRIETTA MARKS, SALLY MARKS
DOB: 12/06/1970
CURRENT RESIDENCE: UNK.
HAIR: BLACK
EYES: BROWN
QUALIFICATIONS:
SHE HAS MADE SUBSTANTIAL PROGRESS IN THE FIELD OF GENETIC REGENERATION AND MUTATION.
PSYCHIC ENERGY PATTERNS RELATING TO MUTANTS. A LOT OF WORK ON FAILED MUTATIONS AND WHAT CAUSES THEM.
WAS SHE INVOLVED IN THE X-23 PROGRAM?
SHE WAS STILL IN SCHOOL THEN. LATER SHE WENT ON TO WORK FOR ALCHEMAX. NOW SHE'S MISSING.
I CAME ACROSS THIS IN RELATION TO A FEW INVESTIGATIONS OF MISSING SCIENTISTS CONNECTED TO WORK ON GENETIC REGENERATION. WHICH YOU ARE NOW PURSUING...
YES.
YOUR EXPERIENCE WAS THE WORST SIDE OF SCIENCE.
YOU THINK?
THIS WORK CREATED YOU, AND THE WORLD IS BETTER WITH YOU IN IT. BUT ORGANIZATIONS LIKE ALCHEMAX ARE MODELS OF THE ABUSE OF POWER. THEY ARE NOT SCIENCE. SCIENCE SEEKS TO UNDERSTAND FORCES, NOT CONTROL THEM.
SO THAT'S WHY WHAT YOU'RE DOING NOW IS IMPORTANT, AND I WANT TO HELP YOU.
I DON'T KNOW IF THIS IS ANYTHING WORTH PURSUING, BUT IT RELATES TO ALCHEMAX, SO I BROUGHT IT TO YOU.
THANK YOU, HANK.

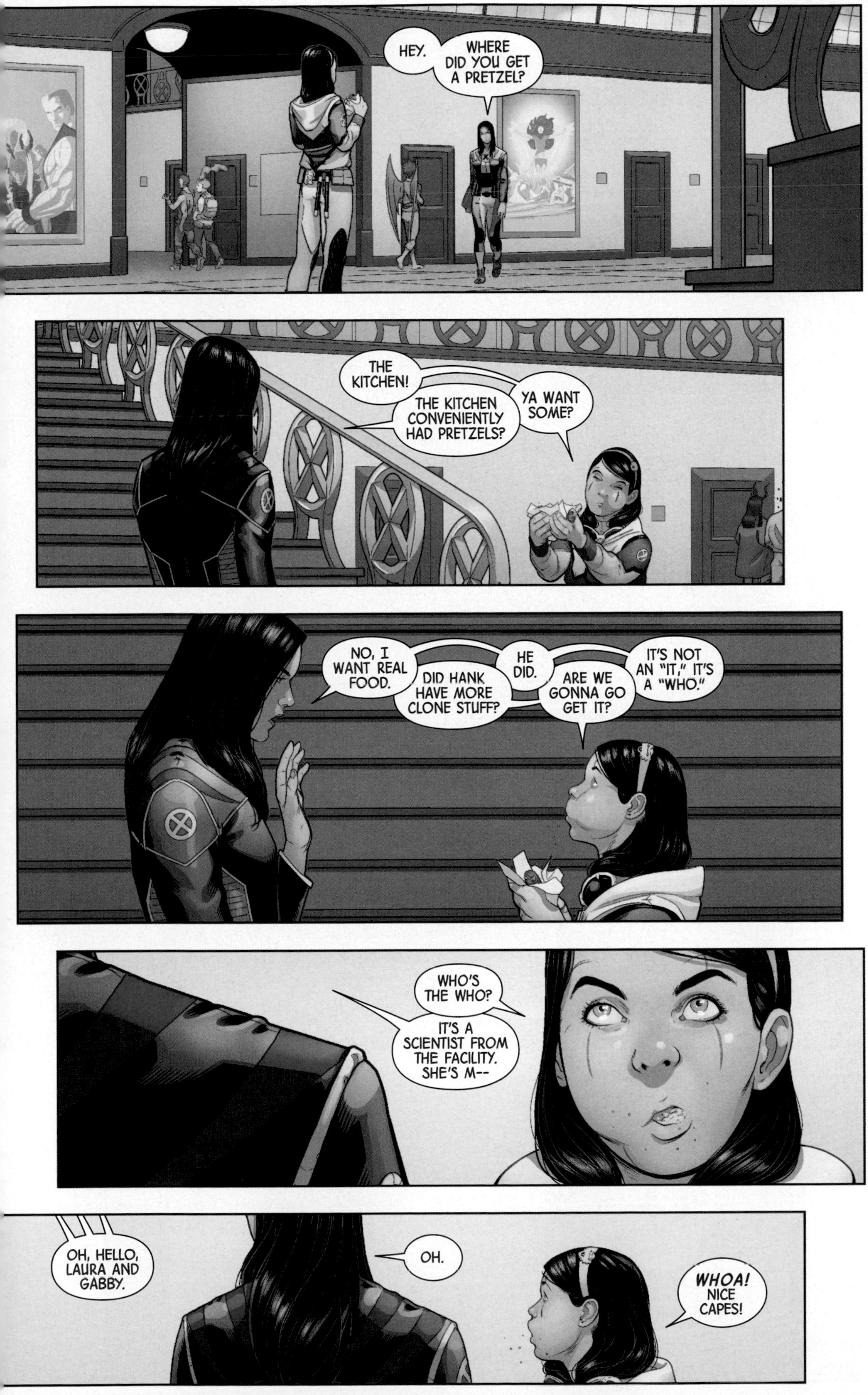
HEY.
WHERE DID YOU GET A PRETZEL?
THE KITCHEN!
YA WANT SOME?
THE KITCHEN CONVENIENTLY HAD PRETZELS?
NO, I WANT REAL FOOD.
DID HANK HAVE MORE CLONE STUFF?
HE DID.
ARE WE GONNA GO GET IT?
IT'S NOT AN "IT," IT'S A "WHO."
WHO'S THE WHO?
IT'S A SCIENTIST FROM THE FACILITY. SHE'S M--
OH, HELLO, LAURA AND GABBY.
OH.
WHOA! NICE CAPES!

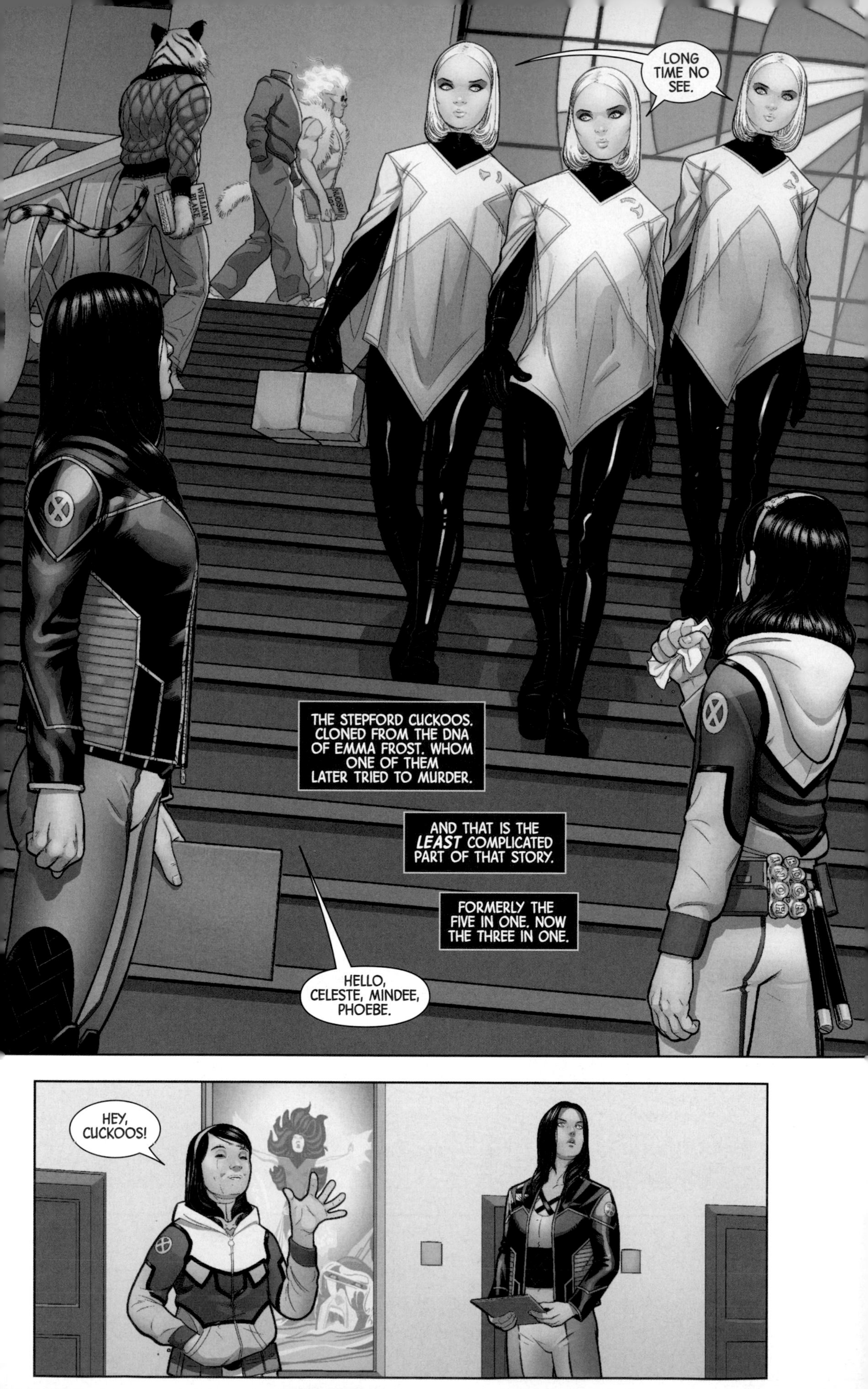
WILLIAM BLAKE
LONG TIME NO SEE.
THE STEPFORD CUCKOOS. CLONED FROM THE DNA OF EMMA FROST. WHOM ONE OF THEM LATER TRIED TO MURDER.
AND THAT IS THE *LEAST* COMPLICATED PART OF THAT STORY.
FORMERLY THE FIVE IN ONE. NOW THE THREE IN ONE.
HELLO, CELESTE, MINDEE, PHOEBE.
HEY, CUCKOOS!

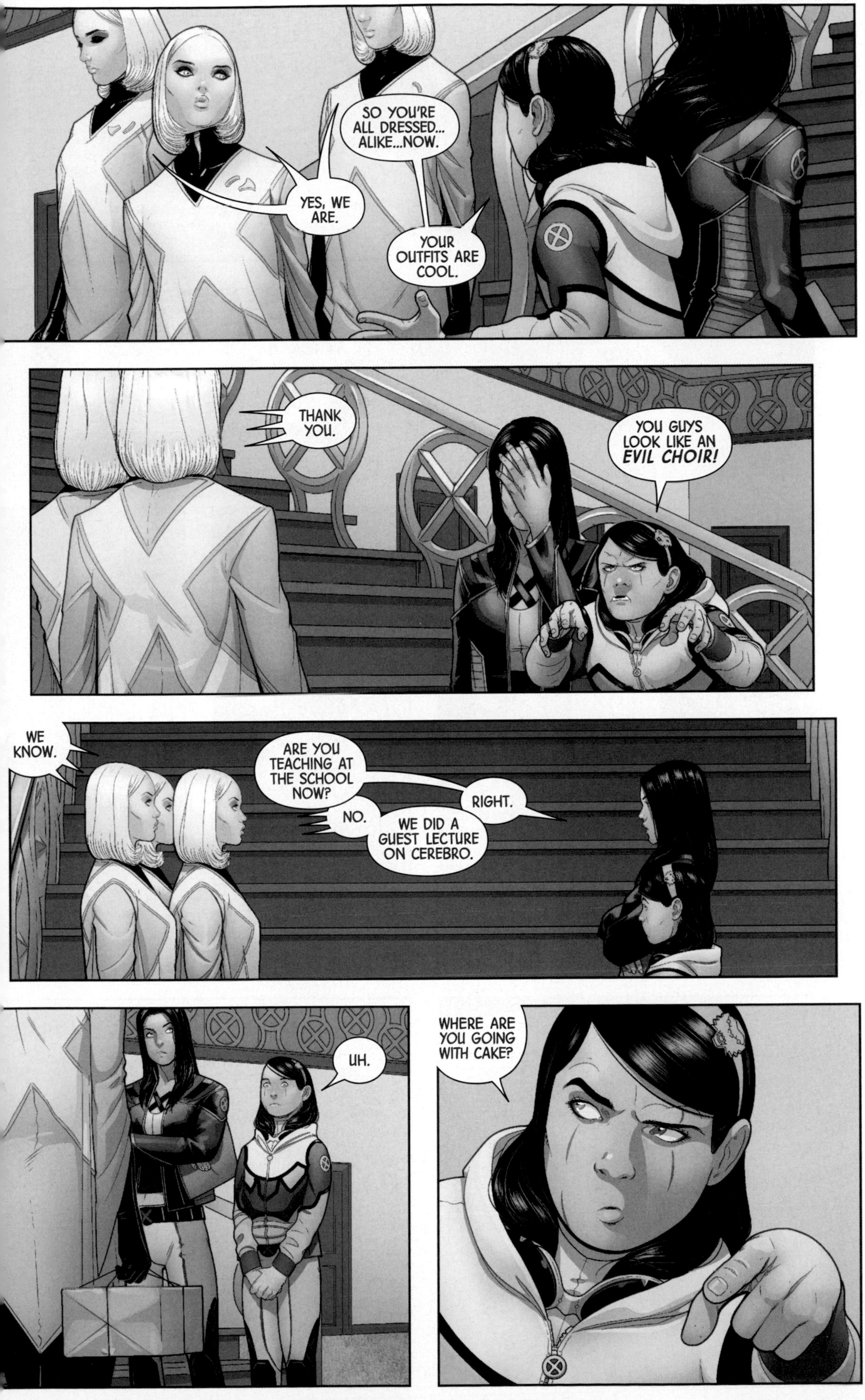
SO YOU'RE ALL DRESSED... ALIKE...NOW.
YES, WE ARE.
YOUR OUTFITS ARE COOL.
THANK YOU.
YOU GUYS LOOK LIKE AN EVIL CHOIR!
WE KNOW.
ARE YOU TEACHING AT THE SCHOOL NOW?
NO.
WE DID A GUEST LECTURE ON CEREBRO.
RIGHT.
UH.
WHERE ARE YOU GOING WITH CAKE?

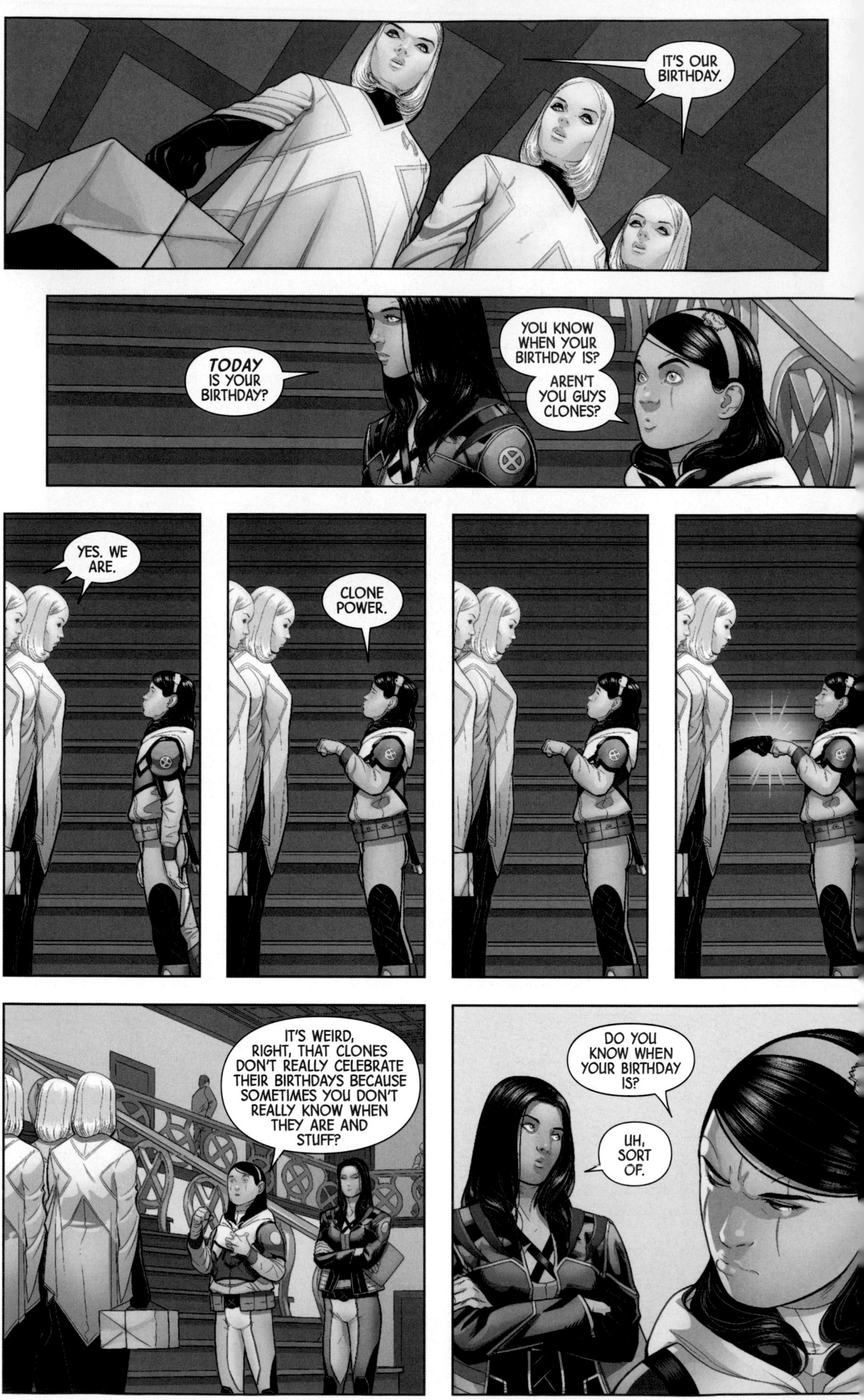
IT'S OUR BIRTHDAY.
TODAY IS YOUR BIRTHDAY?
YOU KNOW WHEN YOUR BIRTHDAY IS?
AREN'T YOU GUYS CLONES?
YES. WE ARE.
CLONE POWER.
IT'S WEIRD, RIGHT, THAT CLONES DON'T REALLY CELEBRATE THEIR BIRTHDAYS BECAUSE SOMETIMES YOU DON'T REALLY KNOW WHEN THEY ARE AND STUFF?
DO YOU KNOW WHEN YOUR BIRTHDAY IS?
UH, SORT OF.

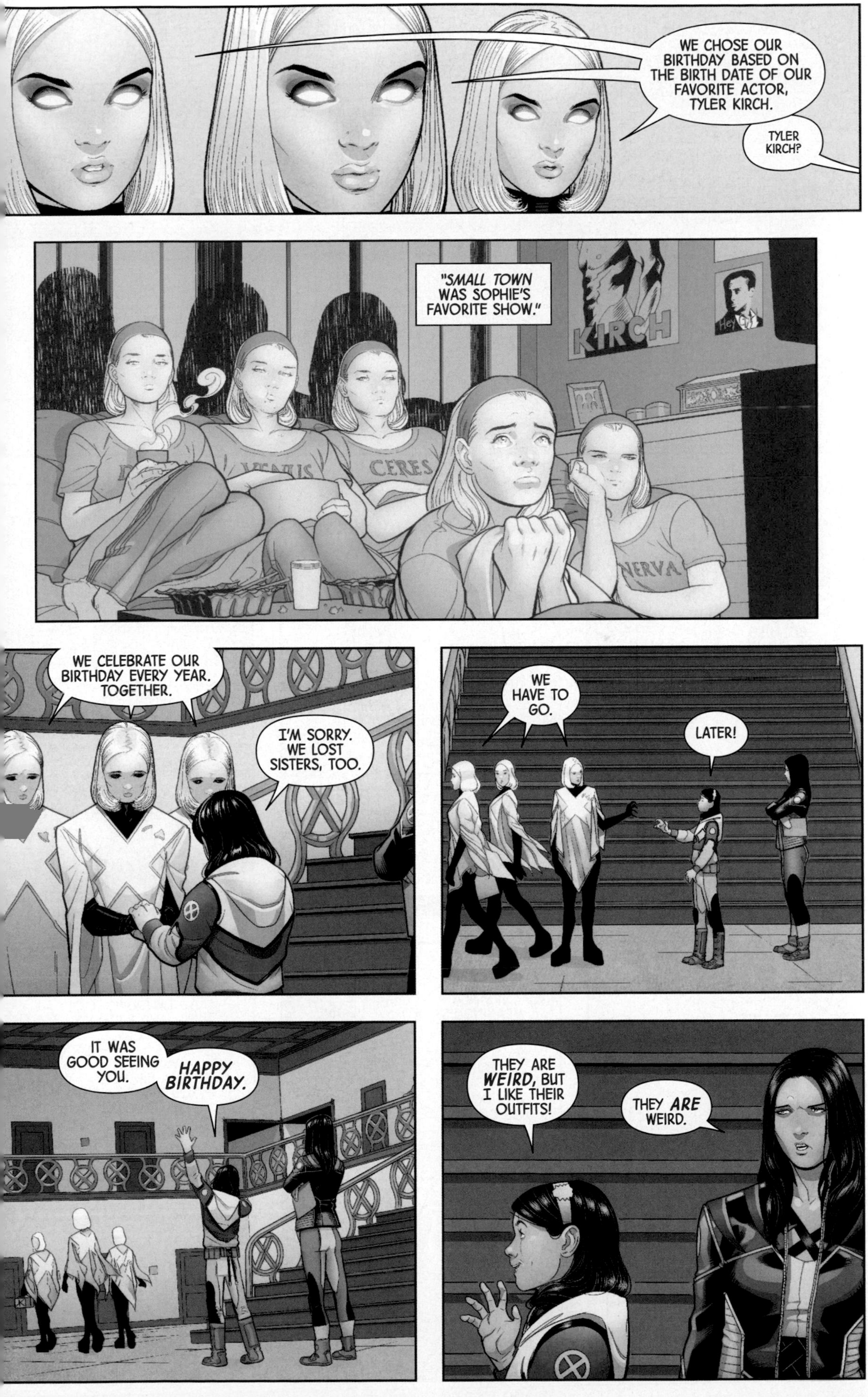
WE CHOSE OUR BIRTHDAY BASED ON THE BIRTH DATE OF OUR FAVORITE ACTOR, TYLER KIRCH.
TYLER KIRCH?
"SMALL TOWN WAS SOPHIE'S FAVORITE SHOW."
KIRCH
CERES
VENUS
NERVA
WE CELEBRATE OUR BIRTHDAY EVERY YEAR. TOGETHER.
I'M SORRY. WE LOST SISTERS, TOO.
WE HAVE TO GO.
LATER!
IT WAS GOOD SEEING YOU.
HAPPY BIRTHDAY.
THEY ARE WEIRD, BUT I LIKE THEIR OUTFITS!
THEY ARE WEIRD.

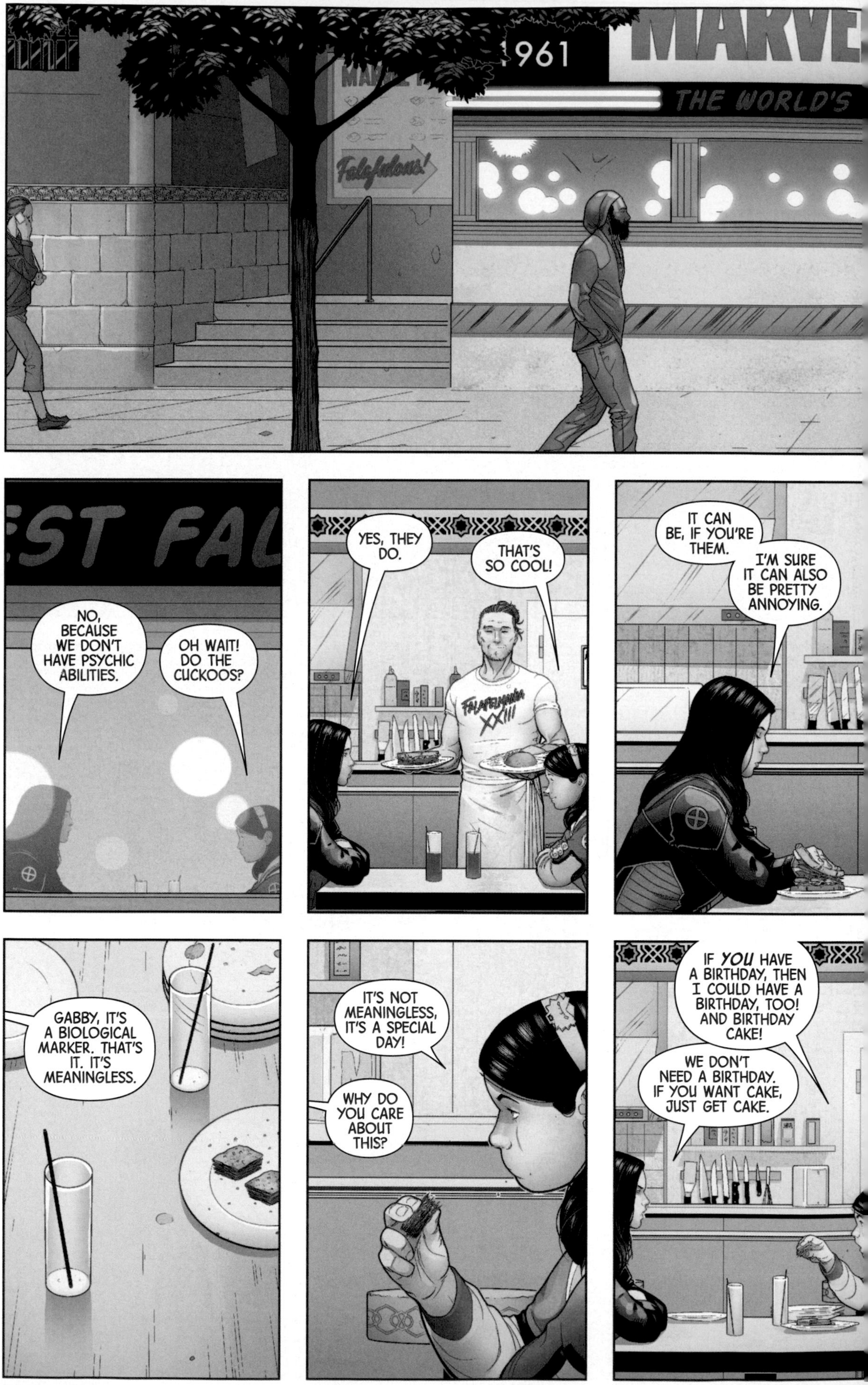
1961
MARVE
THE WORLD'S
Falafelous!
EST FAL
NO, BECAUSE WE DON'T HAVE PSYCHIC ABILITIES.
OH WAIT! DO THE CUCKOOS?
YES, THEY DO.
THAT'S SO COOL!
FALAFELMANIA XXIII
IT CAN BE, IF YOU'RE THEM.
I'M SURE IT CAN ALSO BE PRETTY ANNOYING.
GABBY, IT'S A BIOLOGICAL MARKER. THAT'S IT. IT'S MEANINGLESS.
IT'S NOT MEANINGLESS, IT'S A SPECIAL DAY!
WHY DO YOU CARE ABOUT THIS?
IF *YOU* HAVE A BIRTHDAY, THEN I COULD HAVE A BIRTHDAY, TOO! AND BIRTHDAY CAKE!
WE DON'T NEED A BIRTHDAY. IF YOU WANT CAKE, JUST GET CAKE.

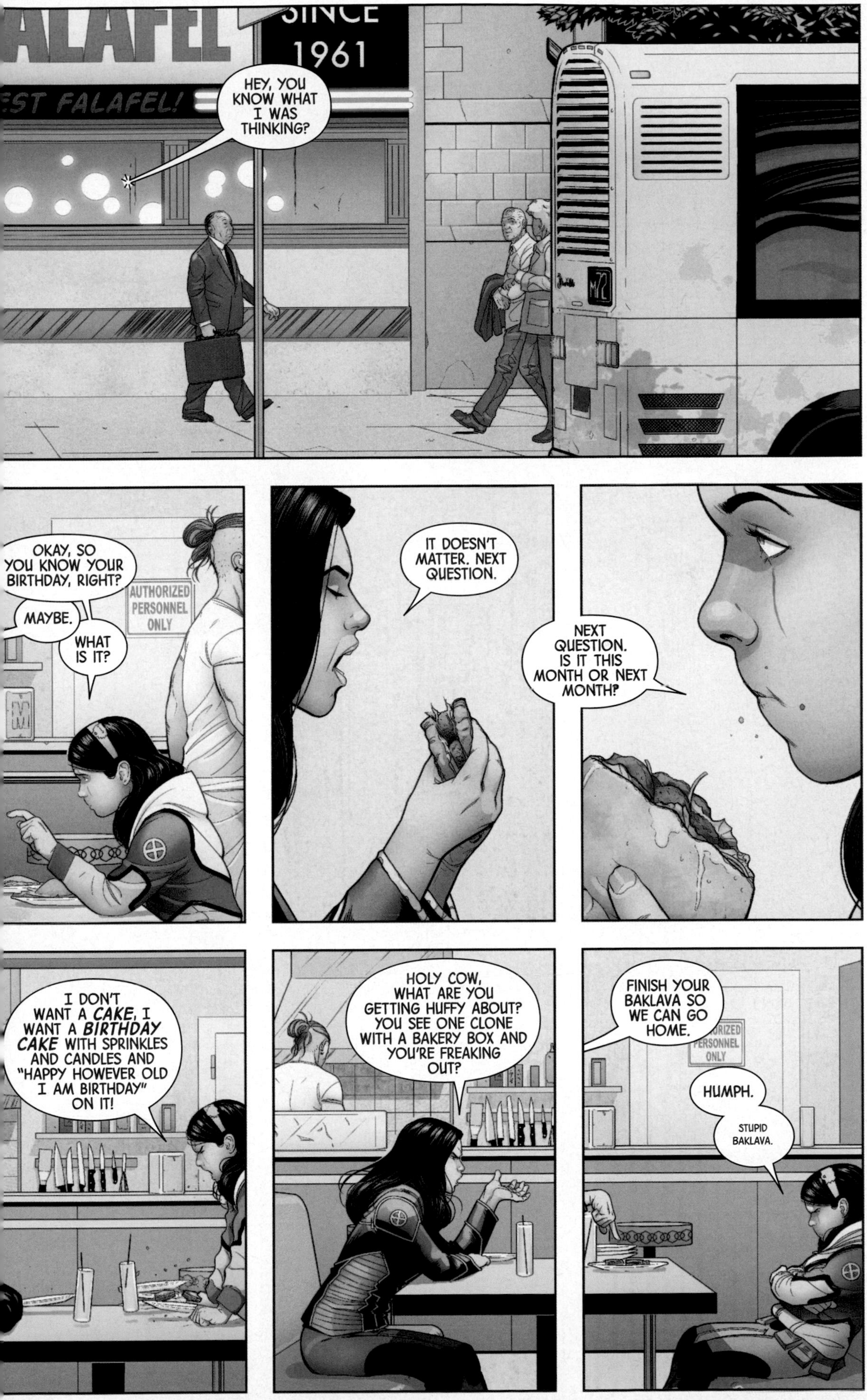
ALAFEL
SINCE 1961
EST FALAFEL!
HEY, YOU KNOW WHAT I WAS THINKING?
OKAY, SO YOU KNOW YOUR BIRTHDAY, RIGHT?
MAYBE.
WHAT IS IT?
AUTHORIZED PERSONNEL ONLY
IT DOESN'T MATTER. NEXT QUESTION.
NEXT QUESTION. IS IT THIS MONTH OR NEXT MONTH?
I DON'T WANT A *CAKE*, I WANT A *BIRTHDAY CAKE* WITH SPRINKLES AND CANDLES AND "HAPPY HOWEVER OLD I AM BIRTHDAY" ON IT!
HOLY COW, WHAT ARE YOU GETTING HUFFY ABOUT? YOU SEE ONE CLONE WITH A BAKERY BOX AND YOU'RE FREAKING OUT?
FINISH YOUR BAKLAVA SO WE CAN GO HOME.
HUMPH.
STUPID BAKLAVA.

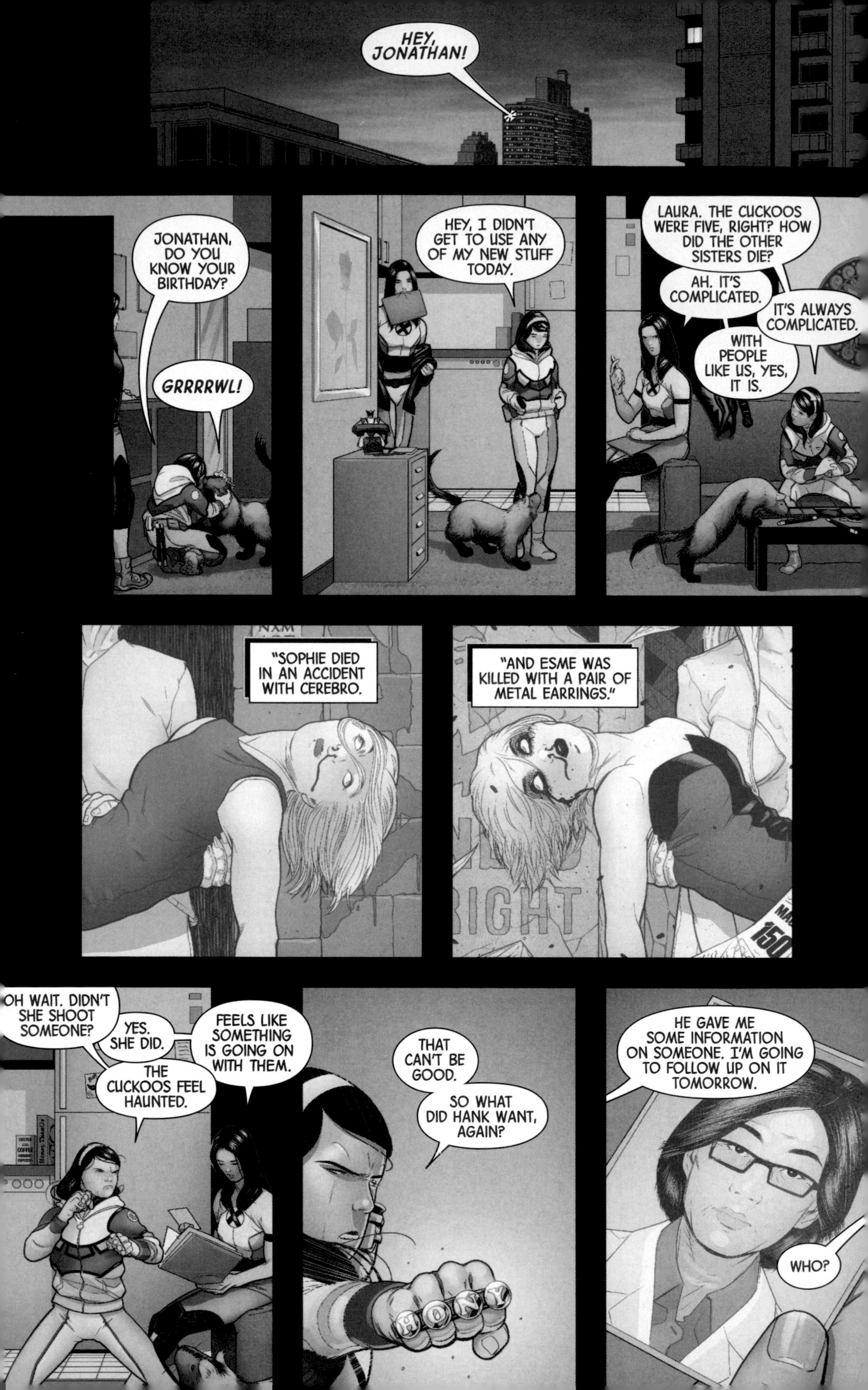
HEY, JONATHAN!
JONATHAN, DO YOU KNOW YOUR BIRTHDAY?
GRRRRWL!
HEY, I DIDN'T GET TO USE ANY OF MY NEW STUFF TODAY.
LAURA. THE CUCKOOS WERE FIVE, RIGHT? HOW DID THE OTHER SISTERS DIE?
AH. IT'S COMPLICATED.
IT'S ALWAYS COMPLICATED.
WITH PEOPLE LIKE US, YES, IT IS.
"SOPHIE DIED IN AN ACCIDENT WITH CEREBRO.
"AND ESME WAS KILLED WITH A PAIR OF METAL EARRINGS."
OH WAIT. DIDN'T SHE SHOOT SOMEONE?
YES. SHE DID.
THE CUCKOOS FEEL HAUNTED.
FEELS LIKE SOMETHING IS GOING ON WITH THEM.
THAT CAN'T BE GOOD.
SO WHAT DID HANK WANT, AGAIN?
HE GAVE ME SOME INFORMATION ON SOMEONE. I'M GOING TO FOLLOW UP ON IT TOMORROW.
WHO?

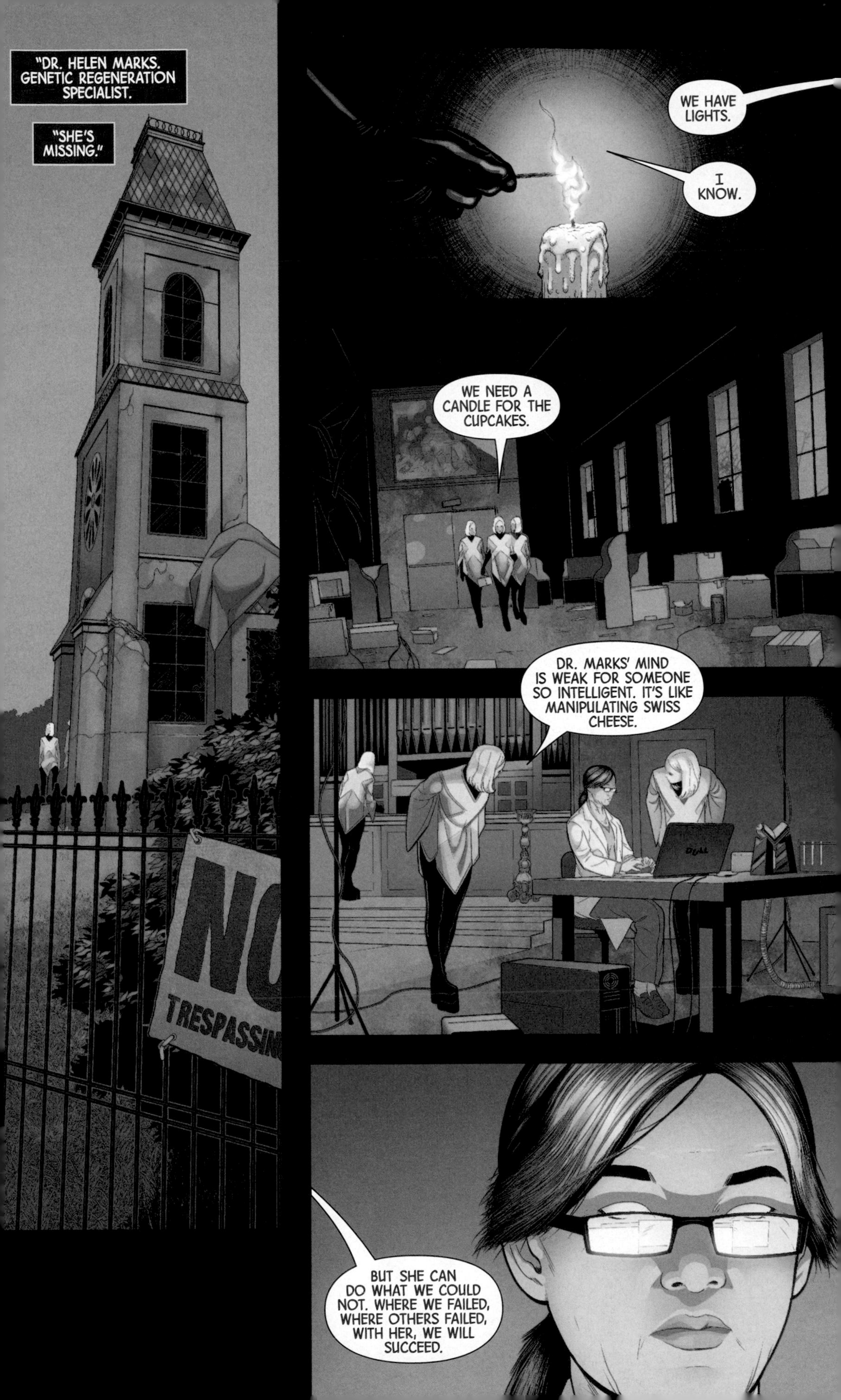
"DR. HELEN MARKS. GENETIC REGENERATION SPECIALIST.
"SHE'S MISSING."
NO TRESPASSING
WE HAVE LIGHTS.
I KNOW.
WE NEED A CANDLE FOR THE CUPCAKES.
DR. MARKS' MIND IS WEAK FOR SOMEONE SO INTELLIGENT. IT'S LIKE MANIPULATING SWISS CHEESE.
BUT SHE CAN DO WHAT WE COULD NOT. WHERE WE FAILED, WHERE OTHERS FAILED, WITH HER, WE WILL SUCCEED.

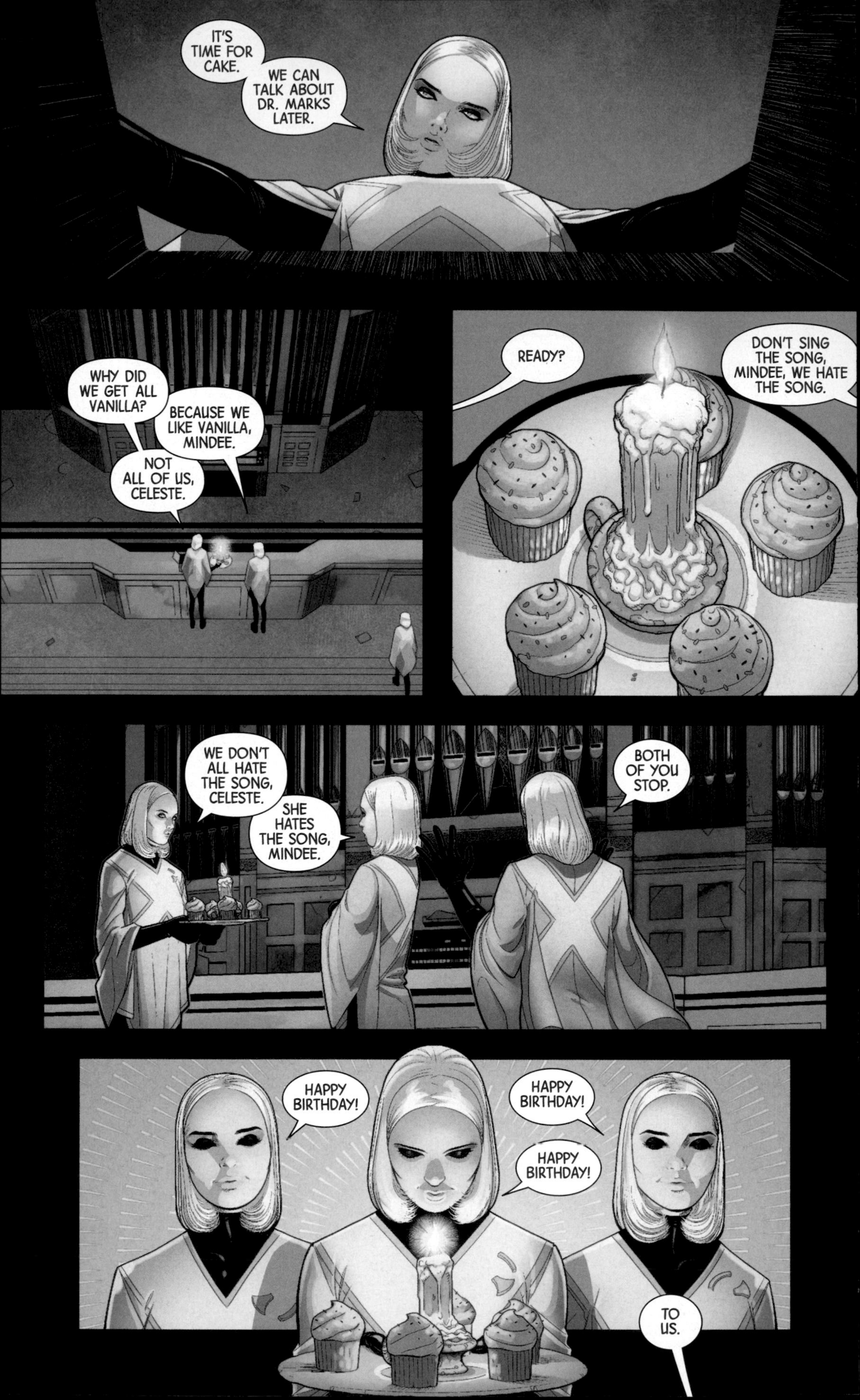

IT'S TIME FOR CAKE.
WE CAN TALK ABOUT DR. MARKS LATER.
WHY DID WE GET ALL VANILLA?
BECAUSE WE LIKE VANILLA, MINDEE.
NOT ALL OF US, CELESTE.
READY?
DON'T SING THE SONG, MINDEE, WE HATE THE SONG.
WE DON'T ALL HATE THE SONG, CELESTE.
SHE HATES THE SONG, MINDEE.
BOTH OF YOU STOP.
HAPPY BIRTHDAY!
HAPPY BIRTHDAY!
HAPPY BIRTHDAY!
TO US.

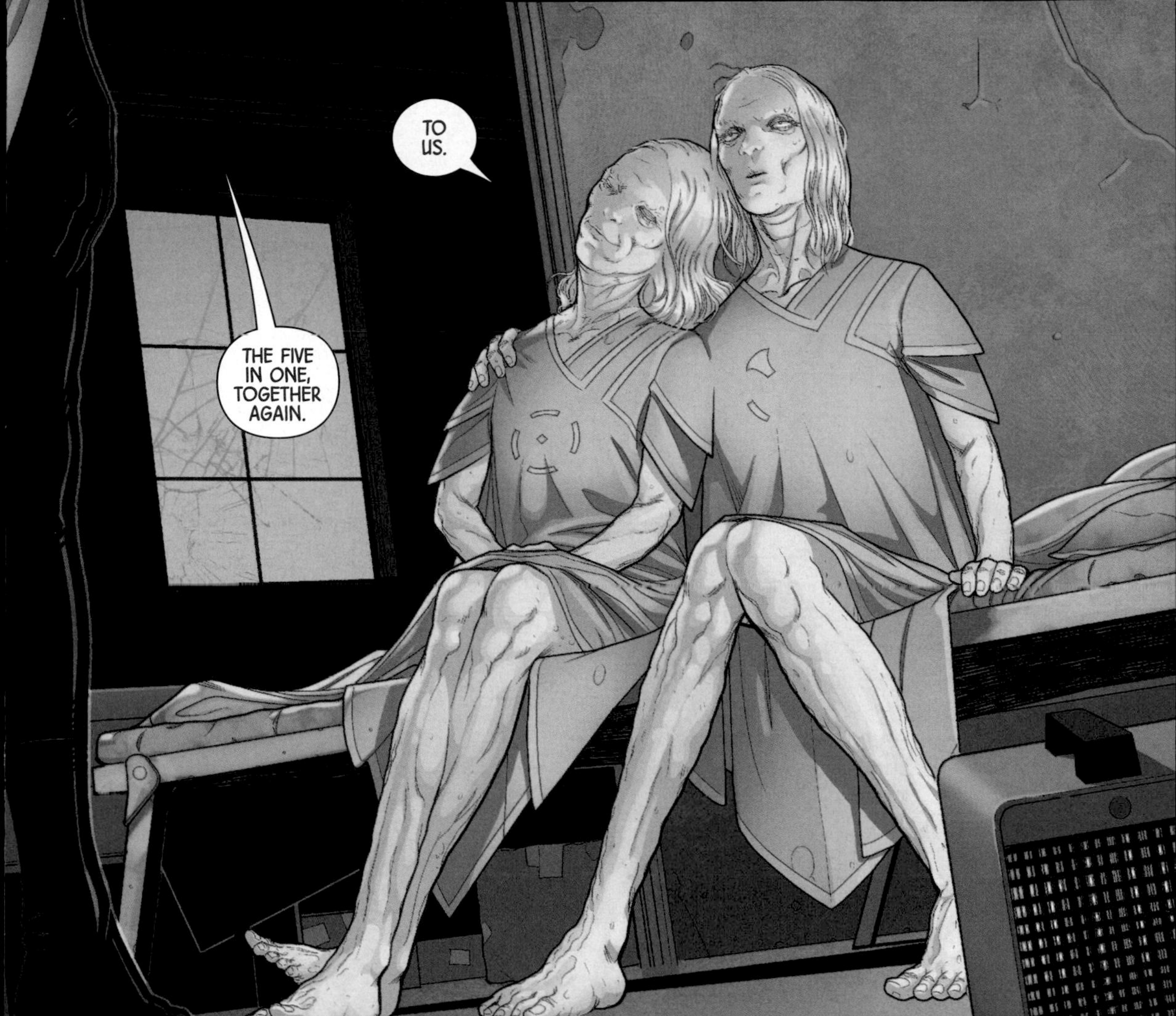
TO US.
THE FIVE IN ONE, TOGETHER AGAIN.

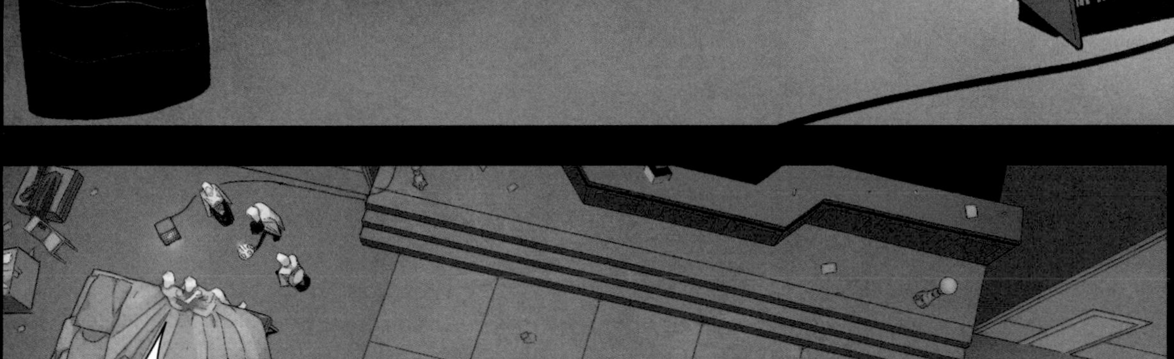
DON'T SING THAT STUPID SONG. I HATE THAT SONG.

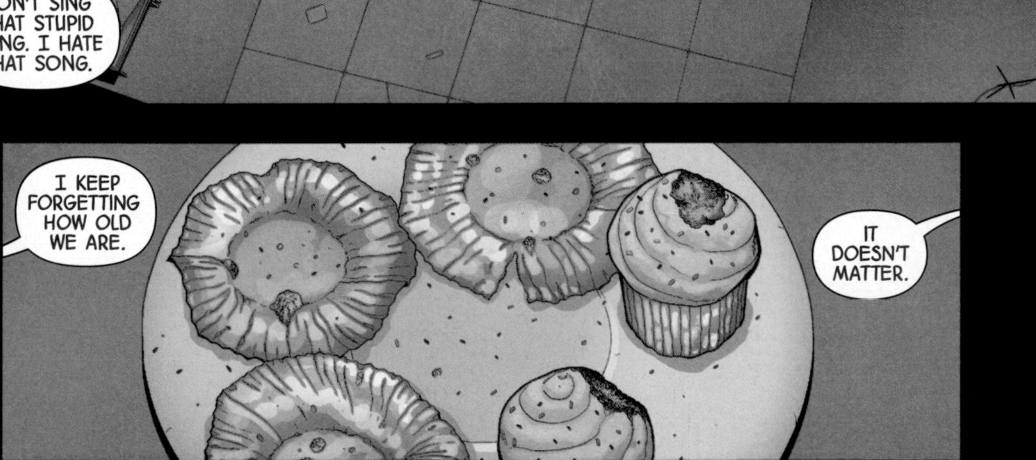
I KEEP FORGETTING HOW OLD WE ARE.
IT DOESN'T MATTER.

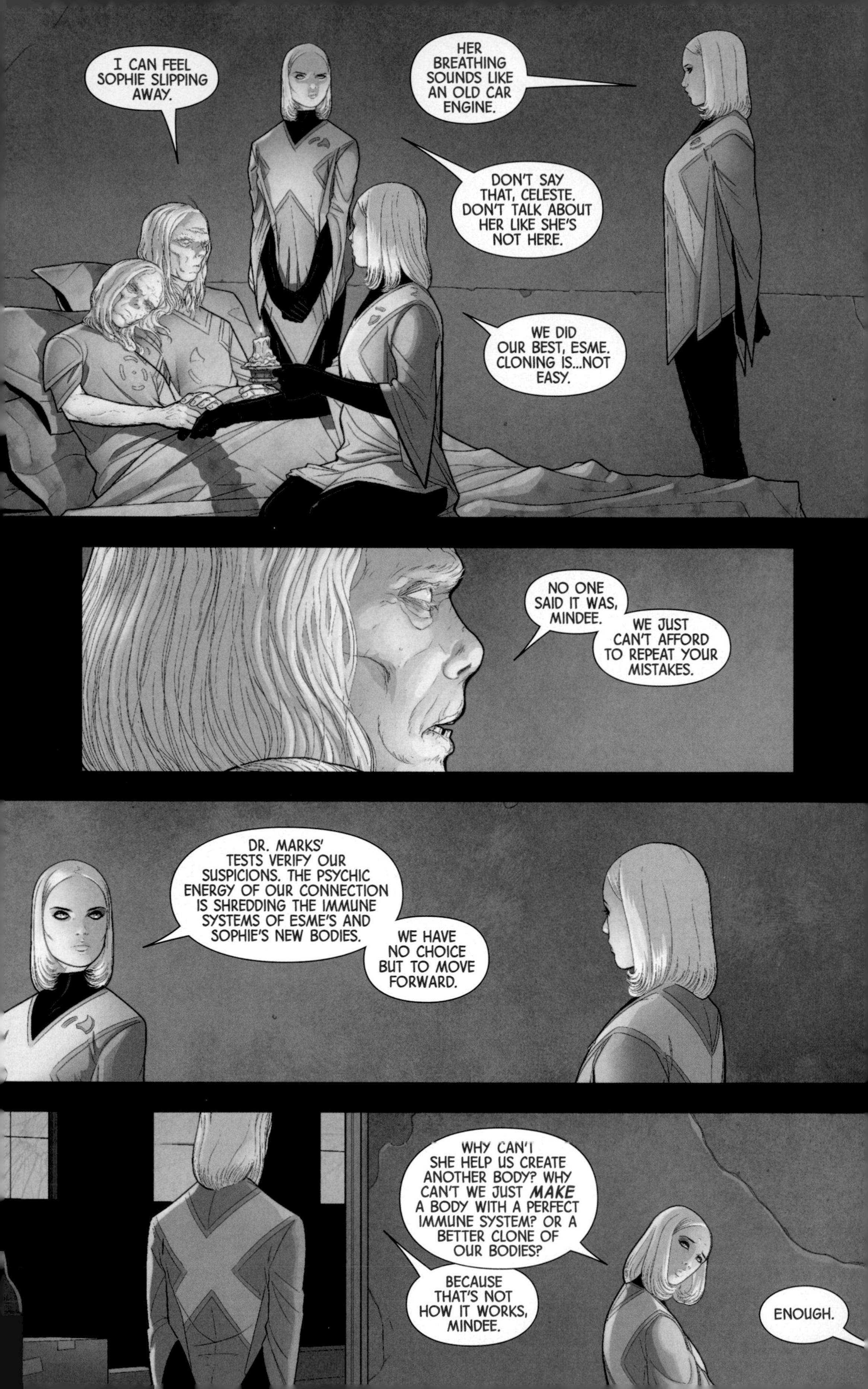
I CAN FEEL SOPHIE SLIPPING AWAY.
HER BREATHING SOUNDS LIKE AN OLD CAR ENGINE.
DON'T SAY THAT, CELESTE. DON'T TALK ABOUT HER LIKE SHE'S NOT HERE.
WE DID OUR BEST, ESME. CLONING IS...NOT EASY.
NO ONE SAID IT WAS, MINDEE.
WE JUST CAN'T AFFORD TO REPEAT YOUR MISTAKES.
DR. MARKS' TESTS VERIFY OUR SUSPICIONS. THE PSYCHIC ENERGY OF OUR CONNECTION IS SHREDDING THE IMMUNE SYSTEMS OF ESME'S AND SOPHIE'S NEW BODIES.
WE HAVE NO CHOICE BUT TO MOVE FORWARD.
WHY CAN'T SHE HELP US CREATE ANOTHER BODY? WHY CAN'T WE JUST *MAKE* A BODY WITH A PERFECT IMMUNE SYSTEM? OR A BETTER CLONE OF OUR BODIES?
BECAUSE THAT'S NOT HOW IT WORKS, MINDEE.
ENOUGH.

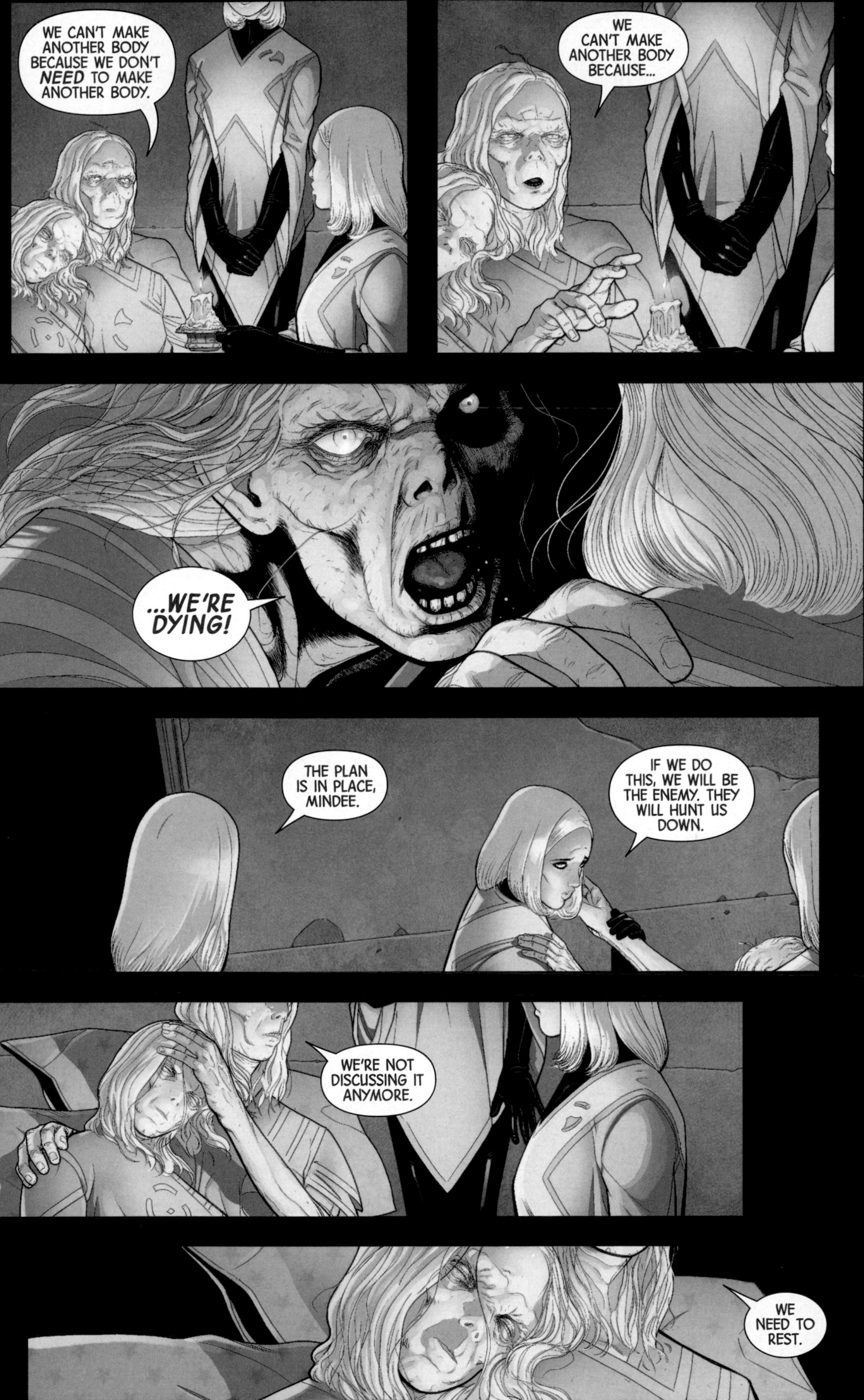
WE CAN'T MAKE ANOTHER BODY BECAUSE WE DON'T *NEED* TO MAKE ANOTHER BODY.
WE CAN'T MAKE ANOTHER BODY BECAUSE...
...WE'RE DYING!
THE PLAN IS IN PLACE, MINDEE.
IF WE DO THIS, WE WILL BE THE ENEMY. THEY WILL HUNT US DOWN.
WE'RE NOT DISCUSSING IT ANYMORE.
WE NEED TO REST.

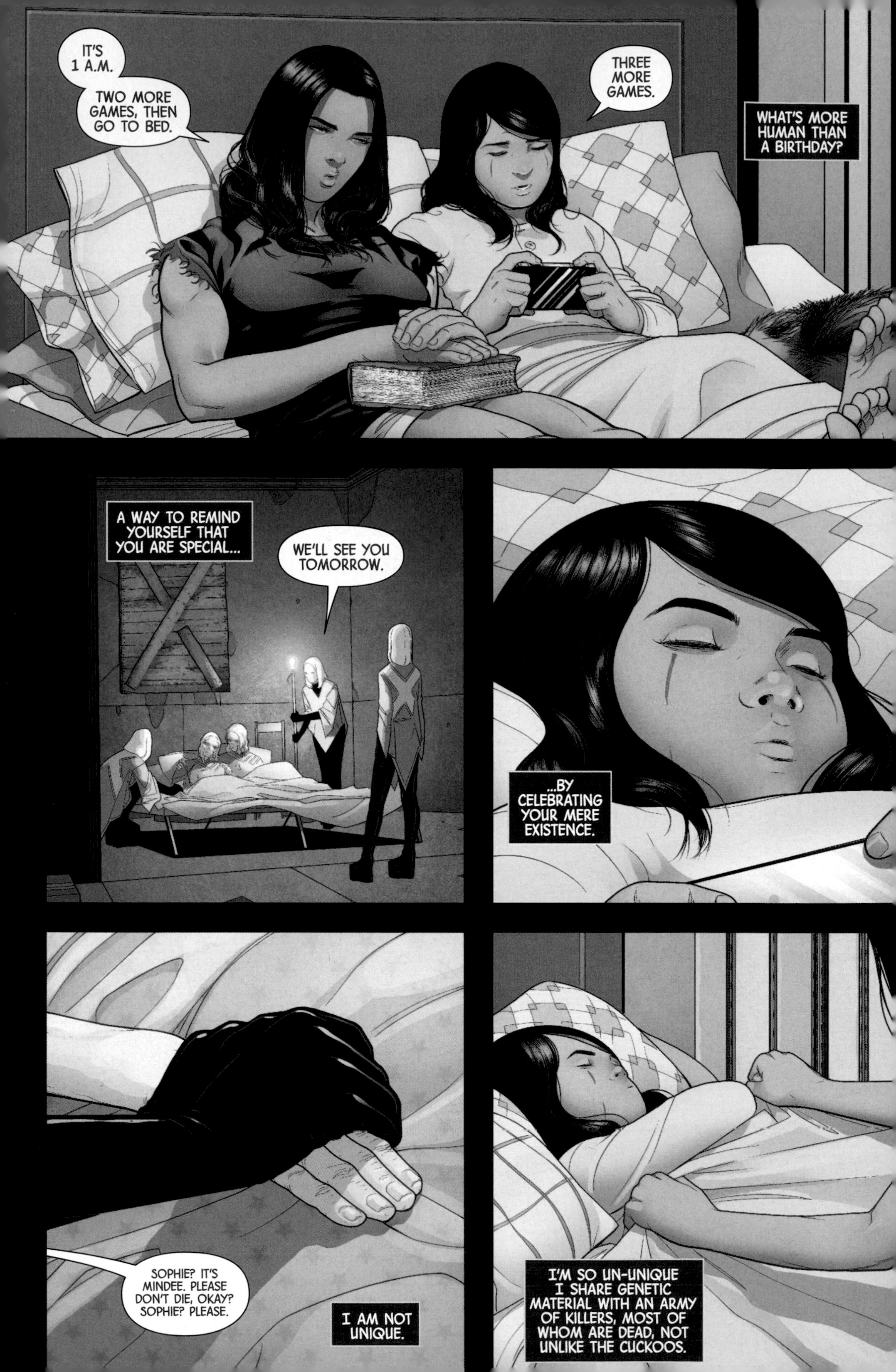
IT'S 1 A.M.
TWO MORE GAMES, THEN GO TO BED.
THREE MORE GAMES.
WHAT'S MORE HUMAN THAN A BIRTHDAY?
A WAY TO REMIND YOURSELF THAT YOU ARE SPECIAL...
WE'LL SEE YOU TOMORROW.
...BY CELEBRATING YOUR MERE EXISTENCE.
SOPHIE? IT'S MINDEE. PLEASE DON'T DIE, OKAY? SOPHIE? PLEASE.
I AM NOT UNIQUE.
I'M SO UN-UNIQUE I SHARE GENETIC MATERIAL WITH AN ARMY OF KILLERS, MOST OF WHOM ARE DEAD, NOT UNLIKE THE CUCKOOS.

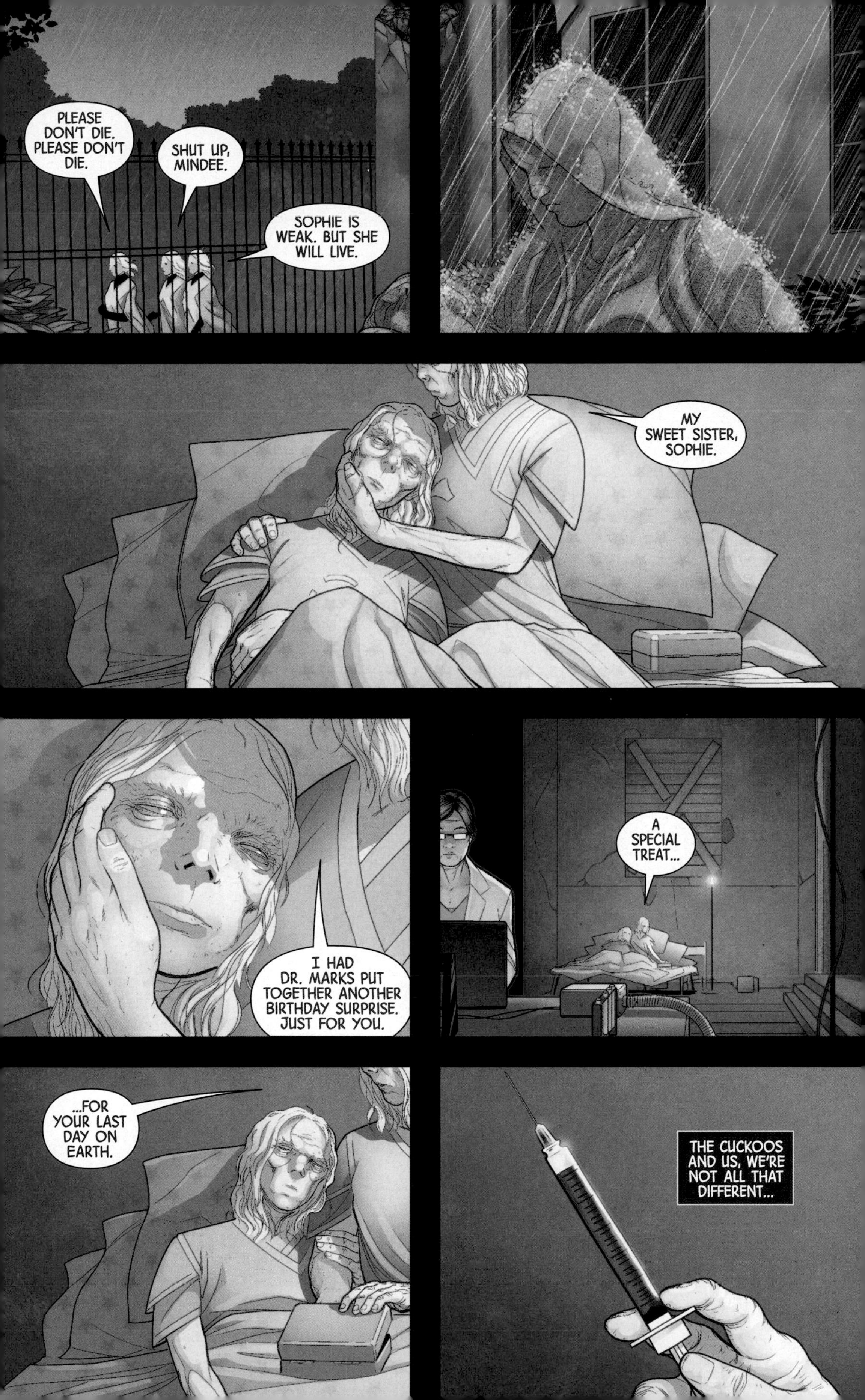
PLEASE DON'T DIE. PLEASE DON'T DIE.
SHUT UP, MINDEE.
SOPHIE IS WEAK. BUT SHE WILL LIVE.
MY SWEET SISTER, SOPHIE.
I HAD DR. MARKS PUT TOGETHER ANOTHER BIRTHDAY SURPRISE. JUST FOR YOU.
A SPECIAL TREAT...
...FOR YOUR LAST DAY ON EARTH.
THE CUCKOOS AND US, WE'RE NOT ALL THAT DIFFERENT...

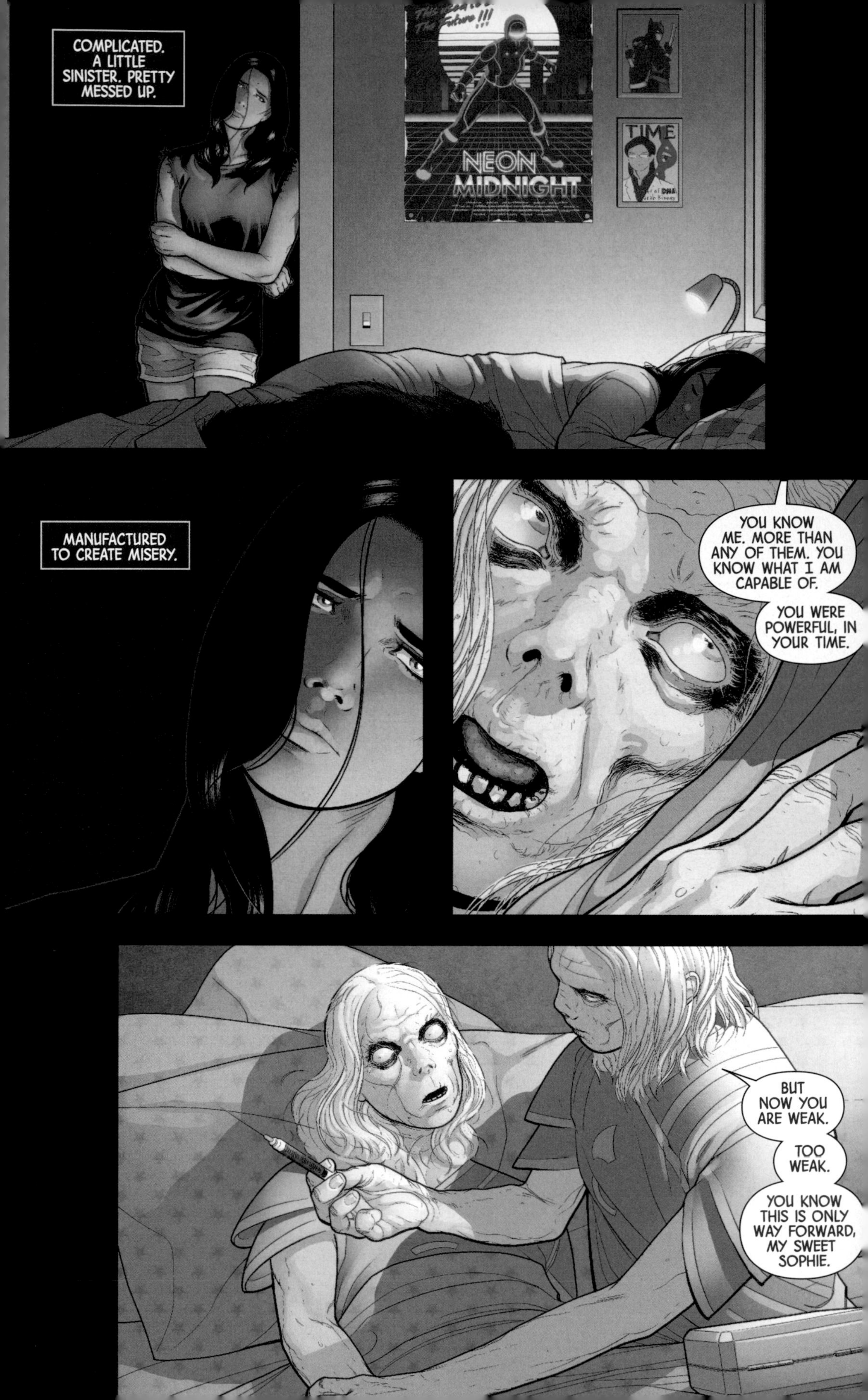
COMPLICATED. A LITTLE SINISTER. PRETTY MESSED UP.
NEON MIDNIGHT
TIME
MANUFACTURED TO CREATE MISERY.
YOU KNOW ME. MORE THAN ANY OF THEM. YOU KNOW WHAT I AM CAPABLE OF.
YOU WERE POWERFUL, IN YOUR TIME.
BUT NOW YOU ARE WEAK.
TOO WEAK.
YOU KNOW THIS IS ONLY WAY FORWARD, MY SWEET SOPHIE.

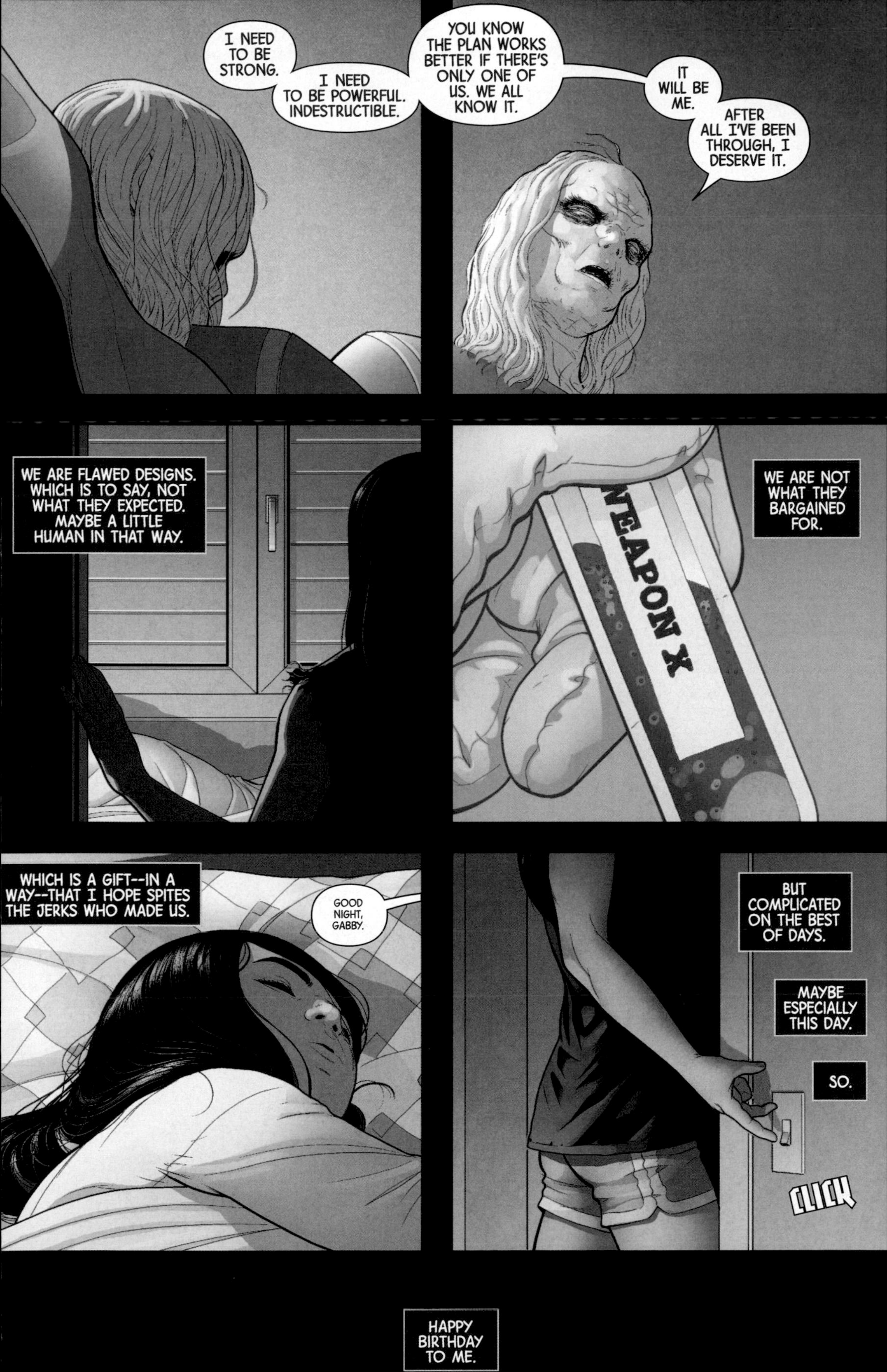
I NEED TO BE STRONG.
I NEED TO BE POWERFUL. INDESTRUCTIBLE.
YOU KNOW THE PLAN WORKS BETTER IF THERE'S ONLY ONE OF US. WE ALL KNOW IT.
IT WILL BE ME.
AFTER ALL I'VE BEEN THROUGH, I DESERVE IT.
WE ARE FLAWED DESIGNS. WHICH IS TO SAY, NOT WHAT THEY EXPECTED. MAYBE A LITTLE HUMAN IN THAT WAY.
WE ARE NOT WHAT THEY BARGAINED FOR.
WEAPON X
WHICH IS A GIFT--IN A WAY--THAT I HOPE SPITES THE JERKS WHO MADE US.
GOOD NIGHT, GABBY.
BUT COMPLICATED ON THE BEST OF DAYS.
MAYBE ESPECIALLY THIS DAY.
SO.
CLICK
HAPPY BIRTHDAY TO ME.

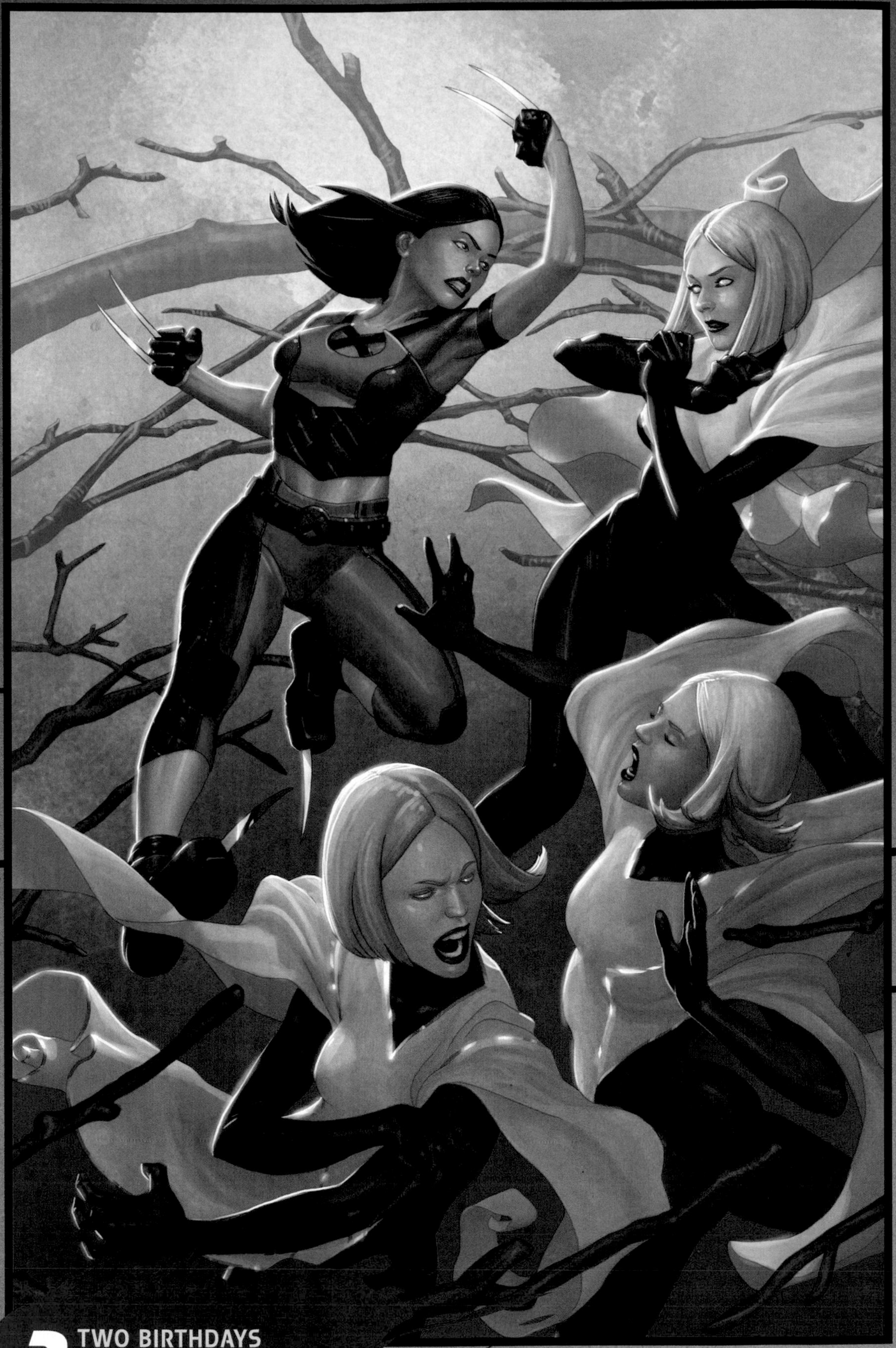

2 TWO BIRTHDAYS AND THREE FUNERALS
PART 2

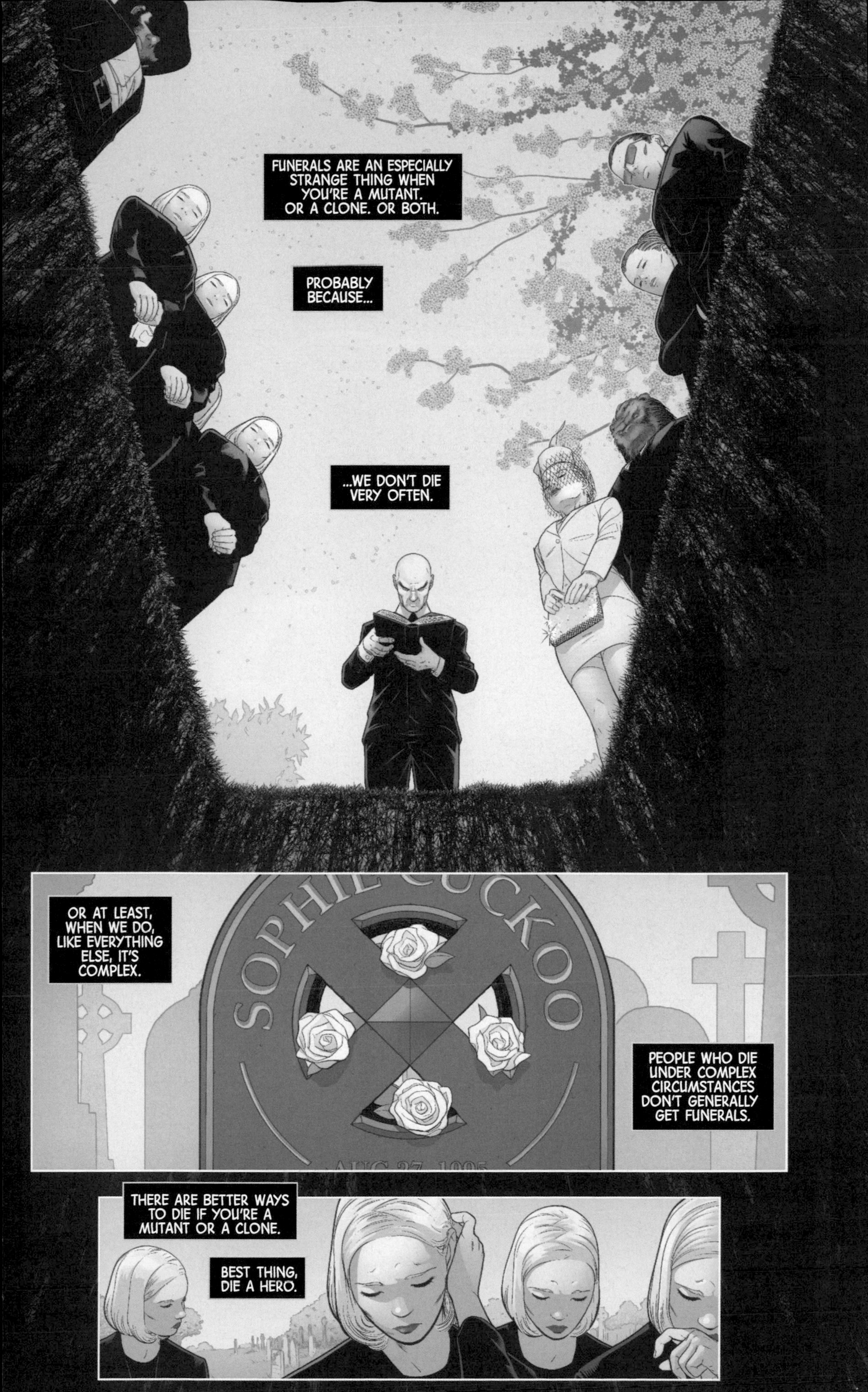
FUNERALS ARE AN ESPECIALLY STRANGE THING WHEN YOU'RE A MUTANT. OR A CLONE. OR BOTH.
PROBABLY BECAUSE...
...WE DON'T DIE VERY OFTEN.
OR AT LEAST, WHEN WE DO, LIKE EVERYTHING ELSE, IT'S COMPLEX.
SOPHIE CUCKOO
PEOPLE WHO DIE UNDER COMPLEX CIRCUMSTANCES DON'T GENERALLY GET FUNERALS.
THERE ARE BETTER WAYS TO DIE IF YOU'RE A MUTANT OR A CLONE.
BEST THING, DIE A HERO.

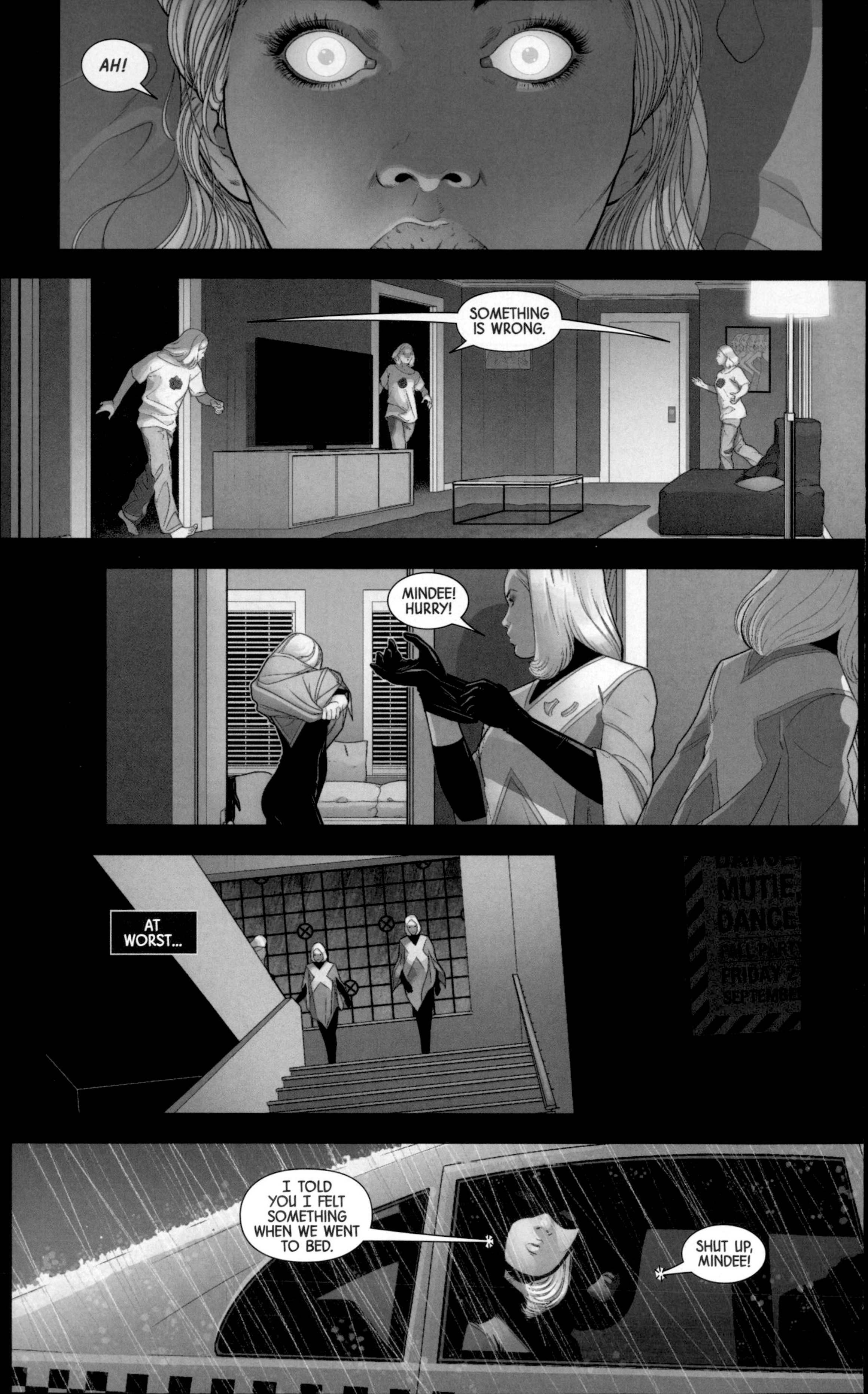
AH!
SOMETHING IS WRONG.
MINDEE! HURRY!
AT WORST...
I TOLD YOU I FELT SOMETHING WHEN WE WENT TO BED.
SHUT UP, MINDEE!

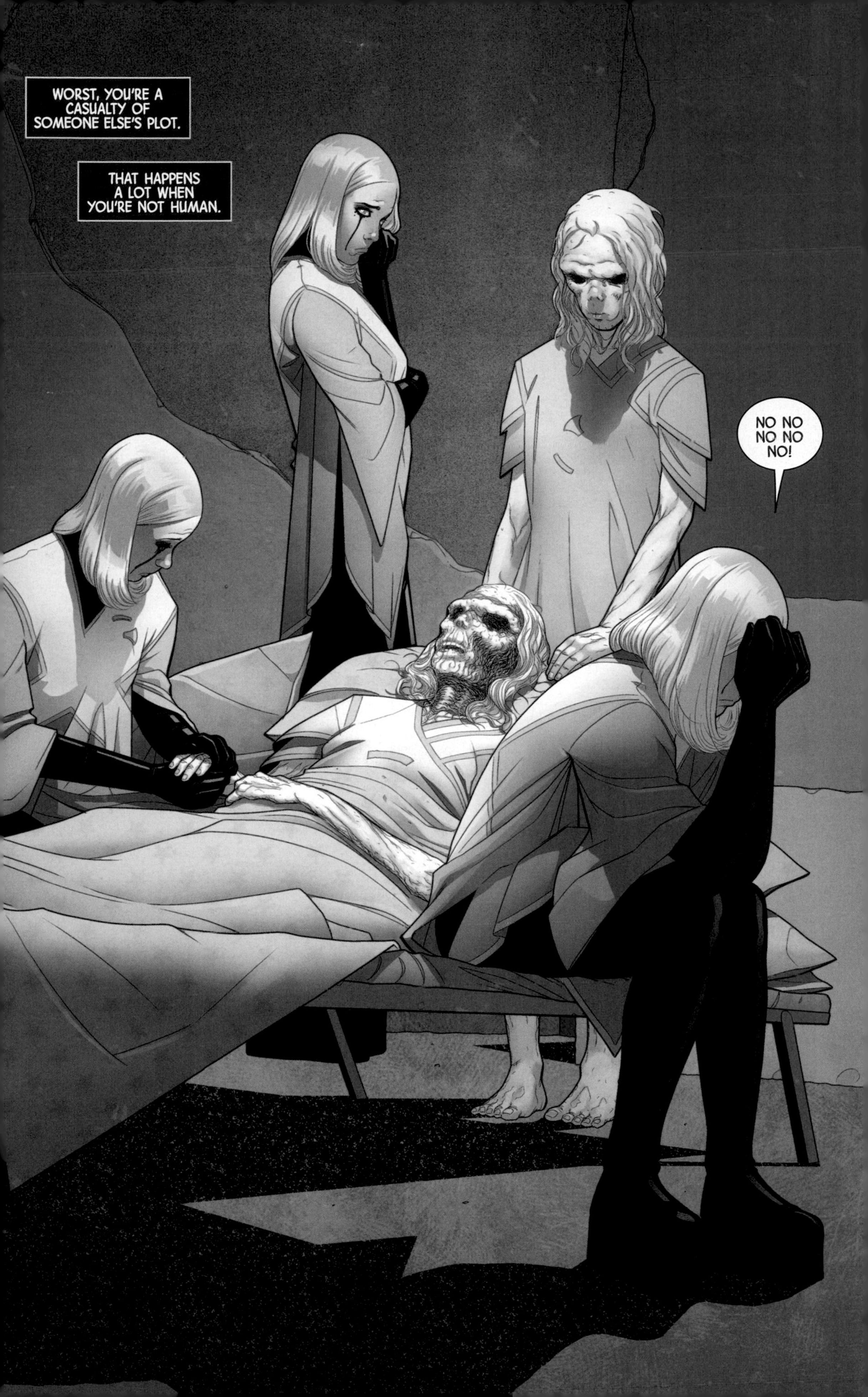
WORST, YOU'RE A CASUALTY OF SOMEONE ELSE'S PLOT.
THAT HAPPENS A LOT WHEN YOU'RE NOT HUMAN.
NO NO NO NO NO!

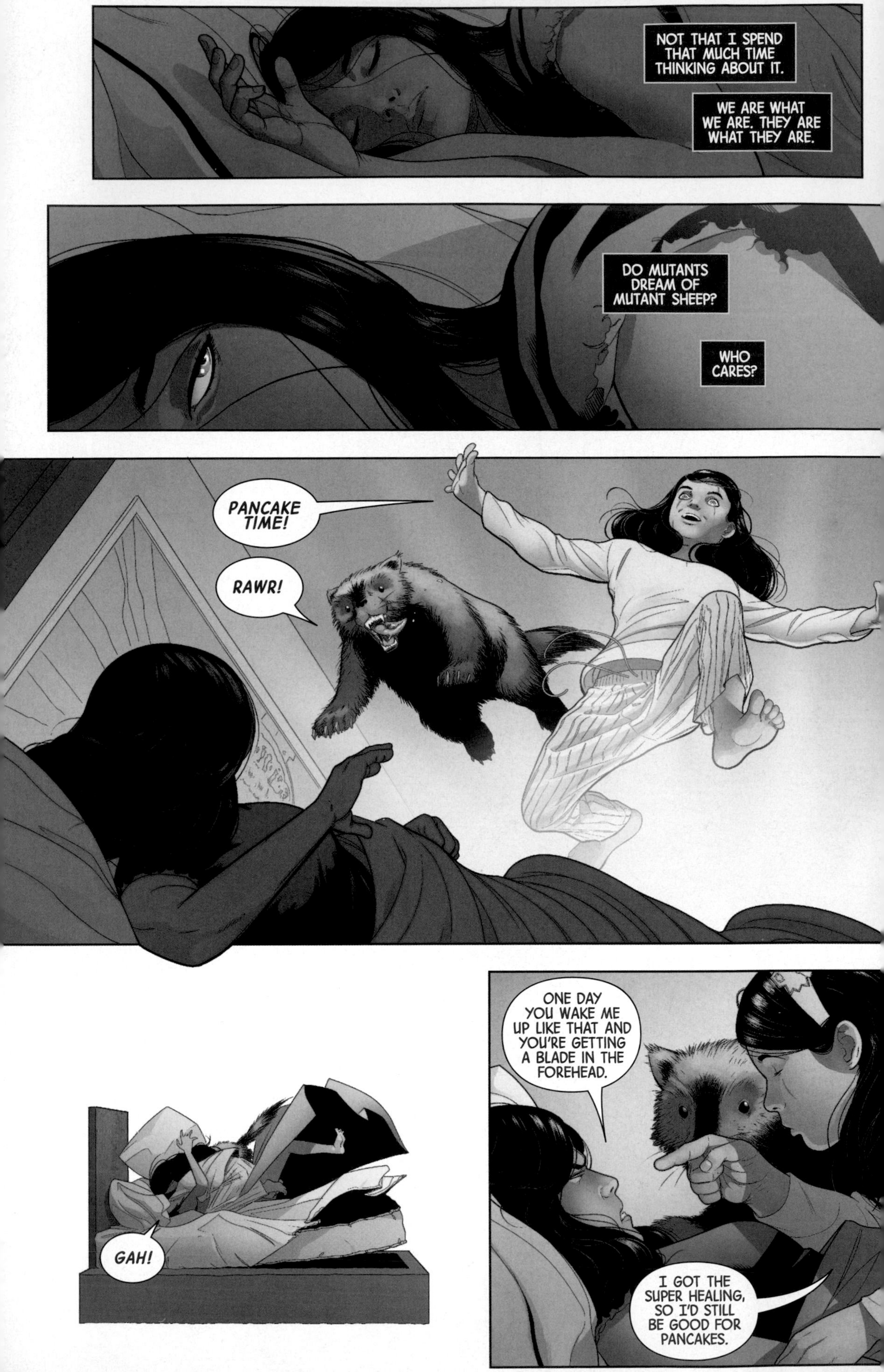
NOT THAT I SPEND THAT MUCH TIME THINKING ABOUT IT.
WE ARE WHAT WE ARE. THEY ARE WHAT THEY ARE.
DO MUTANTS DREAM OF MUTANT SHEEP?
WHO CARES?
PANCAKE TIME!
RAWR!
GAH!
ONE DAY YOU WAKE ME UP LIKE THAT AND YOU'RE GETTING A BLADE IN THE FOREHEAD.
I GOT THE SUPER HEALING, SO I'D STILL BE GOOD FOR PANCAKES.

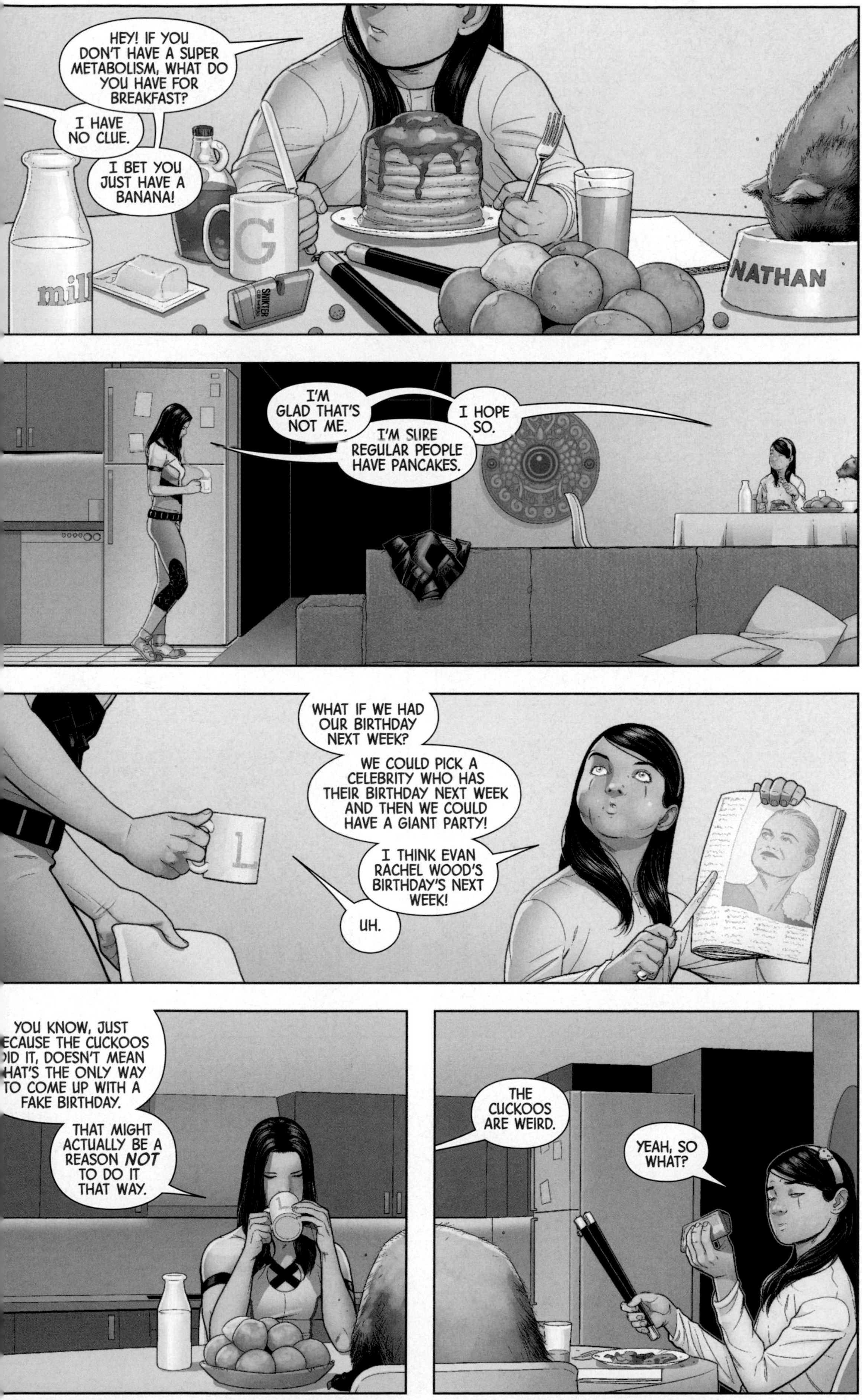
HEY! IF YOU DON'T HAVE A SUPER METABOLISM, WHAT DO YOU HAVE FOR BREAKFAST?
I HAVE NO CLUE.
I BET YOU JUST HAVE A BANANA!
NATHAN
I'M GLAD THAT'S NOT ME.
I HOPE SO.
I'M SURE REGULAR PEOPLE HAVE PANCAKES.
WHAT IF WE HAD OUR BIRTHDAY NEXT WEEK?
WE COULD PICK A CELEBRITY WHO HAS THEIR BIRTHDAY NEXT WEEK AND THEN WE COULD HAVE A GIANT PARTY!
I THINK EVAN RACHEL WOOD'S BIRTHDAY'S NEXT WEEK!
UH.
YOU KNOW, JUST BECAUSE THE CUCKOOS DID IT, DOESN'T MEAN THAT'S THE ONLY WAY TO COME UP WITH A FAKE BIRTHDAY.
THAT MIGHT ACTUALLY BE A REASON NOT TO DO IT THAT WAY.
THE CUCKOOS ARE WEIRD.
YEAH, SO WHAT?

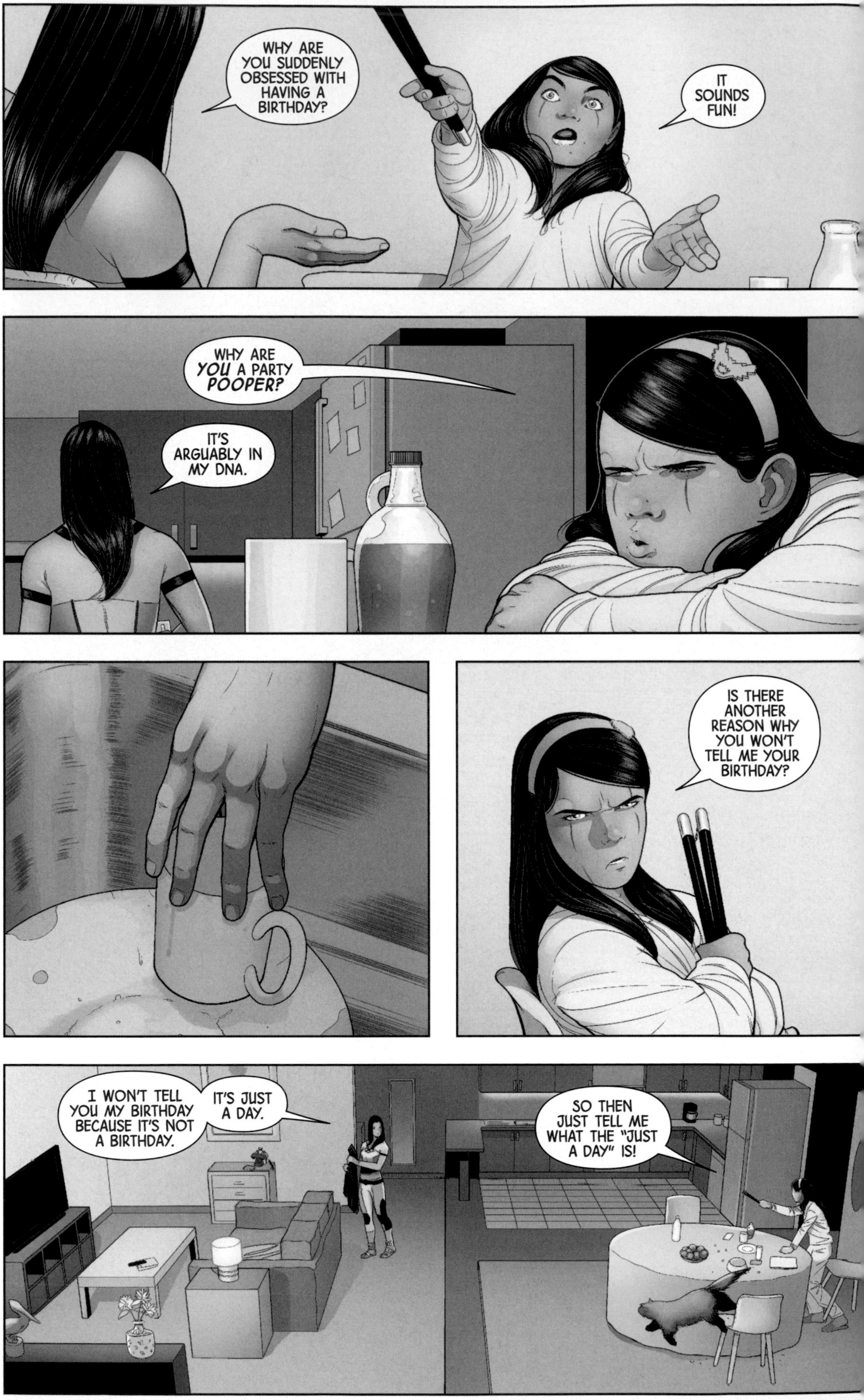
WHY ARE YOU SUDDENLY OBSESSED WITH HAVING A BIRTHDAY?
IT SOUNDS FUN!
WHY ARE YOU A PARTY POOPER?
IT'S ARGUABLY IN MY DNA.
IS THERE ANOTHER REASON WHY YOU WON'T TELL ME YOUR BIRTHDAY?
I WON'T TELL YOU MY BIRTHDAY BECAUSE IT'S NOT A BIRTHDAY.
IT'S JUST A DAY.
SO THEN JUST TELL ME WHAT THE "JUST A DAY" IS!

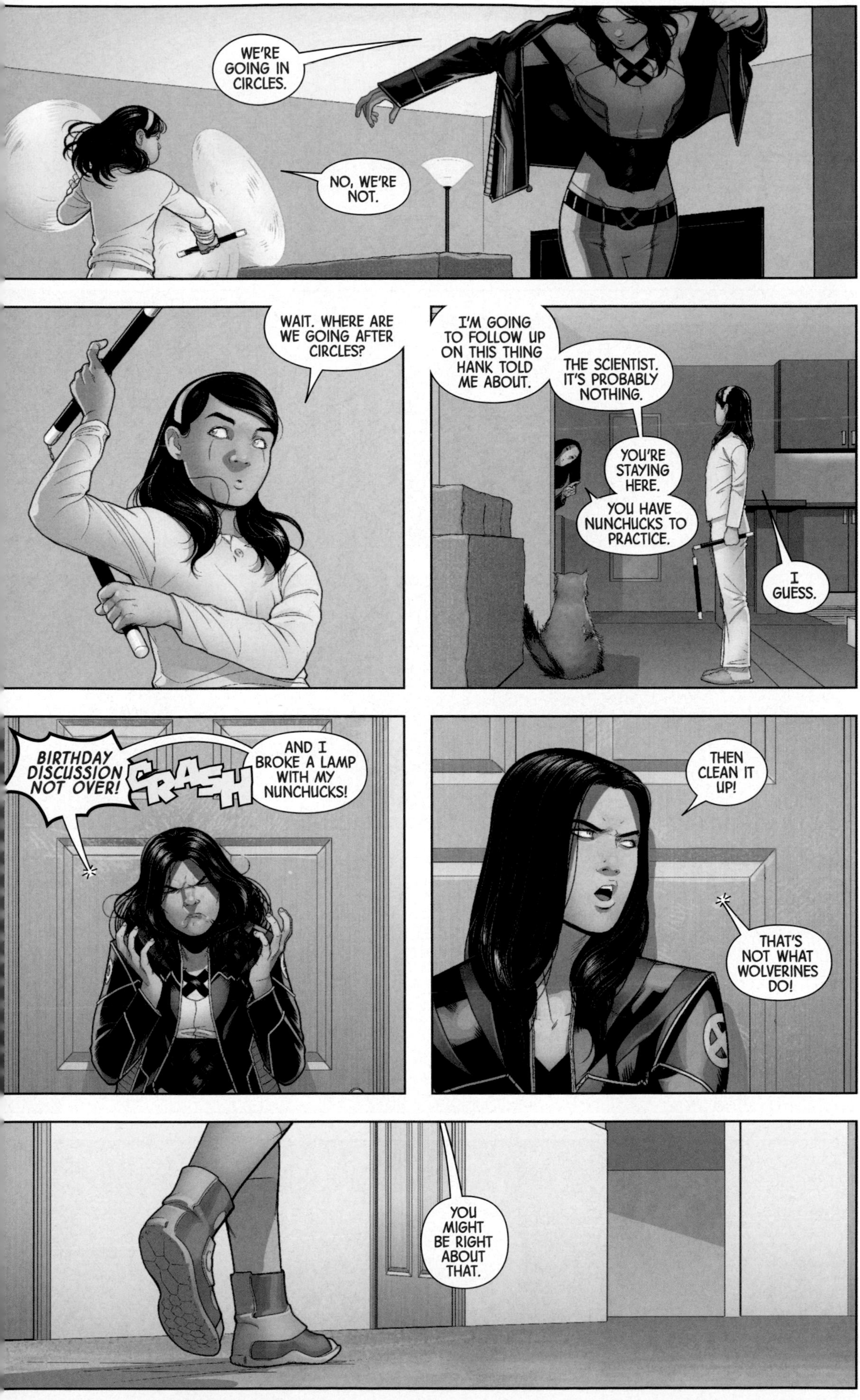

WE'RE GOING IN CIRCLES.
NO, WE'RE NOT.
WAIT. WHERE ARE WE GOING AFTER CIRCLES?
I'M GOING TO FOLLOW UP ON THIS THING HANK TOLD ME ABOUT.
THE SCIENTIST. IT'S PROBABLY NOTHING.
YOU'RE STAYING HERE.
YOU HAVE NUNCHUCKS TO PRACTICE.
I GUESS.
CRASH
AND I BROKE A LAMP WITH MY NUNCHUCKS!
BIRTHDAY DISCUSSION NOT OVER!
THEN CLEAN IT UP!
THAT'S NOT WHAT WOLVERINES DO!
YOU MIGHT BE RIGHT ABOUT THAT.

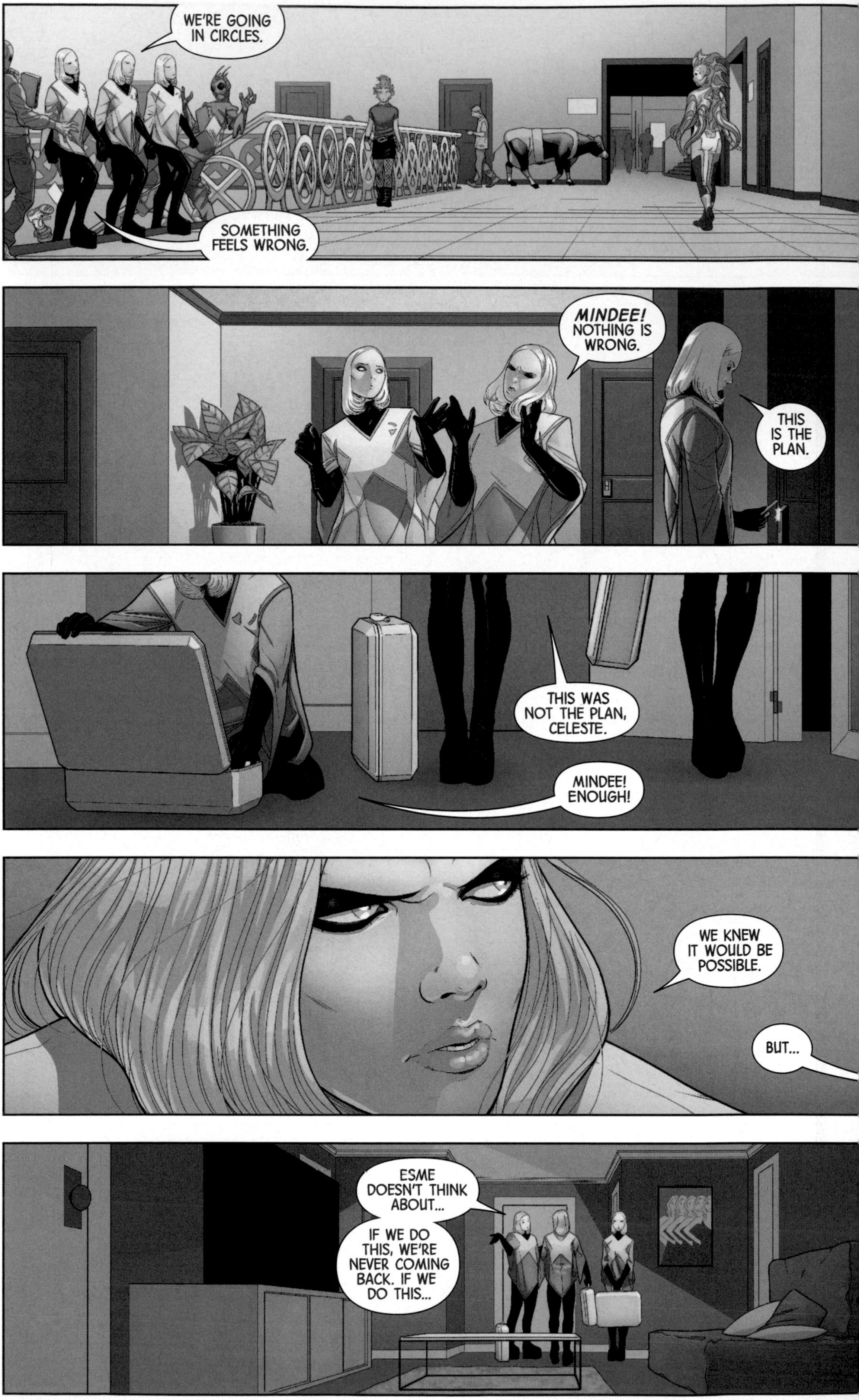
WE'RE GOING IN CIRCLES.
SOMETHING FEELS WRONG.
MINDEE! NOTHING IS WRONG.
THIS IS THE PLAN.
THIS WAS NOT THE PLAN, CELESTE.
MINDEE! ENOUGH!
WE KNEW IT WOULD BE POSSIBLE.
BUT...
ESME DOESN'T THINK ABOUT...
IF WE DO THIS, WE'RE NEVER COMING BACK. IF WE DO THIS...

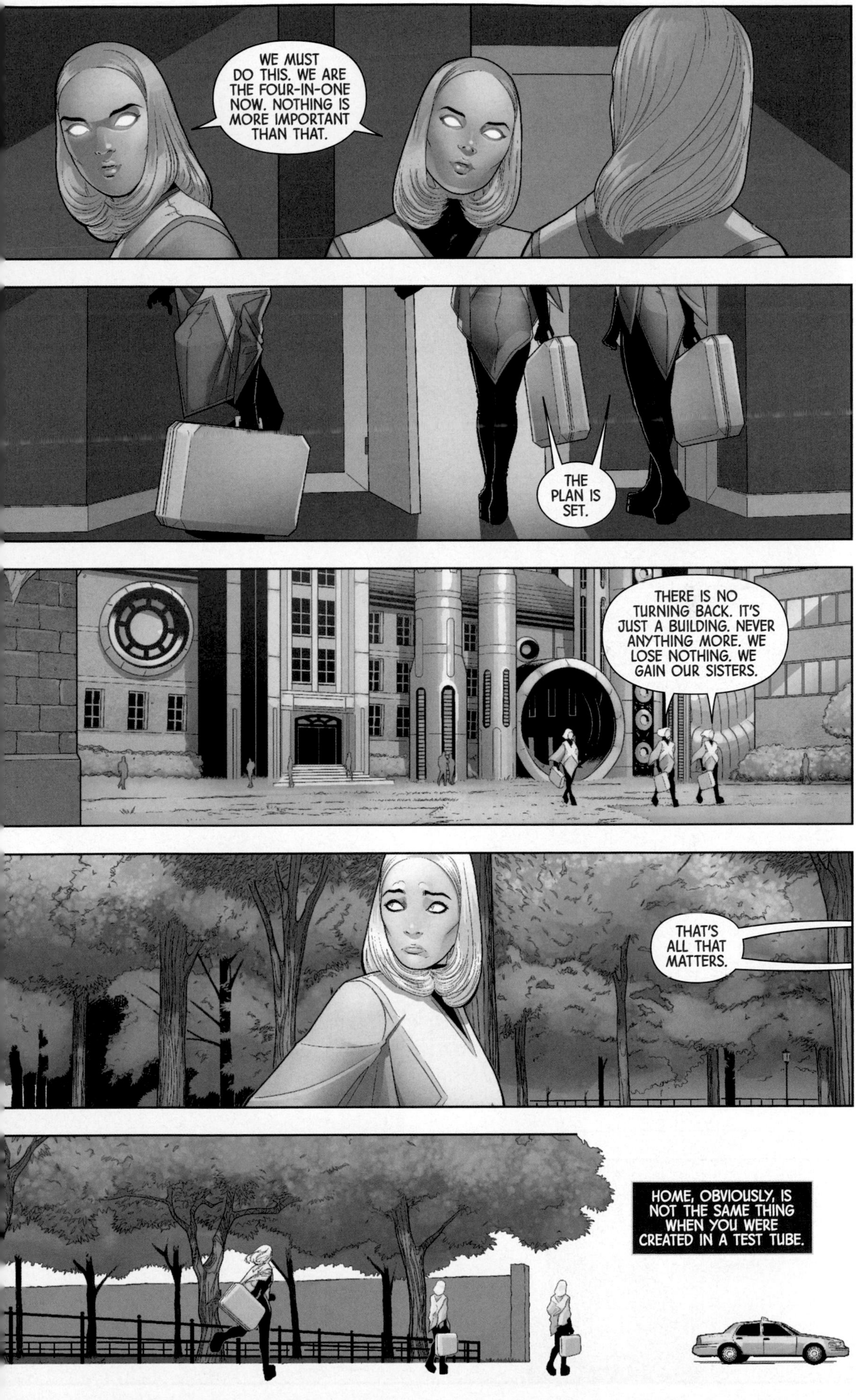
WE MUST DO THIS. WE ARE THE FOUR-IN-ONE NOW. NOTHING IS MORE IMPORTANT THAN THAT.
THE PLAN IS SET.
THERE IS NO TURNING BACK. IT'S JUST A BUILDING. NEVER ANYTHING MORE. WE LOSE NOTHING. WE GAIN OUR SISTERS.
THAT'S ALL THAT MATTERS.
HOME, OBVIOUSLY, IS NOT THE SAME THING WHEN YOU WERE CREATED IN A TEST TUBE.

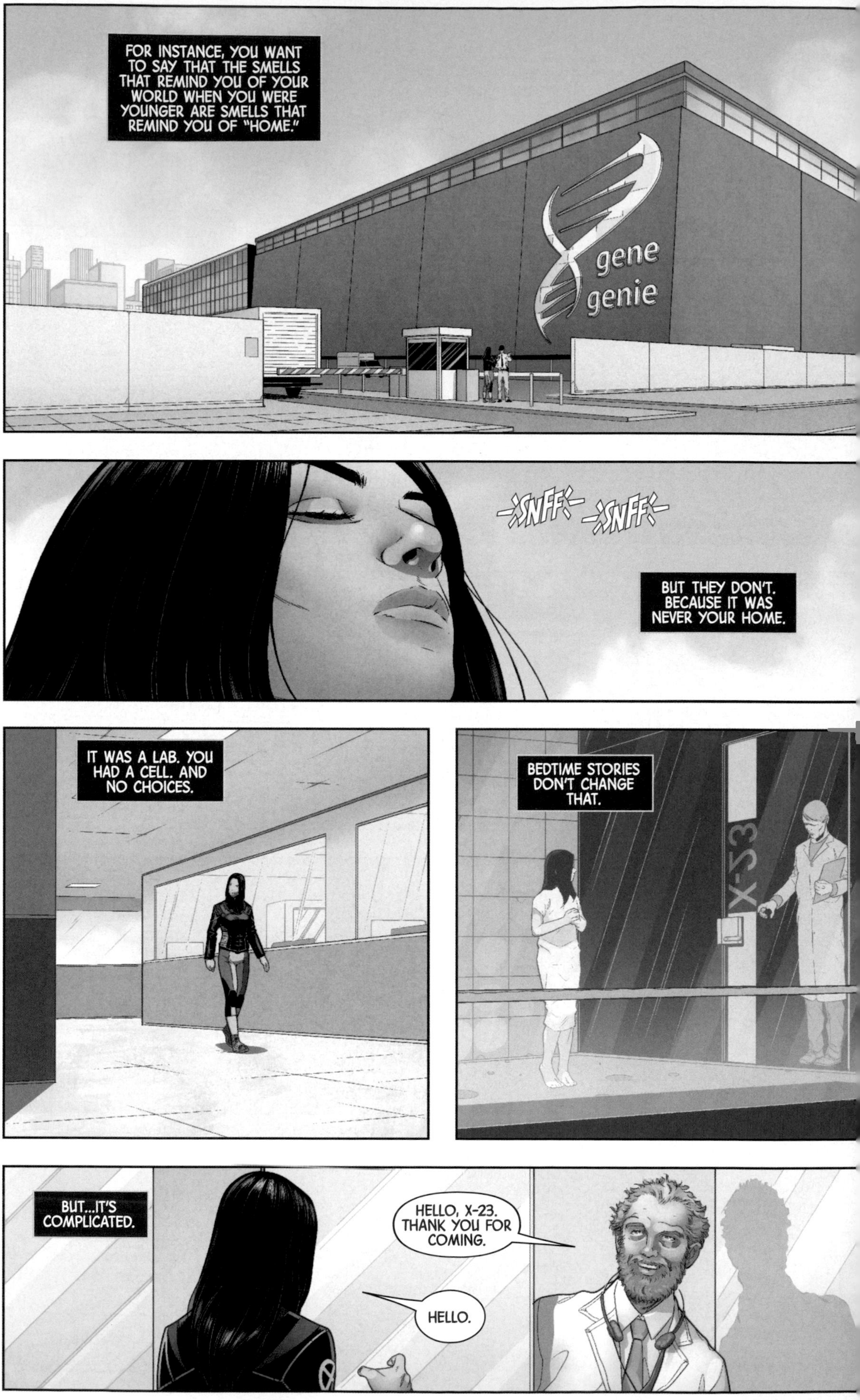
FOR INSTANCE, YOU WANT TO SAY THAT THE SMELLS THAT REMIND YOU OF YOUR WORLD WHEN YOU WERE YOUNGER ARE SMELLS THAT REMIND YOU OF "HOME."
gene genie
SNFF SNFF
BUT THEY DON'T. BECAUSE IT WAS NEVER YOUR HOME.
IT WAS A LAB. YOU HAD A CELL. AND NO CHOICES.
BEDTIME STORIES DON'T CHANGE THAT.
X-53
BUT...IT'S COMPLICATED.
HELLO, X-23. THANK YOU FOR COMING.
HELLO.

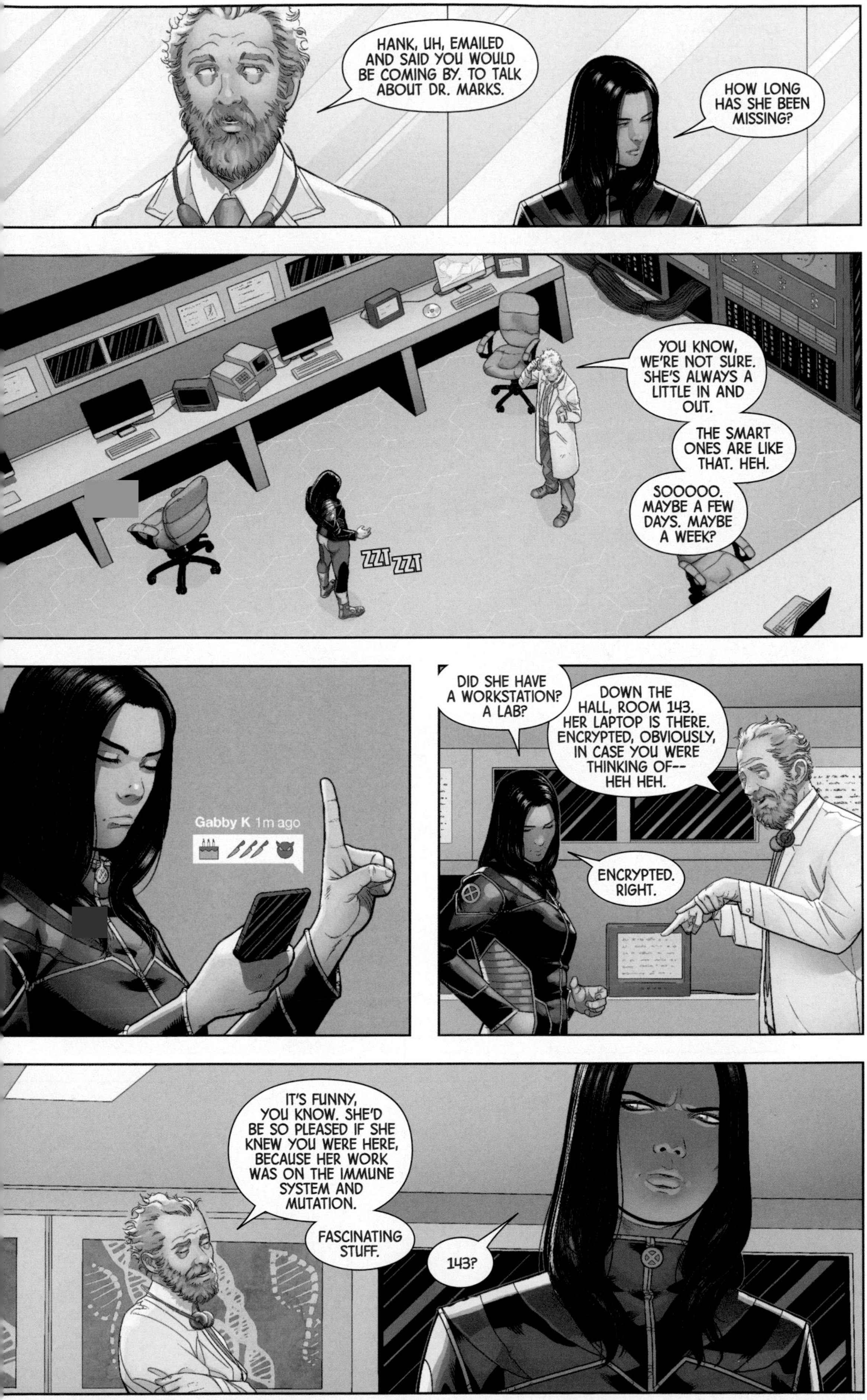
HANK, UH, EMAILED AND SAID YOU WOULD BE COMING BY. TO TALK ABOUT DR. MARKS.
HOW LONG HAS SHE BEEN MISSING?
YOU KNOW, WE'RE NOT SURE. SHE'S ALWAYS A LITTLE IN AND OUT.
THE SMART ONES ARE LIKE THAT. HEH.
SOOOOO. MAYBE A FEW DAYS. MAYBE A WEEK?
ZZZT ZZZT
Gabby K 1m ago
DID SHE HAVE A WORKSTATION? A LAB?
DOWN THE HALL, ROOM 143. HER LAPTOP IS THERE. ENCRYPTED, OBVIOUSLY, IN CASE YOU WERE THINKING OF-- HEH HEH.
ENCRYPTED. RIGHT.
IT'S FUNNY, YOU KNOW. SHE'D BE SO PLEASED IF SHE KNEW YOU WERE HERE, BECAUSE HER WORK WAS ON THE IMMUNE SYSTEM AND MUTATION.
FASCINATING STUFF.
143?

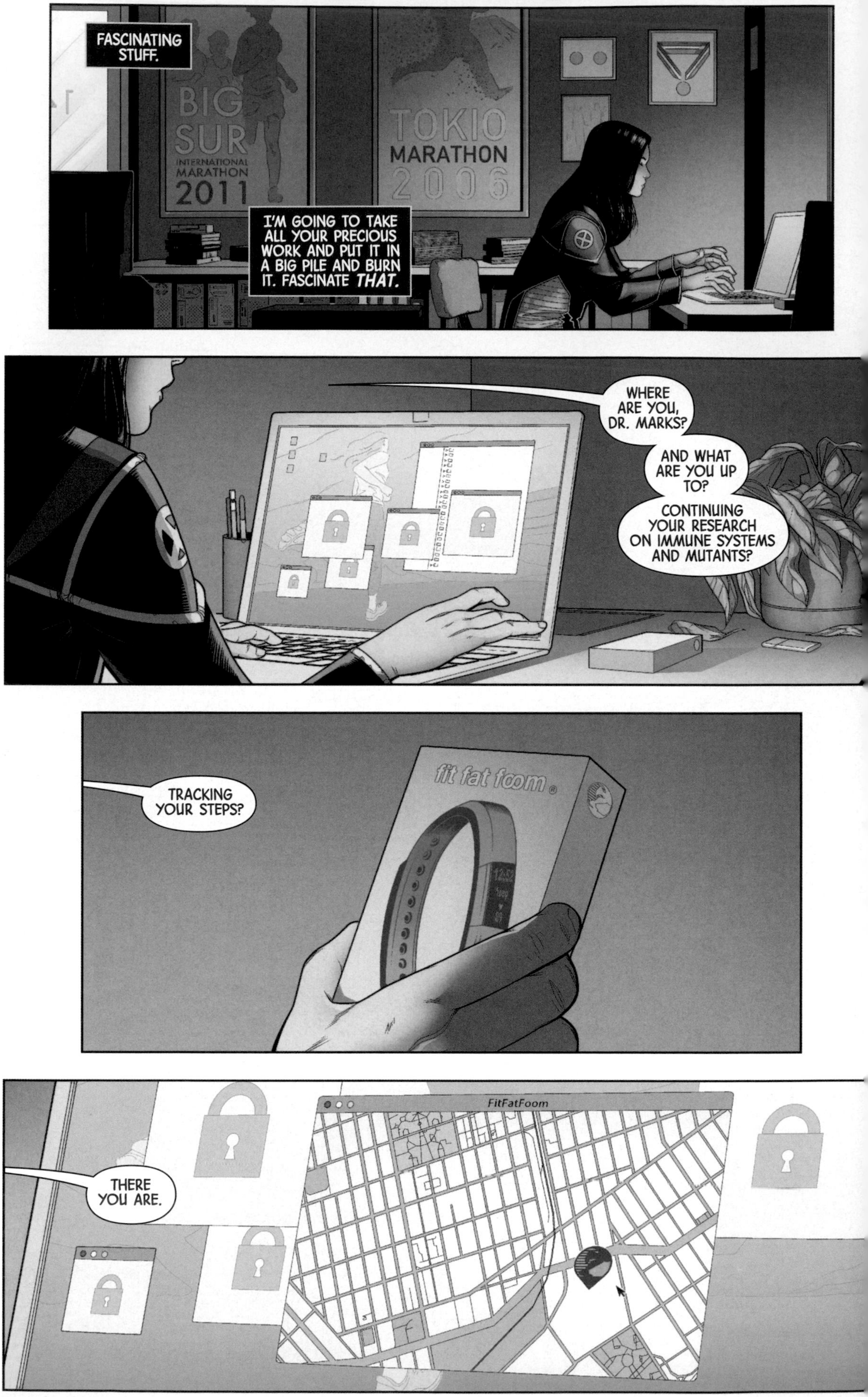
FASCINATING STUFF.
BIG SUR INTERNATIONAL MARATHON 2011
TOKIO MARATHON 2006
I'M GOING TO TAKE ALL YOUR PRECIOUS WORK AND PUT IT IN A BIG PILE AND BURN IT. FASCINATE *THAT.*
WHERE ARE YOU, DR. MARKS?
AND WHAT ARE YOU UP TO?
CONTINUING YOUR RESEARCH ON IMMUNE SYSTEMS AND MUTANTS?
fit fat foom
TRACKING YOUR STEPS?
FitFatFoom
THERE YOU ARE.

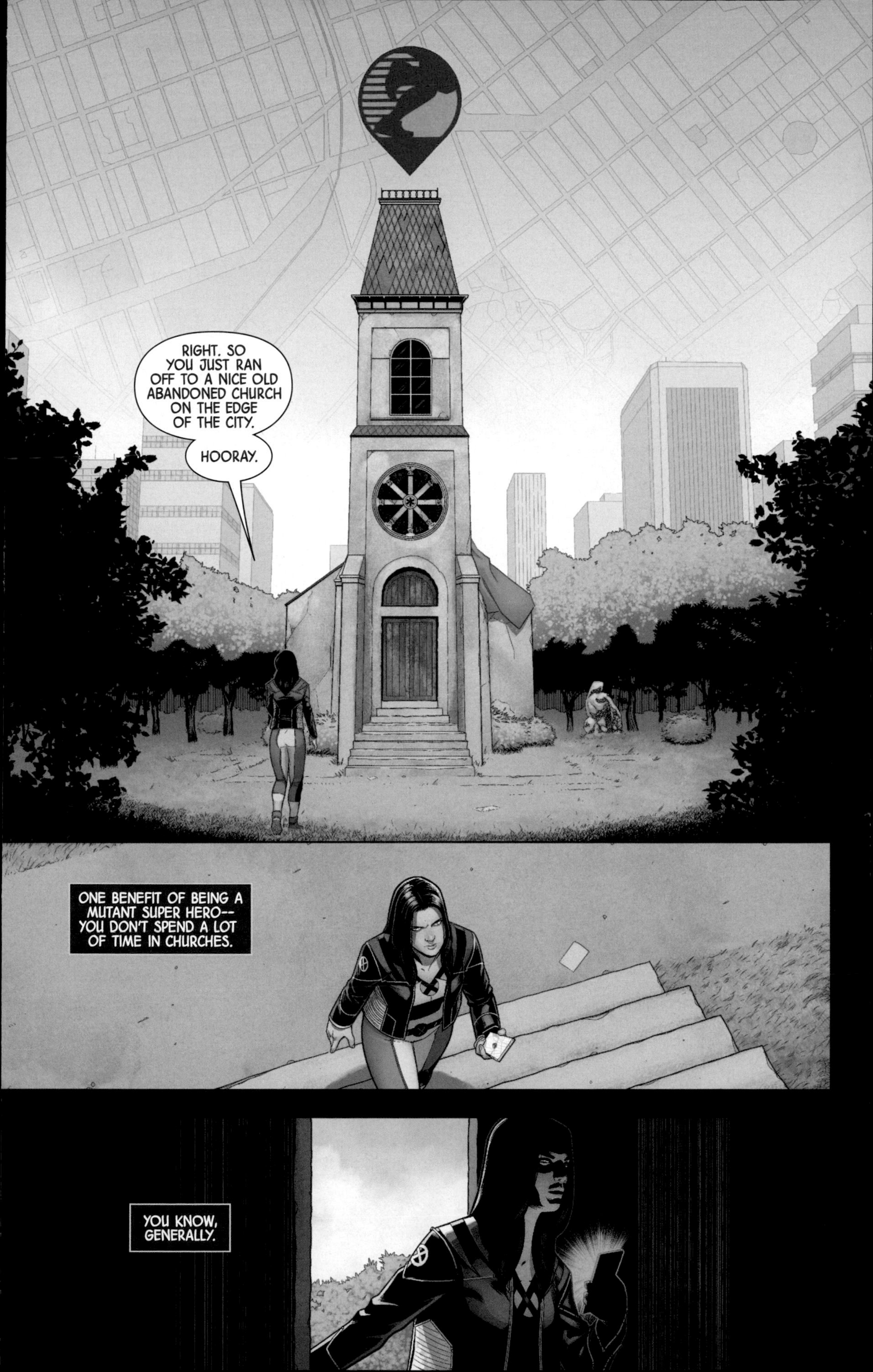
RIGHT. SO YOU JUST RAN OFF TO A NICE OLD ABANDONED CHURCH ON THE EDGE OF THE CITY.
HOORAY.
ONE BENEFIT OF BEING A MUTANT SUPER HERO-- YOU DON'T SPEND A LOT OF TIME IN CHURCHES.
YOU KNOW, GENERALLY.

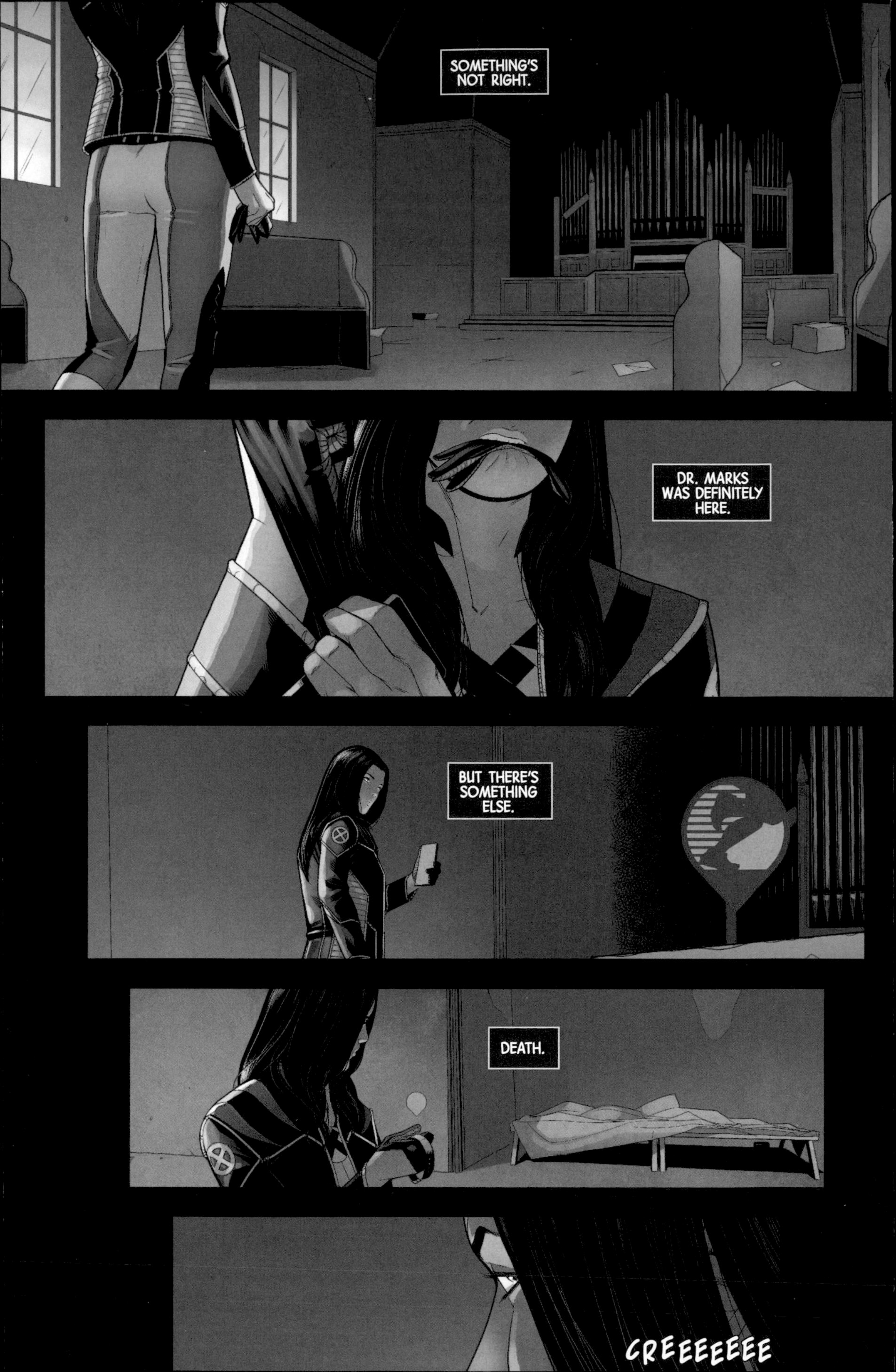
SOMETHING'S NOT RIGHT.
DR. MARKS WAS DEFINITELY HERE.
BUT THERE'S SOMETHING ELSE.
DEATH.
CREEEEEEE

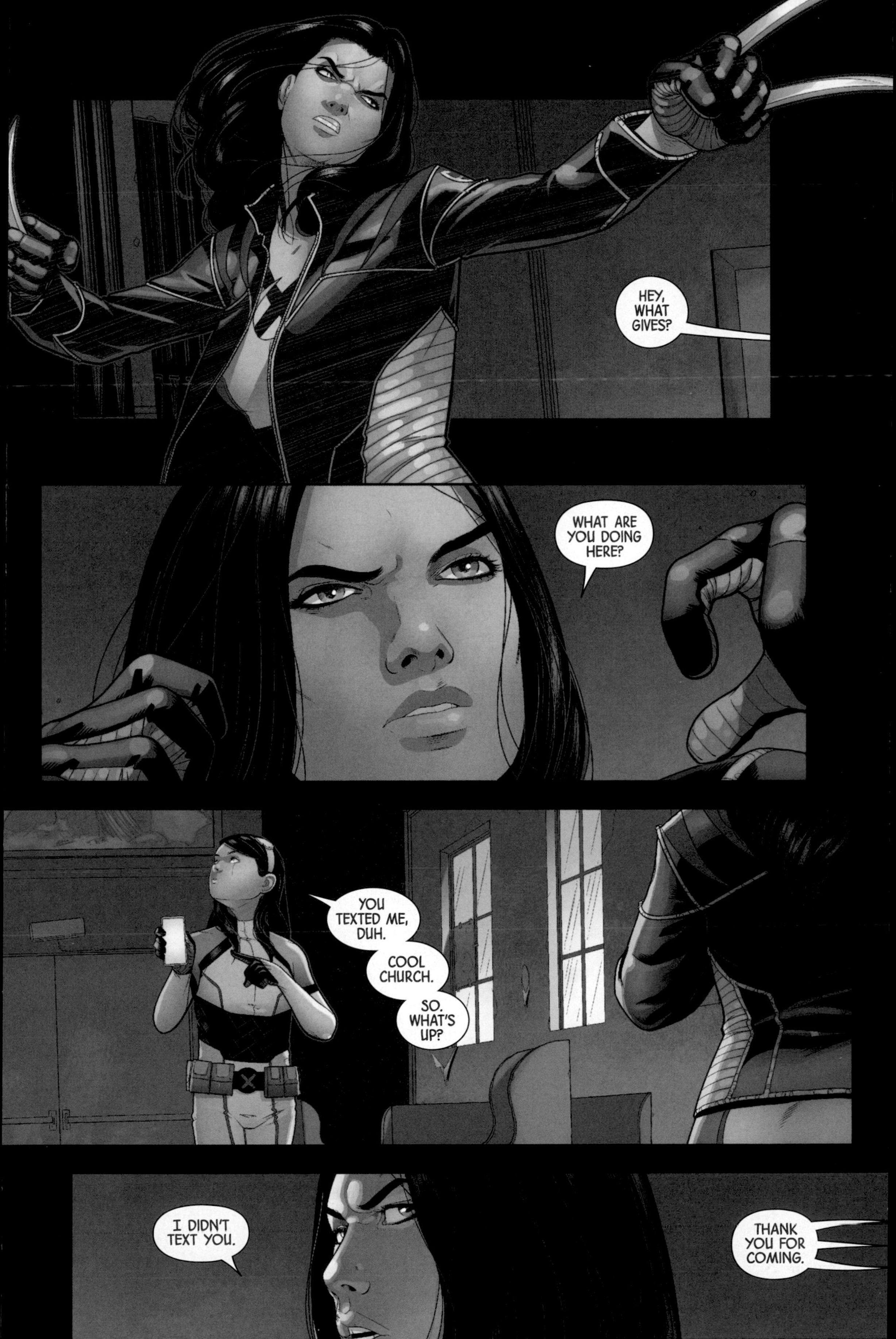
HEY, WHAT GIVES?
WHAT ARE YOU DOING HERE?
YOU TEXTED ME, DUH.
COOL CHURCH.
SO. WHAT'S UP?
I DIDN'T TEXT YOU.
THANK YOU FOR COMING.

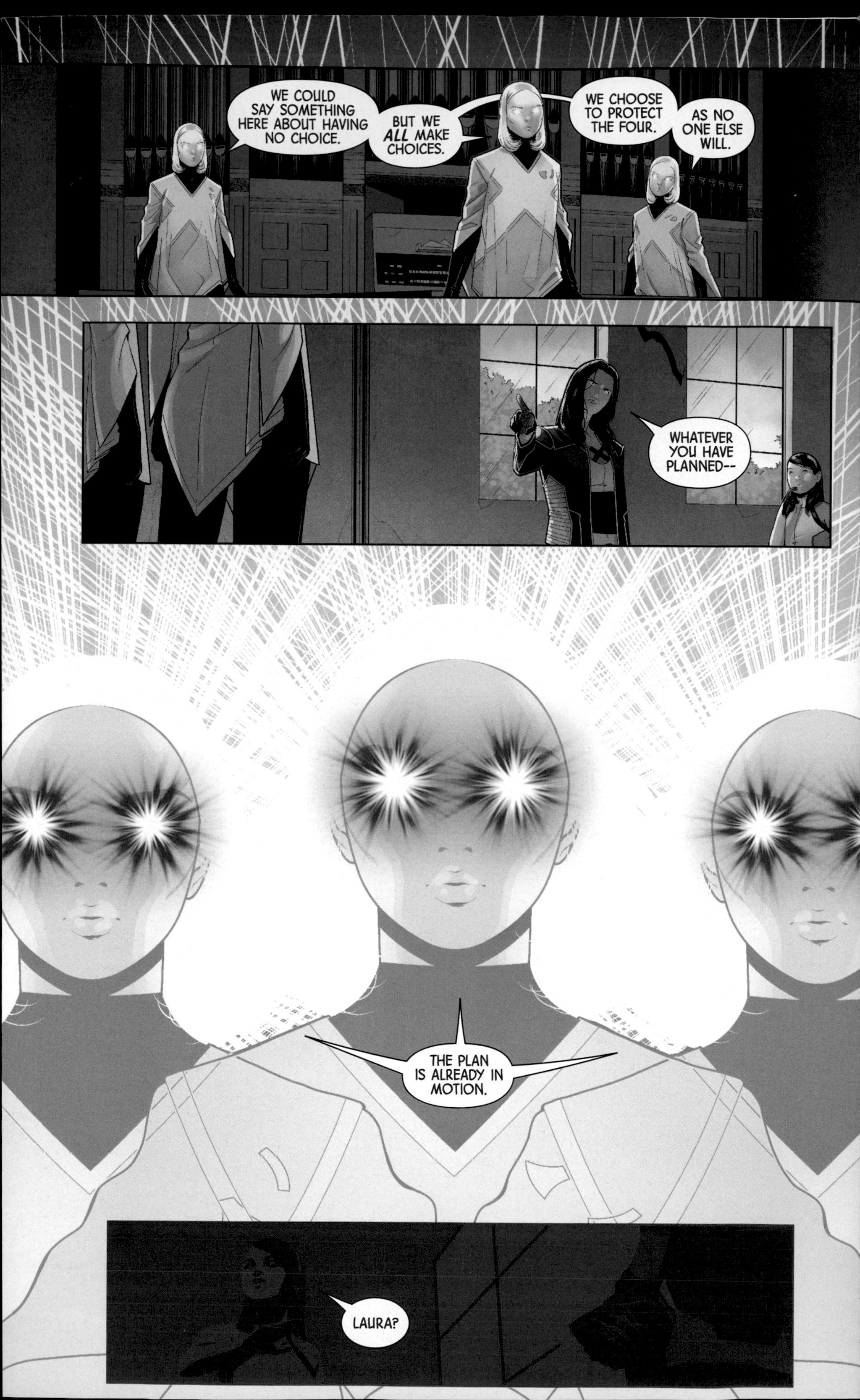
WE COULD SAY SOMETHING HERE ABOUT HAVING NO CHOICE.
BUT WE ALL MAKE CHOICES.
WE CHOOSE TO PROTECT THE FOUR.
AS NO ONE ELSE WILL.
WHATEVER YOU HAVE PLANNED--
THE PLAN IS ALREADY IN MOTION.
LAURA?

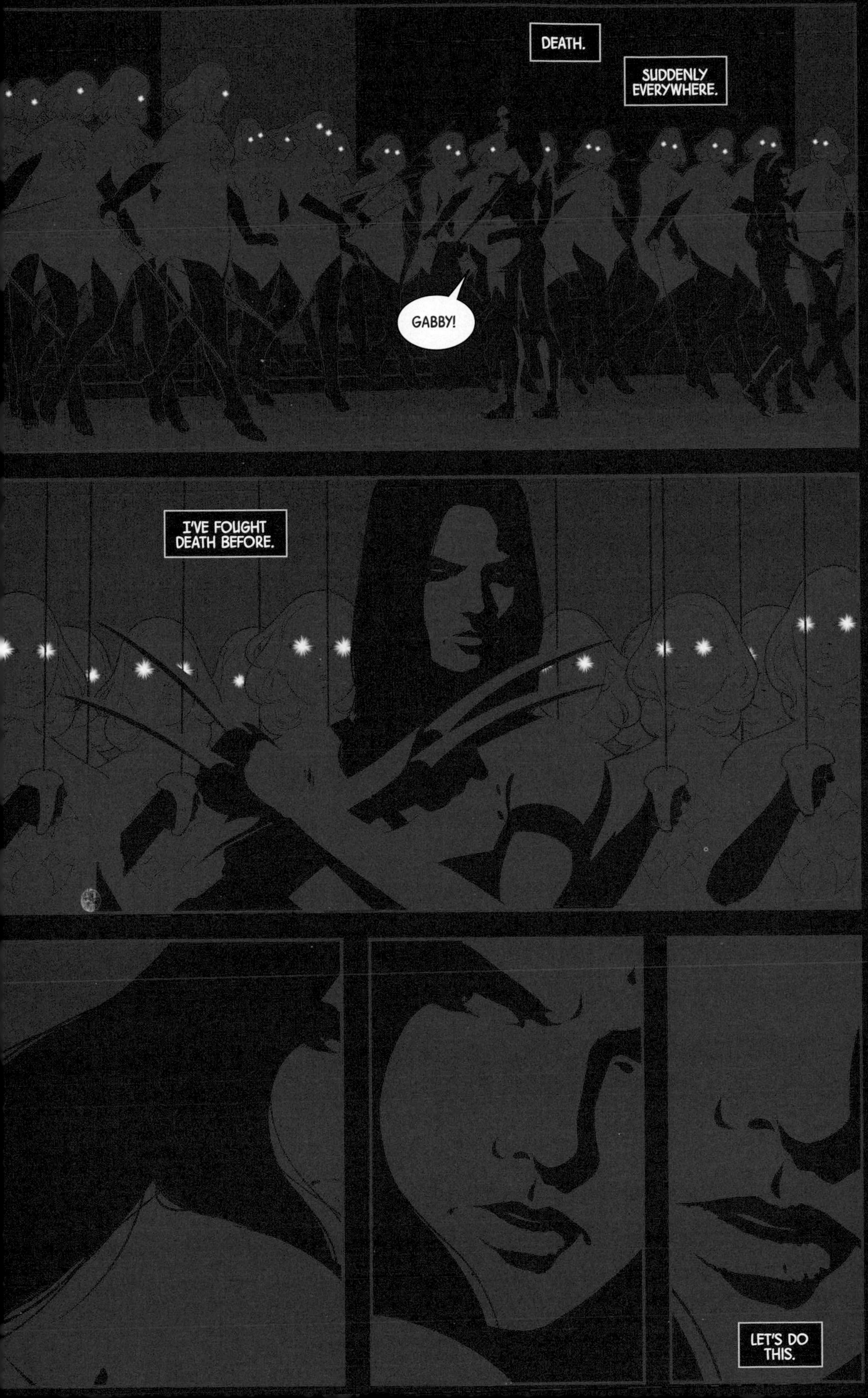
DEATH.
SUDDENLY EVERYWHERE.
GABBY!
I'VE FOUGHT DEATH BEFORE.
LET'S DO THIS.

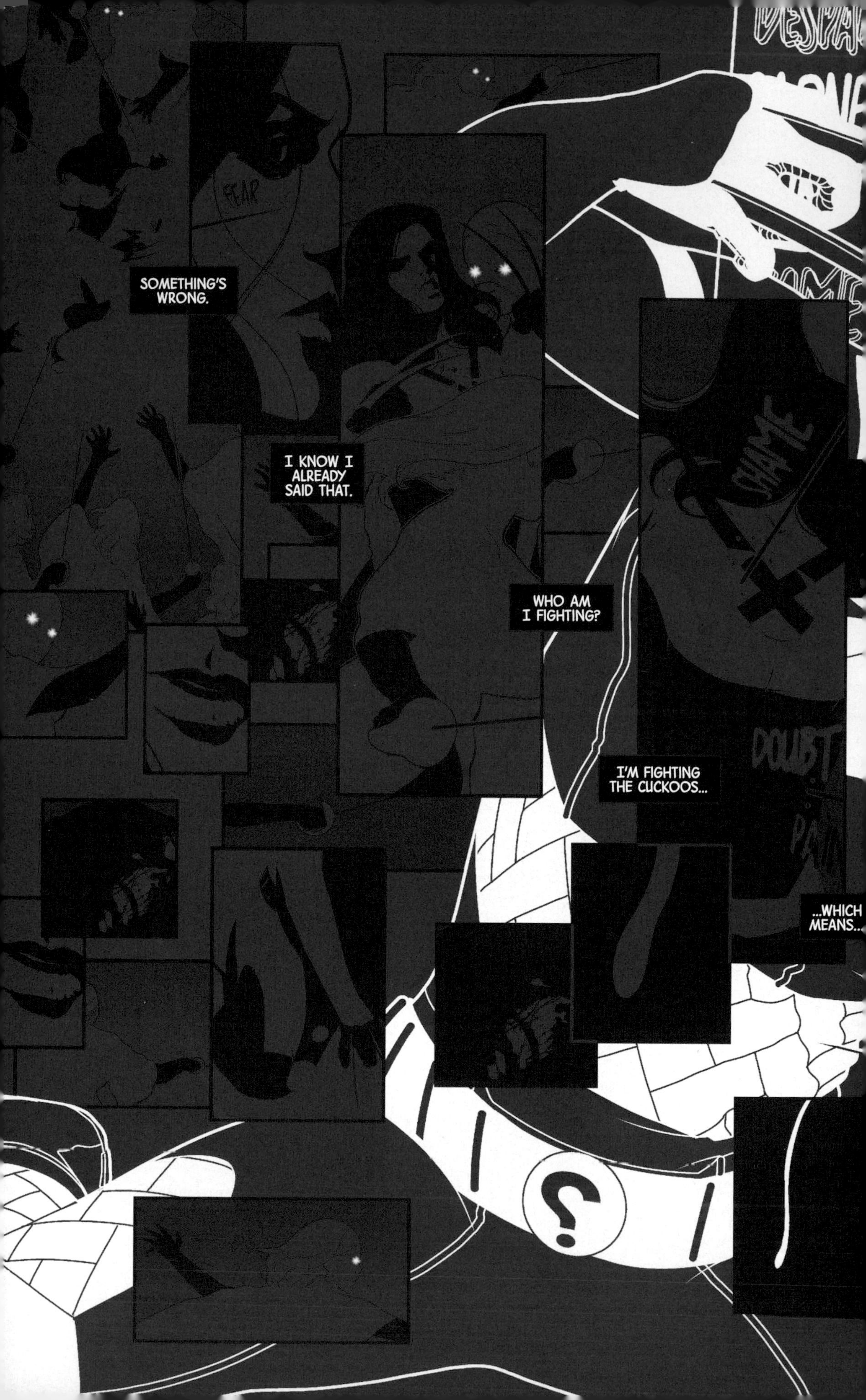
SOMETHING'S WRONG.
I KNOW I ALREADY SAID THAT.
WHO AM I FIGHTING?
I'M FIGHTING THE CUCKOOS...
...WHICH MEANS...
FEAR
SHAME
DOUBT

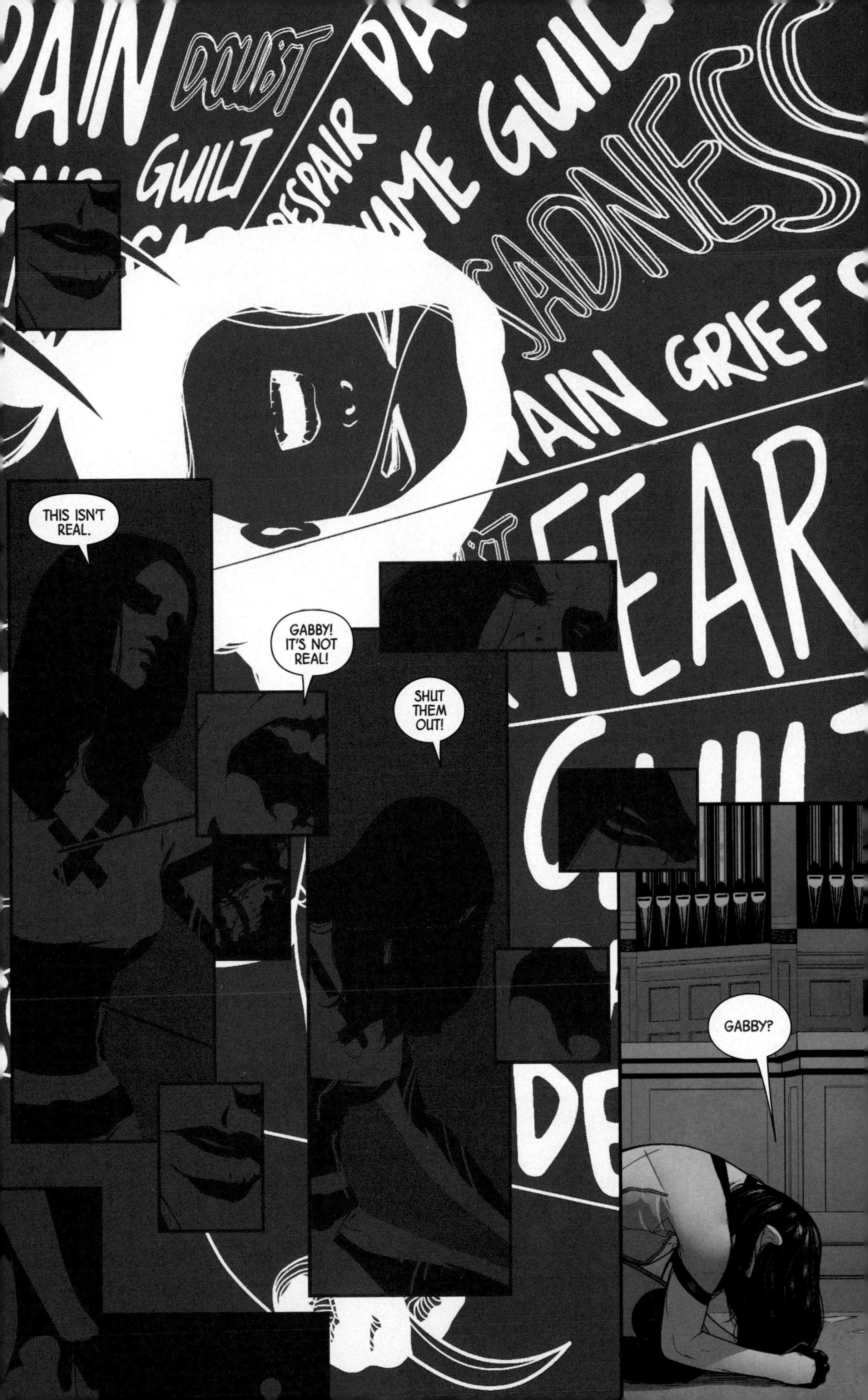

PAIN
DOUBT
GUILT
DESPAIR
PA
SHAME GUIL
SADNESS
PAIN GRIEF
FEAR
THIS ISN'T REAL.
GABBY! IT'S NOT REAL!
SHUT THEM OUT!
GABBY?

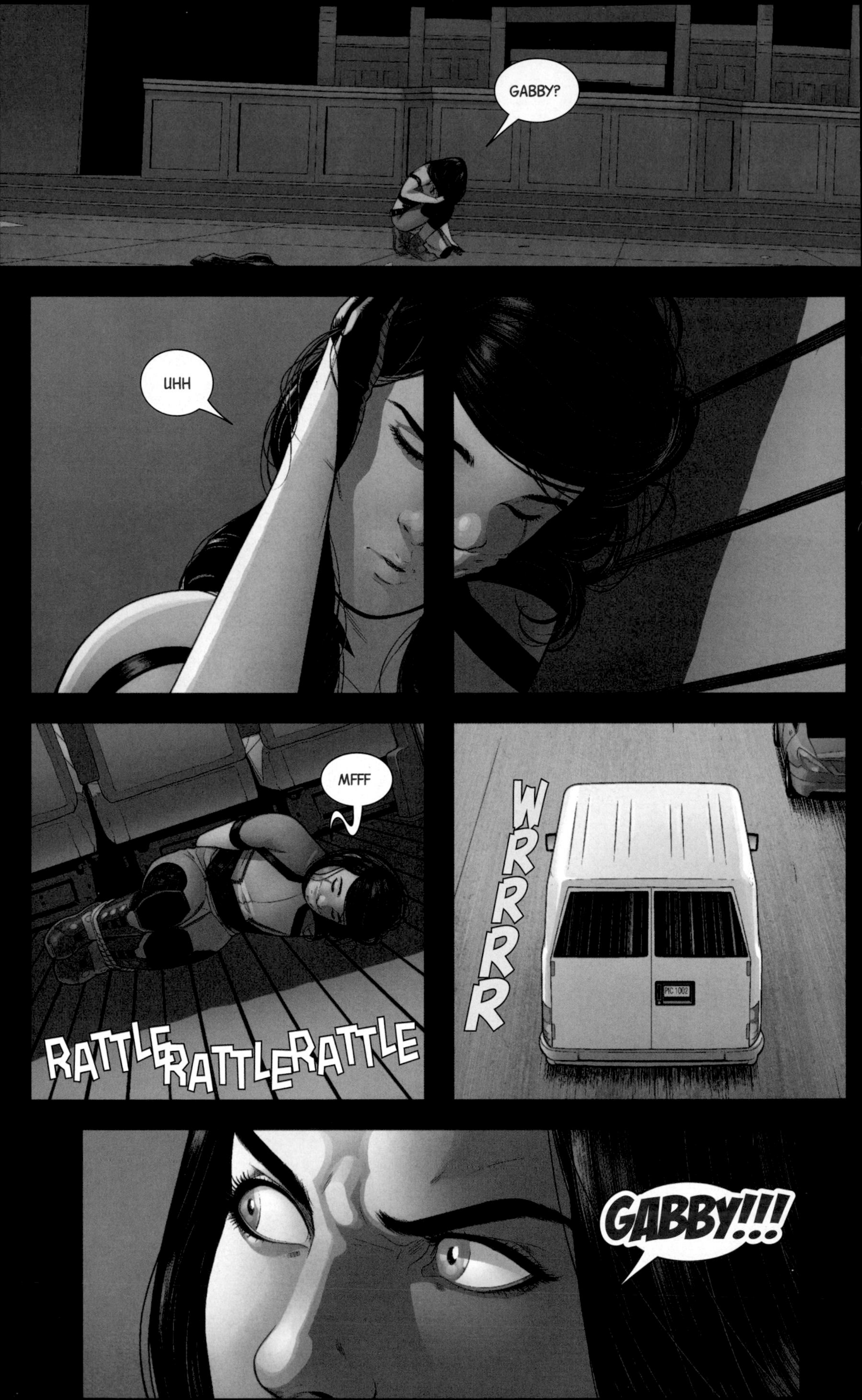
GABBY?
UHH
MFFF
RATTLERATTLERATTLE
WRRRRR
PIC 1002
GABBY!!!

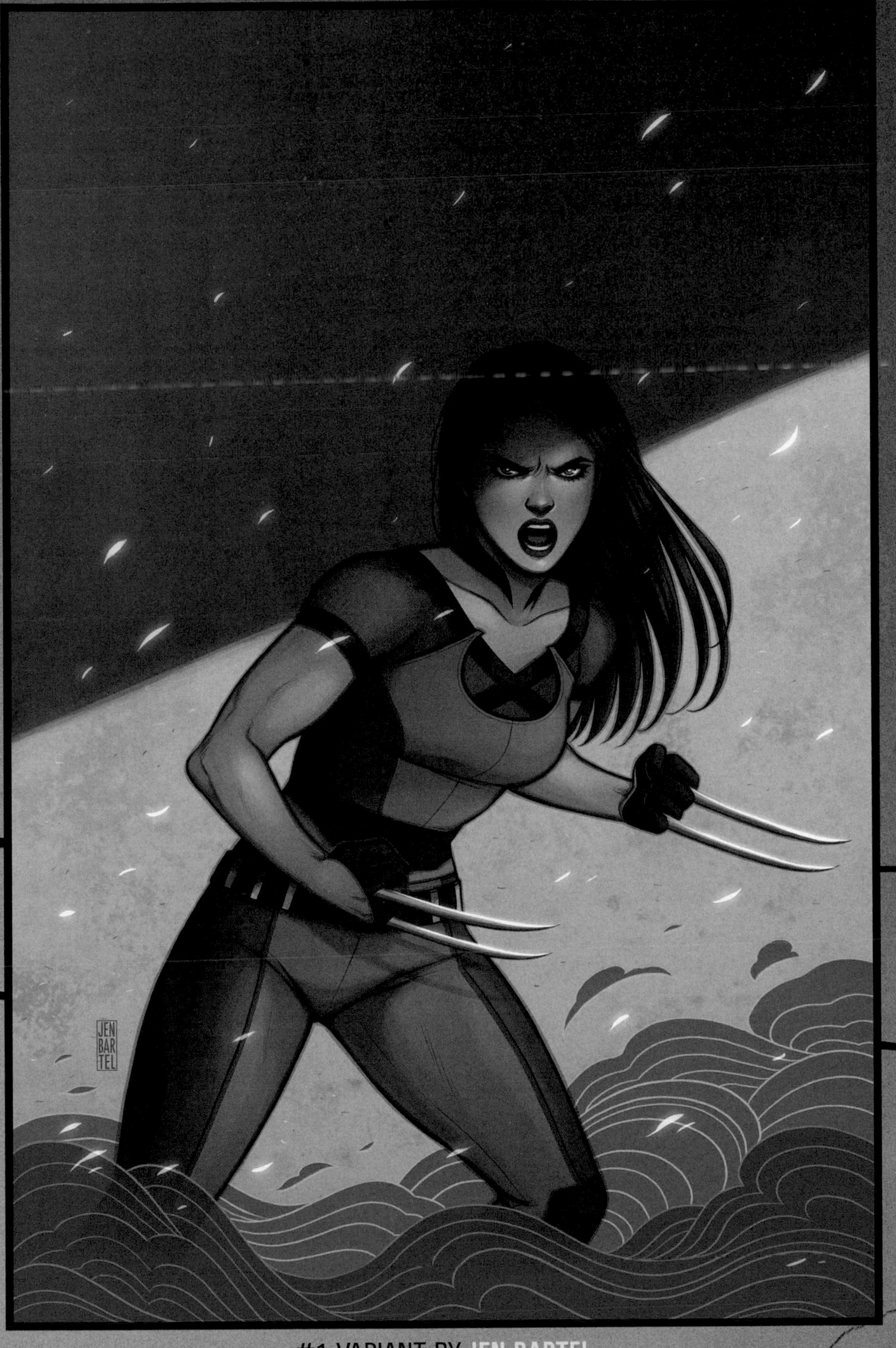
JEN
BAR
TEL

#1 VARIANT BY **JEN BARTEL**

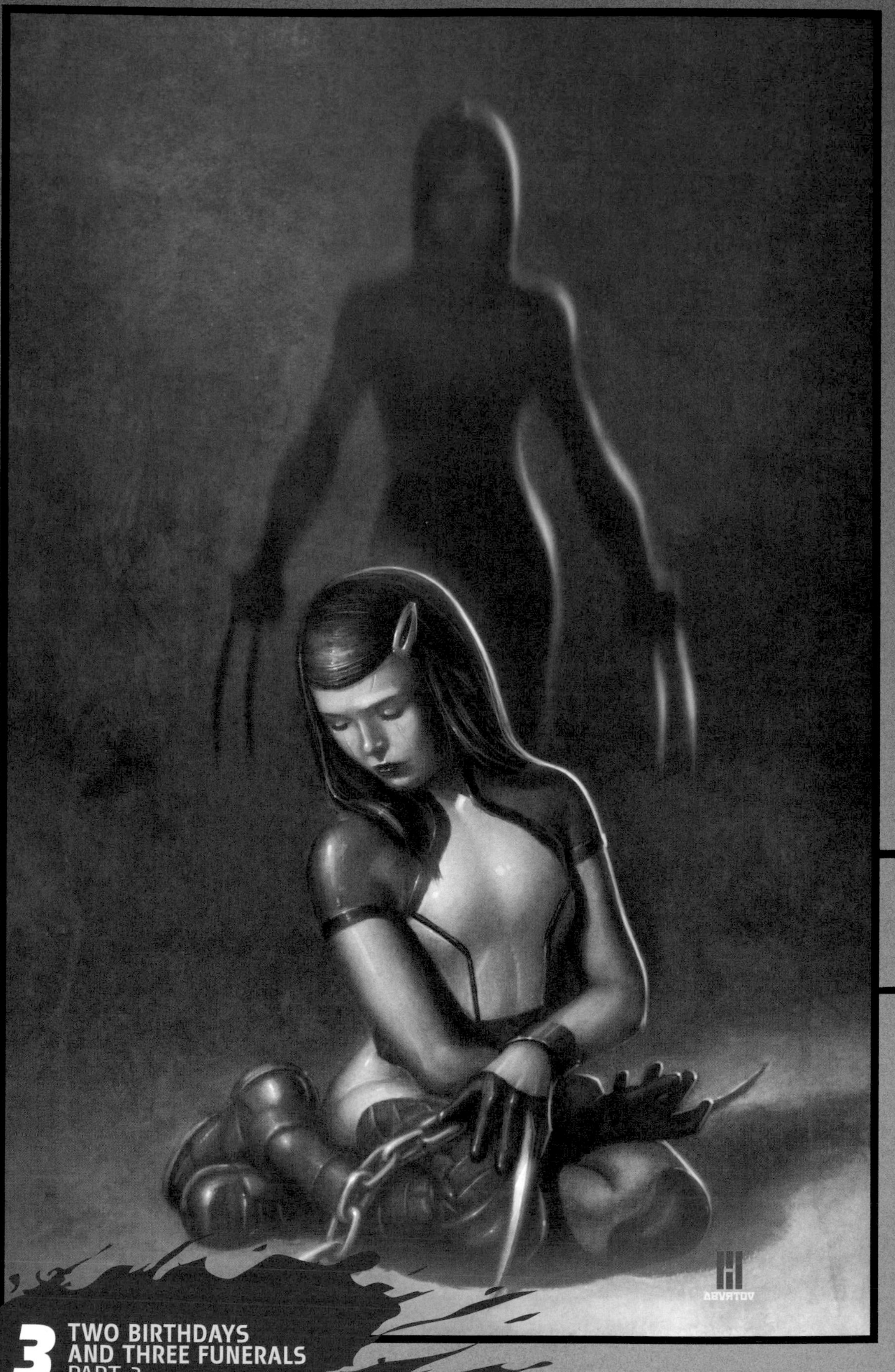

3 TWO BIRTHDAYS AND THREE FUNERALS
PART 3

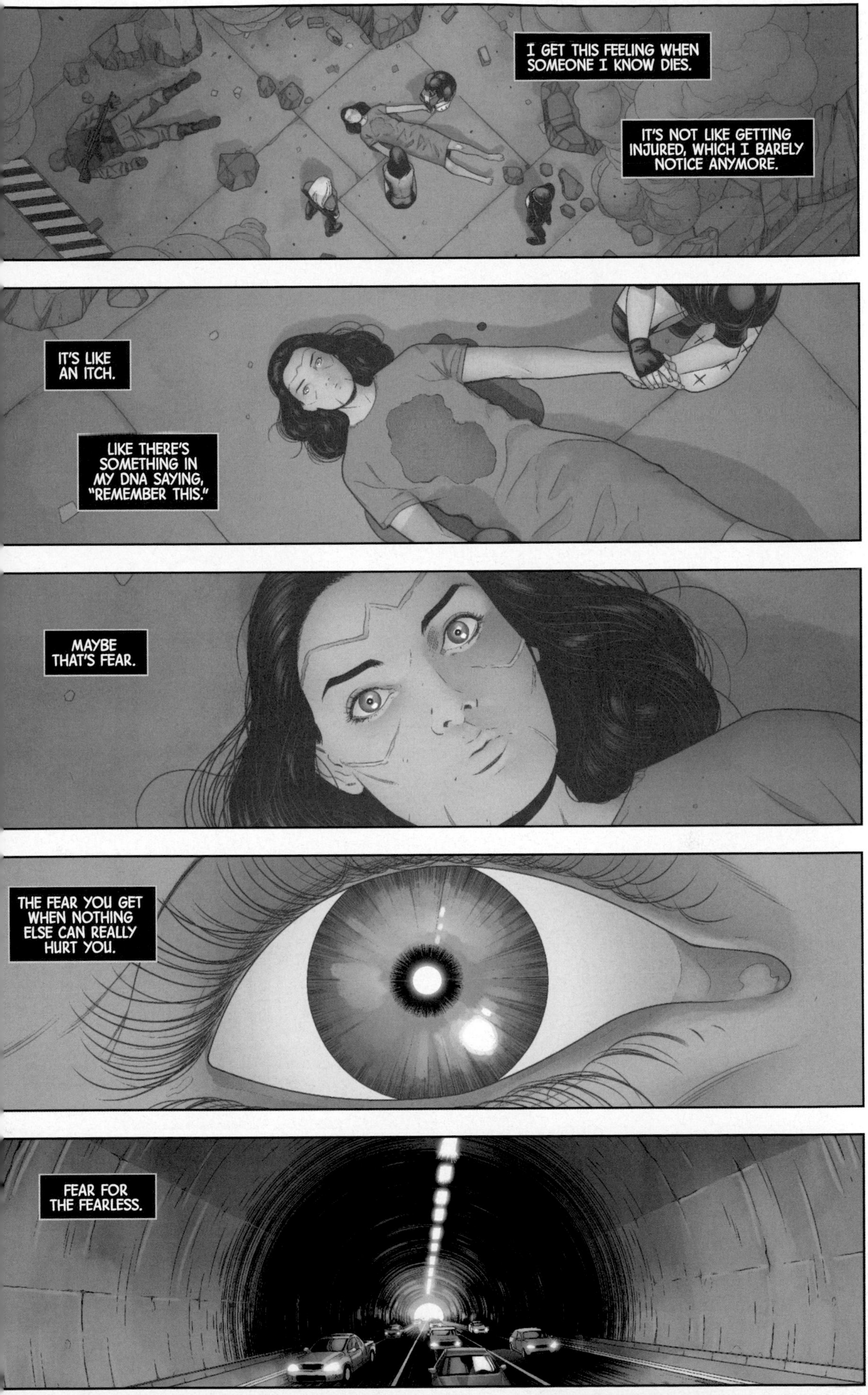
I GET THIS FEELING WHEN SOMEONE I KNOW DIES.
IT'S NOT LIKE GETTING INJURED, WHICH I BARELY NOTICE ANYMORE.
IT'S LIKE AN ITCH.
LIKE THERE'S SOMETHING IN MY DNA SAYING, "REMEMBER THIS."
MAYBE THAT'S FEAR.
THE FEAR YOU GET WHEN NOTHING ELSE CAN REALLY HURT YOU.
FEAR FOR THE FEARLESS.

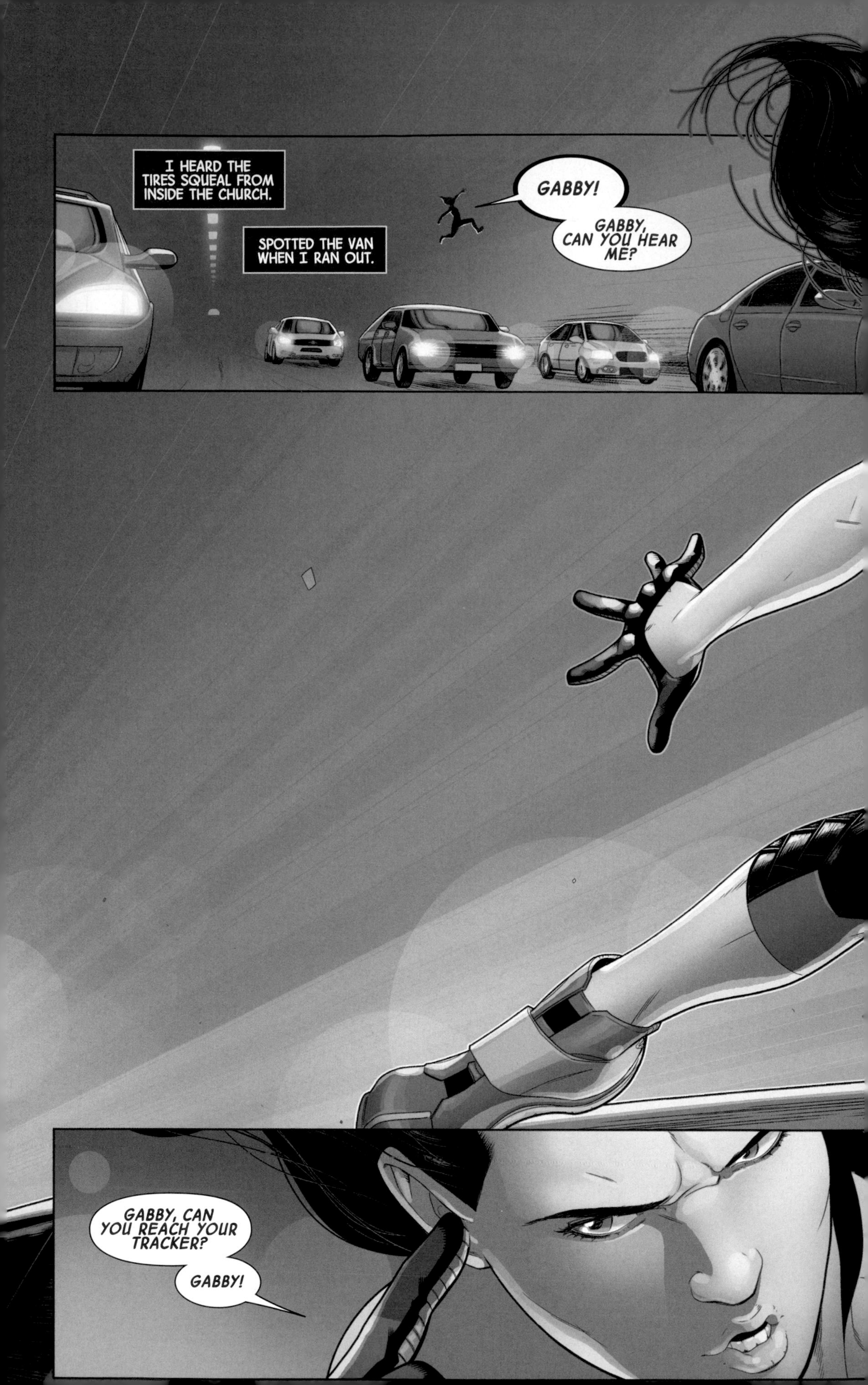
I HEARD THE TIRES SQUEAL FROM INSIDE THE CHURCH.
SPOTTED THE VAN WHEN I RAN OUT.
GABBY!
GABBY, CAN YOU HEAR ME?
GABBY, CAN YOU REACH YOUR TRACKER?
GABBY!

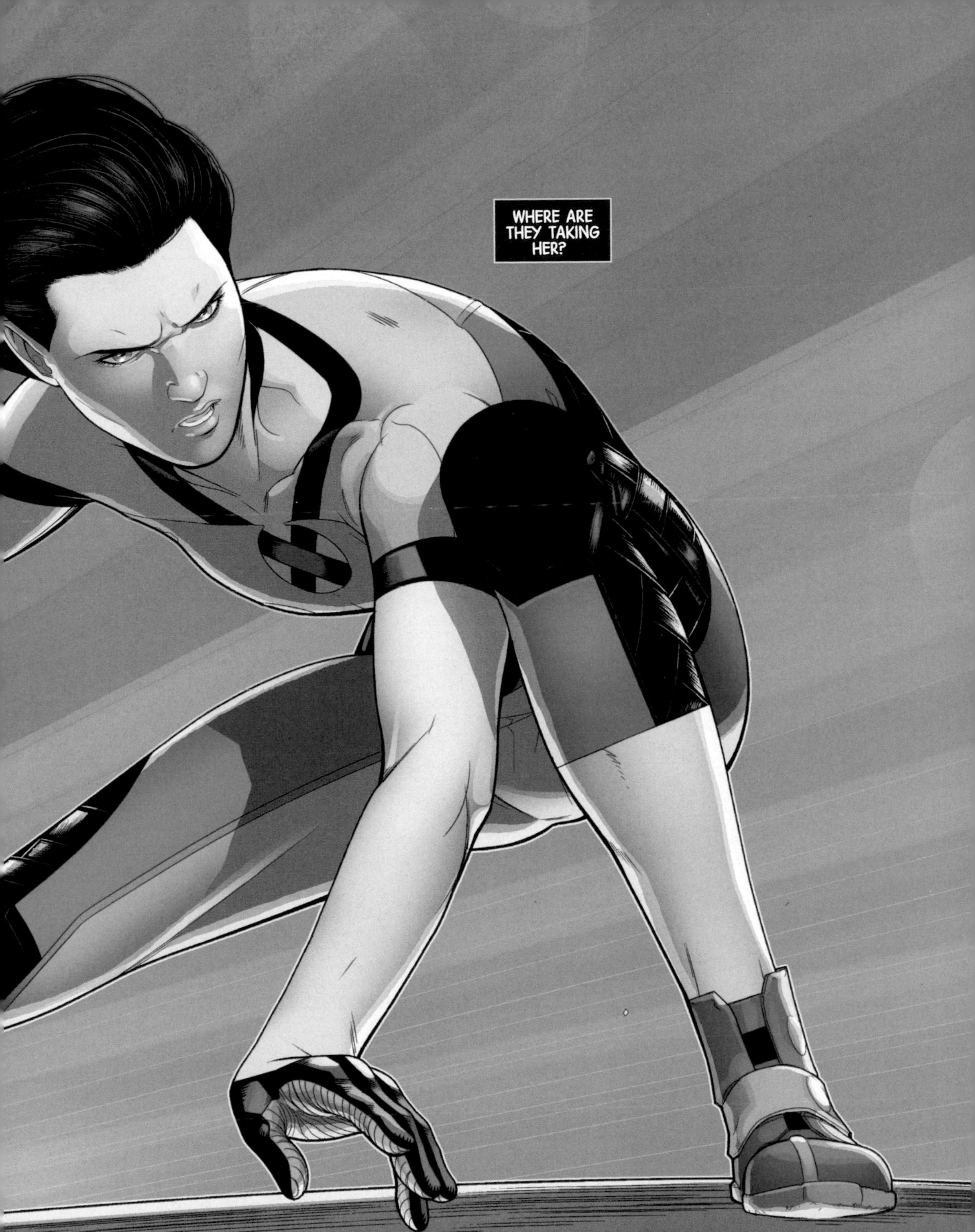
WHERE ARE THEY TAKING HER?
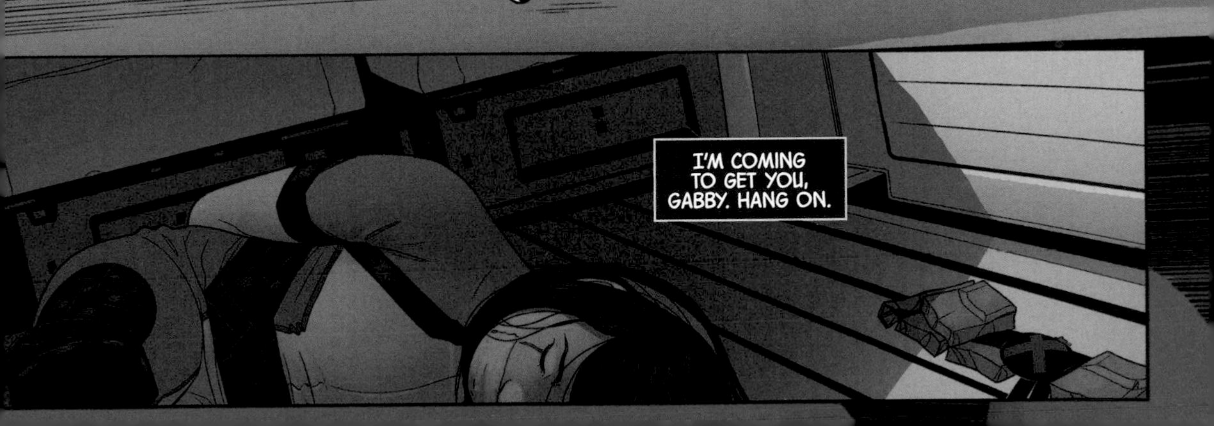
I'M COMING TO GET YOU, GABBY. HANG ON.

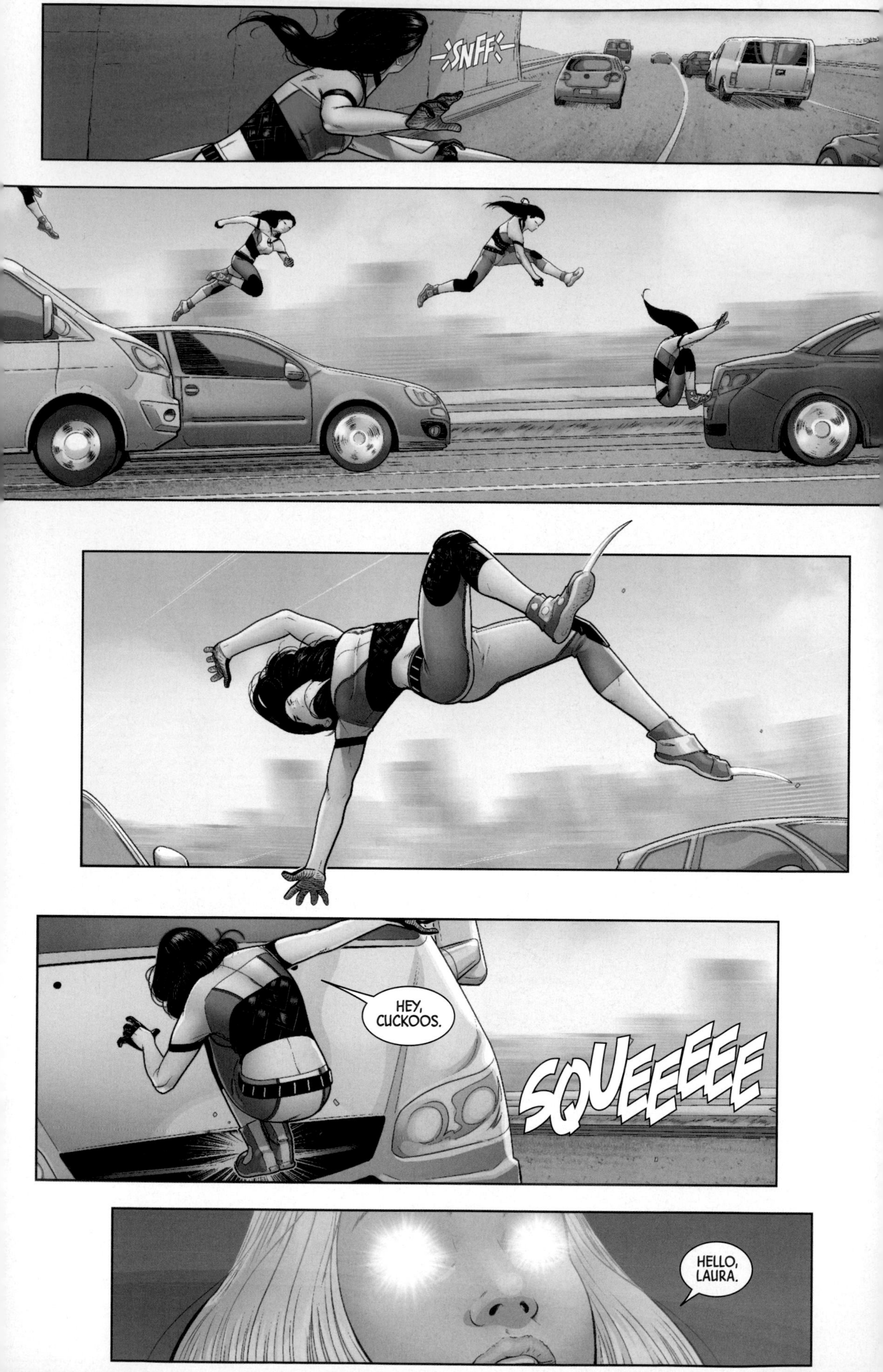
SNFF
HEY, CUCKOOS.
SQUEEEEEE
HELLO, LAURA.

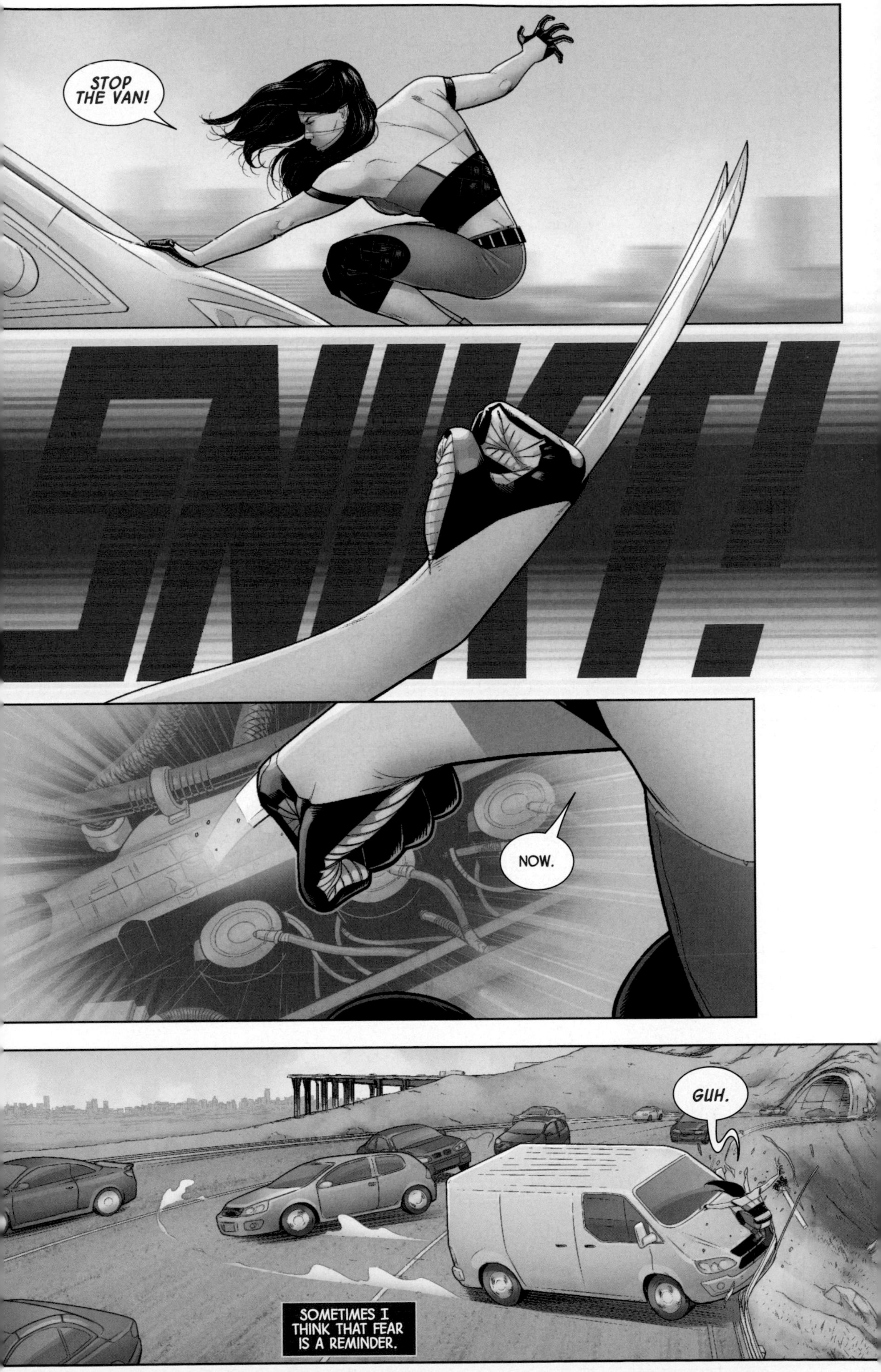
STOP THE VAN!
SNIKT!
NOW.
GUH.
SOMETIMES I THINK THAT FEAR IS A REMINDER.

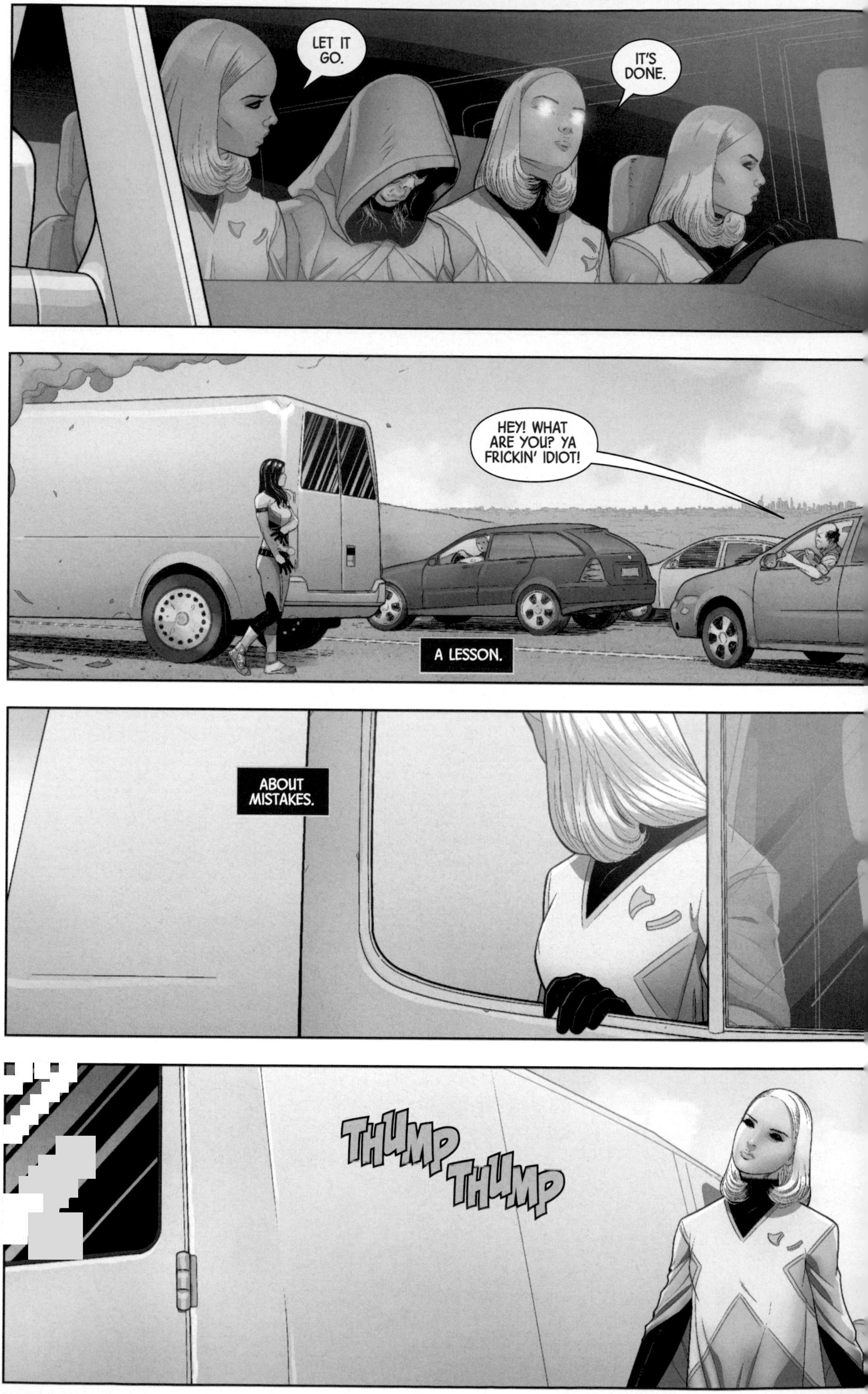
LET IT GO.
IT'S DONE.
HEY! WHAT ARE YOU? YA FRICKIN' IDIOT!
A LESSON.
ABOUT MISTAKES.
THUMP THUMP

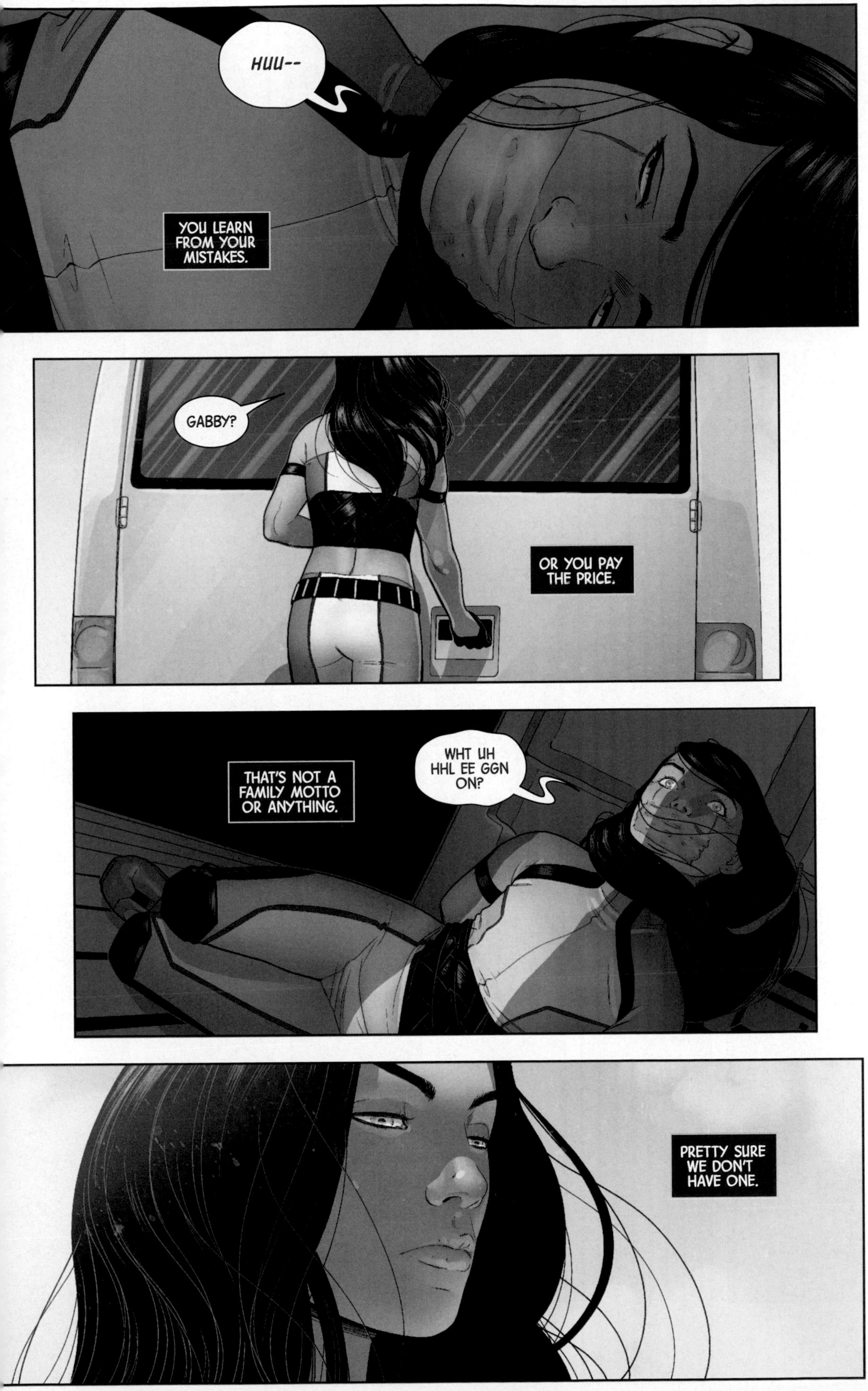
HUU--
YOU LEARN FROM YOUR MISTAKES.
GABBY?
OR YOU PAY THE PRICE.
THAT'S NOT A FAMILY MOTTO OR ANYTHING.
WHT UH HHL EE GGN ON?
PRETTY SURE WE DON'T HAVE ONE.

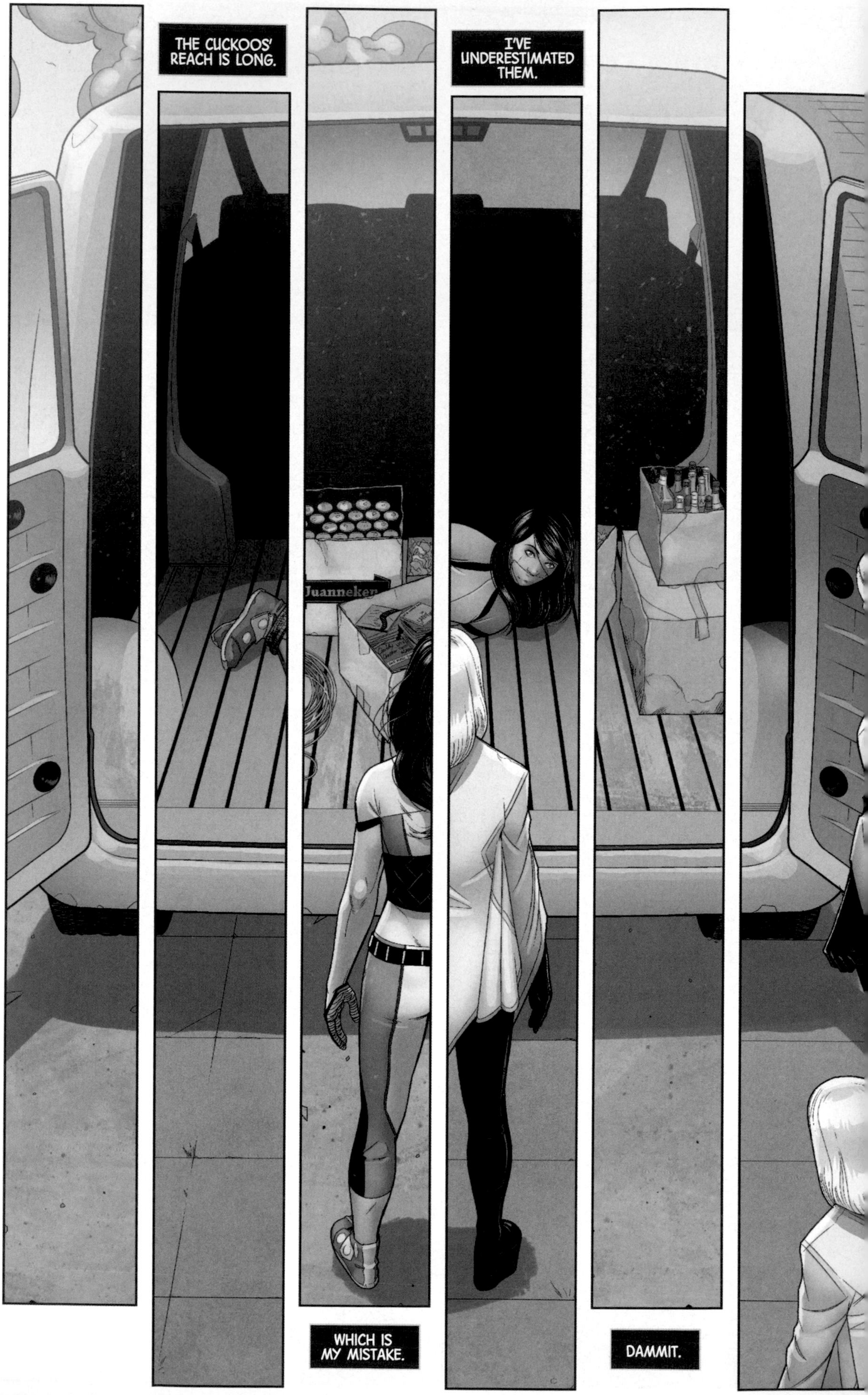
THE CUCKOOS' REACH IS LONG.
I'VE UNDERESTIMATED THEM.
Juanneken
WHICH IS MY MISTAKE.
DAMMIT.

THEY KNEW I WOULD BE TRACKING GABBY'S SCENT.

HEY, MAN. NOT COOL!

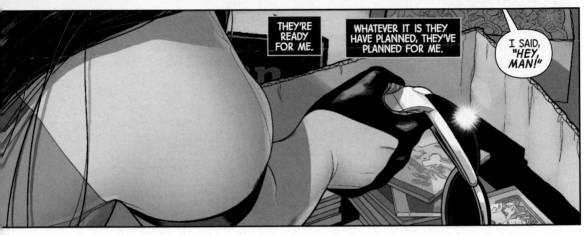

THEY'RE READY FOR ME.

WHATEVER IT IS THEY HAVE PLANNED, THEY'VE PLANNED FOR ME.

I SAID, "HEY MAN!"

I OWE YOU A VAN.

UH. YEAH. THANKS?

NO MORE MISTAKES.

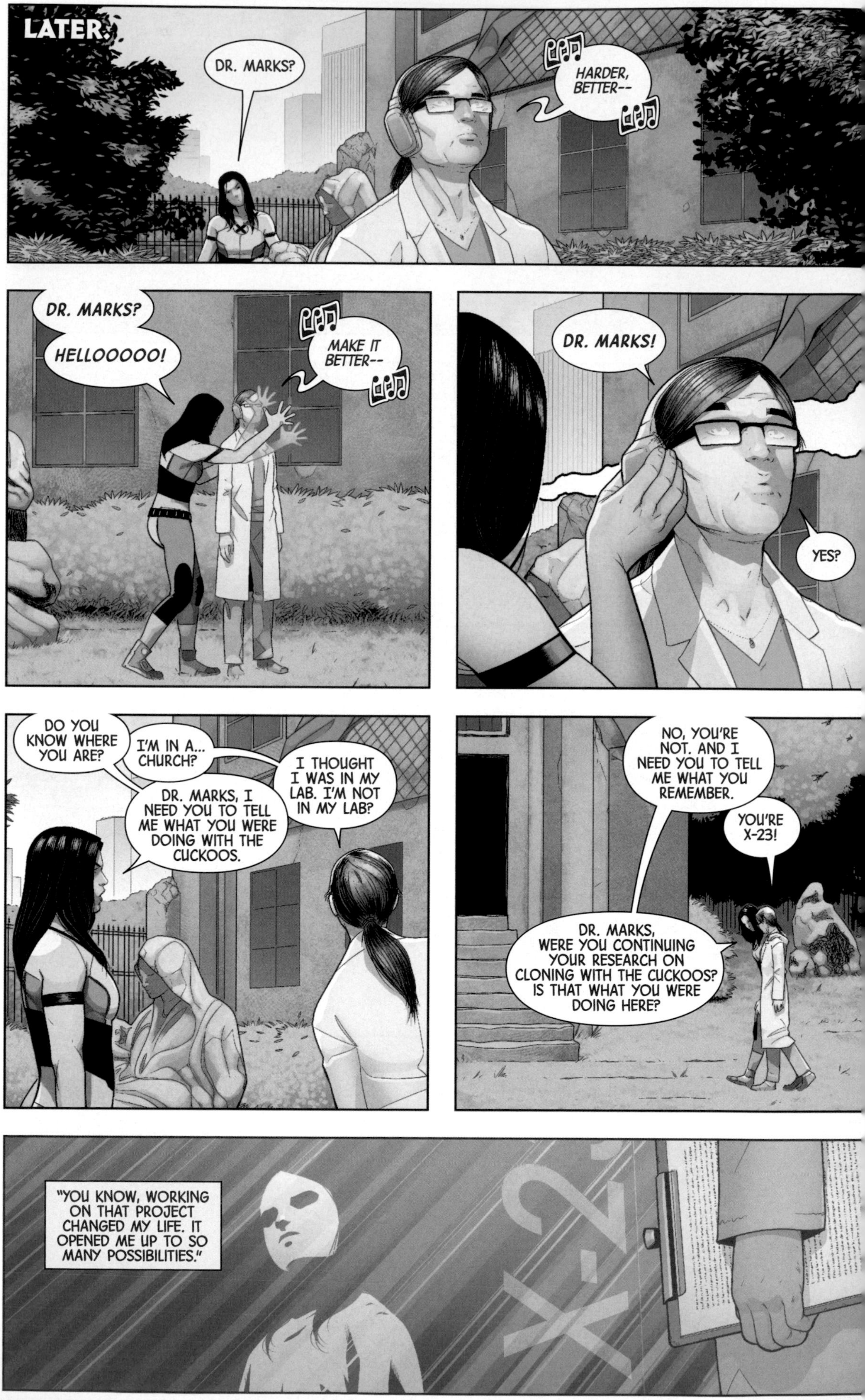
LATER.
DR. MARKS?
HARDER, BETTER--
DR. MARKS?
HELLOOOOO!
MAKE IT BETTER--
DR. MARKS!
YES?
DO YOU KNOW WHERE YOU ARE?
I'M IN A... CHURCH?
DR. MARKS, I NEED YOU TO TELL ME WHAT YOU WERE DOING WITH THE CUCKOOS.
I THOUGHT I WAS IN MY LAB. I'M NOT IN MY LAB?
NO, YOU'RE NOT. AND I NEED YOU TO TELL ME WHAT YOU REMEMBER.
YOU'RE X-23!
DR. MARKS, WERE YOU CONTINUING YOUR RESEARCH ON CLONING WITH THE CUCKOOS? IS THAT WHAT YOU WERE DOING HERE?
"YOU KNOW, WORKING ON THAT PROJECT CHANGED MY LIFE. IT OPENED ME UP TO SO MANY POSSIBILITIES."

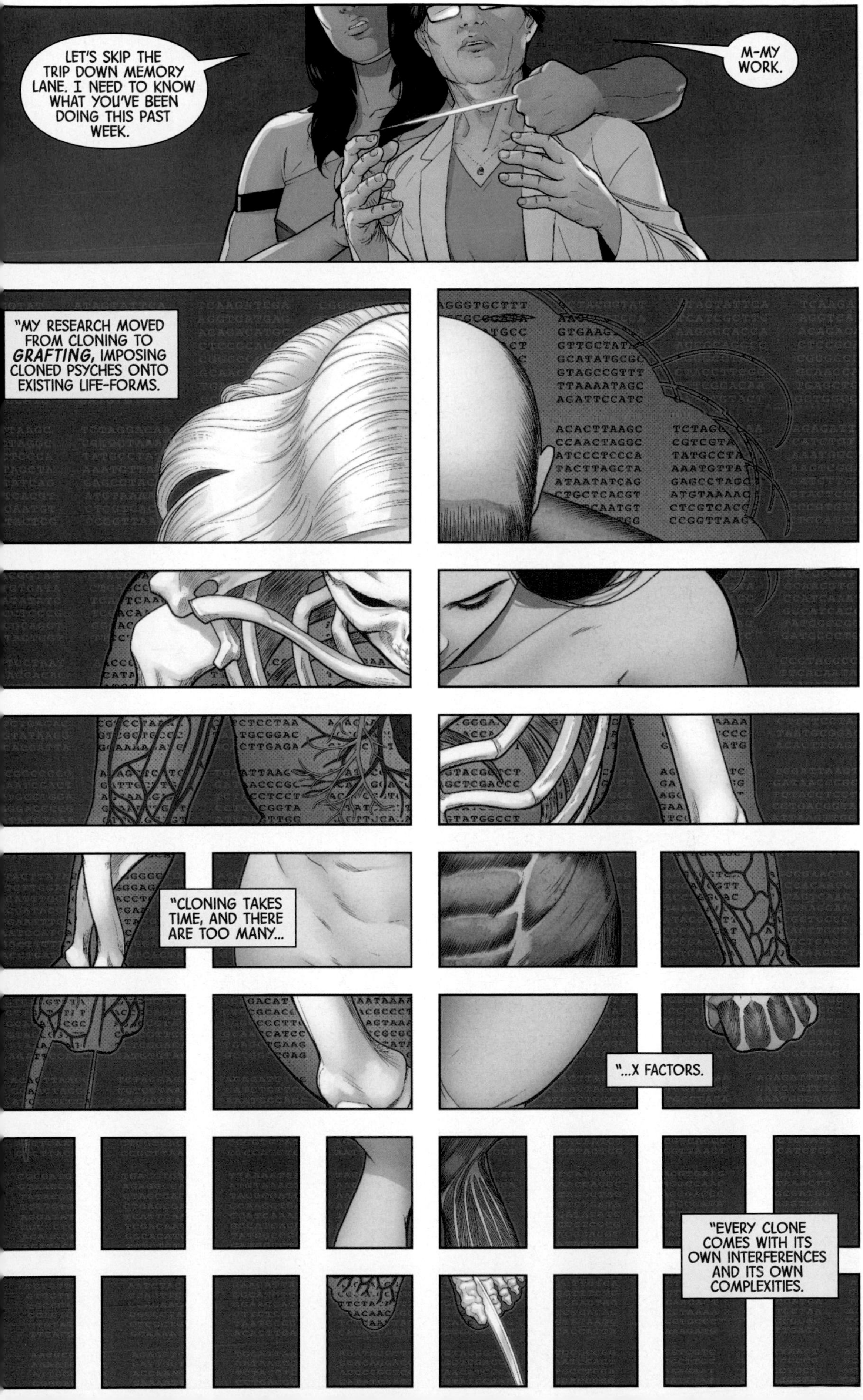
LET'S SKIP THE TRIP DOWN MEMORY LANE. I NEED TO KNOW WHAT YOU'VE BEEN DOING THIS PAST WEEK.
M-MY WORK.
"MY RESEARCH MOVED FROM CLONING TO GRAFTING, IMPOSING CLONED PSYCHES ONTO EXISTING LIFE-FORMS.
"CLONING TAKES TIME, AND THERE ARE TOO MANY...
"...X FACTORS.
"EVERY CLONE COMES WITH ITS OWN INTERFERENCES AND ITS OWN COMPLEXITIES.

"THE TISSUE I WAS GIVEN TO WORK WITH WAS RAPIDLY DISINTEGRATING. PREVIOUS ATTEMPTS TO CLONE SEEMED TO HAVE RESULTED IN COMPROMISED FORMS.

"I SURMISED THAT A PSYCHIC FIELD WAS ACTING AS A KIND OF VIRUS.

"THE PROCESS--THE GRAFTING PROCESS-- TO WORK, TO RESIST THE EFFECTS OF THE PSYCHIC ENERGY-- REQUIRED A STRONG IMMUNE SYSTEM TO STABILIZE IT.

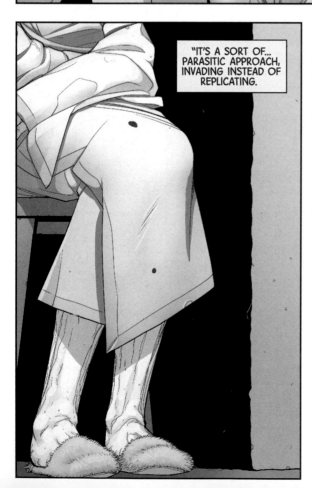

"IT'S A SORT OF... PARASITIC APPROACH, INVADING INSTEAD OF REPLICATING.

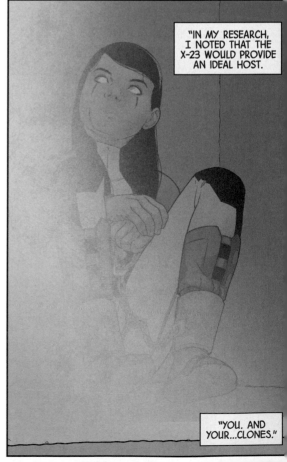

"IN MY RESEARCH, I NOTED THAT THE X-23 WOULD PROVIDE AN IDEAL HOST.

"YOU. AND YOUR...CLONES."

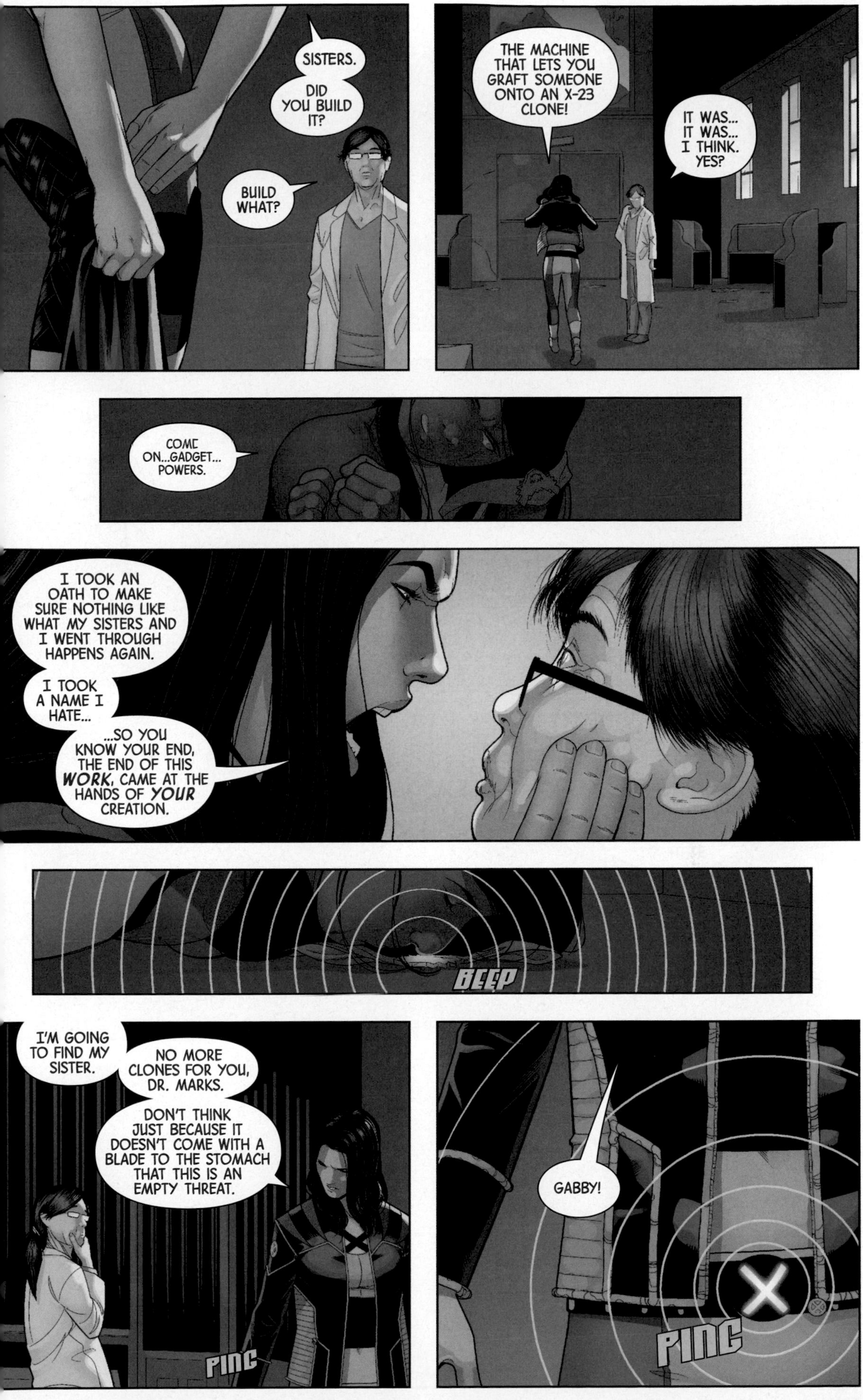

SISTERS.
DID YOU BUILD IT?
BUILD WHAT?
THE MACHINE THAT LETS YOU GRAFT SOMEONE ONTO AN X-23 CLONE!
IT WAS... IT WAS... I THINK. YES?
COME ON...GADGET... POWERS.
I TOOK AN OATH TO MAKE SURE NOTHING LIKE WHAT MY SISTERS AND I WENT THROUGH HAPPENS AGAIN.
I TOOK A NAME I HATE...
...SO YOU KNOW YOUR END, THE END OF THIS *WORK*, CAME AT THE HANDS OF *YOUR* CREATION.
BEEP
I'M GOING TO FIND MY SISTER.
NO MORE CLONES FOR YOU, DR. MARKS.
DON'T THINK JUST BECAUSE IT DOESN'T COME WITH A BLADE TO THE STOMACH THAT THIS IS AN EMPTY THREAT.
PING
GABBY!
PING

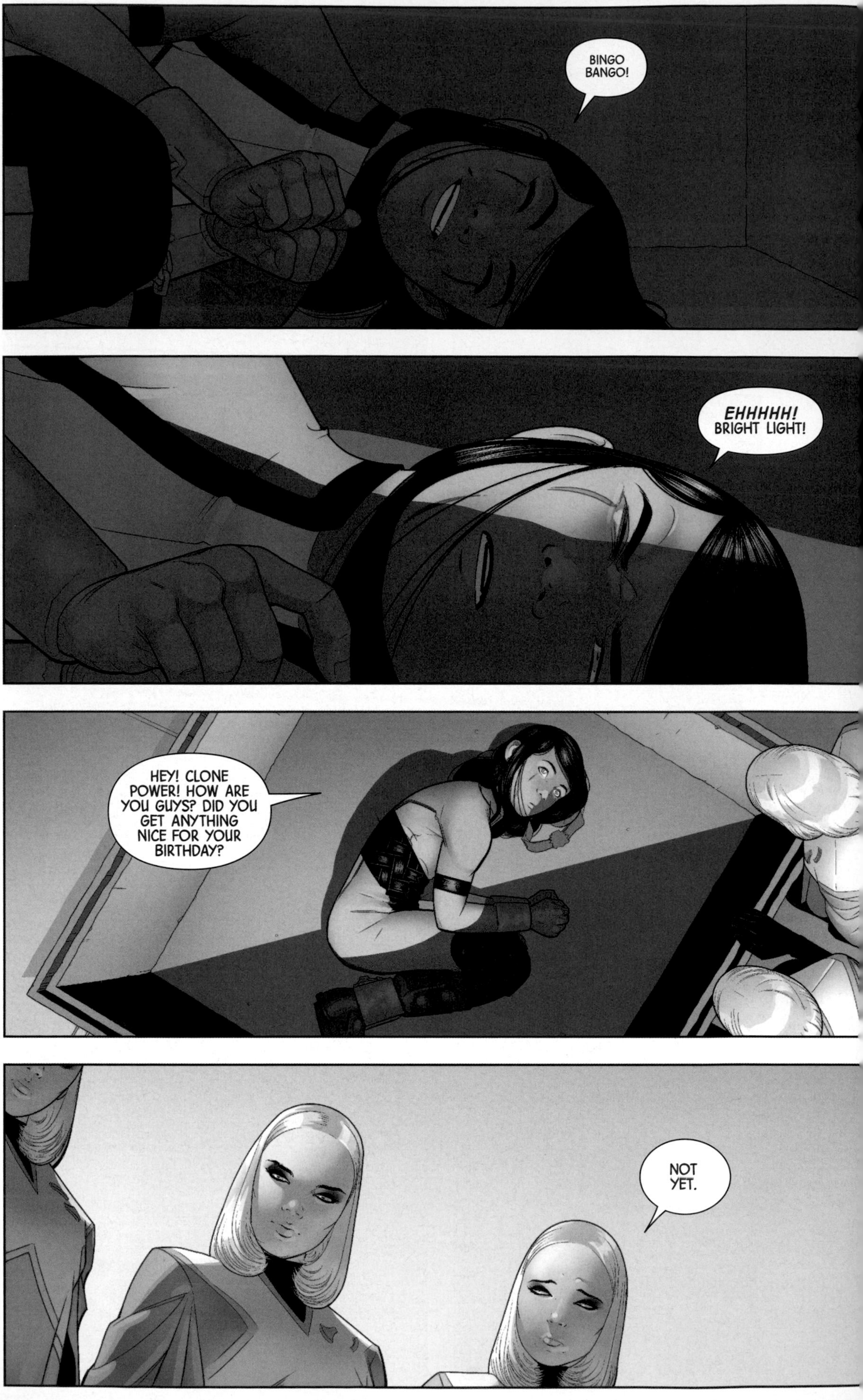
BINGO BANGO!
EHHHHH! BRIGHT LIGHT!
HEY! CLONE POWER! HOW ARE YOU GUYS? DID YOU GET ANYTHING NICE FOR YOUR BIRTHDAY?
NOT YET.

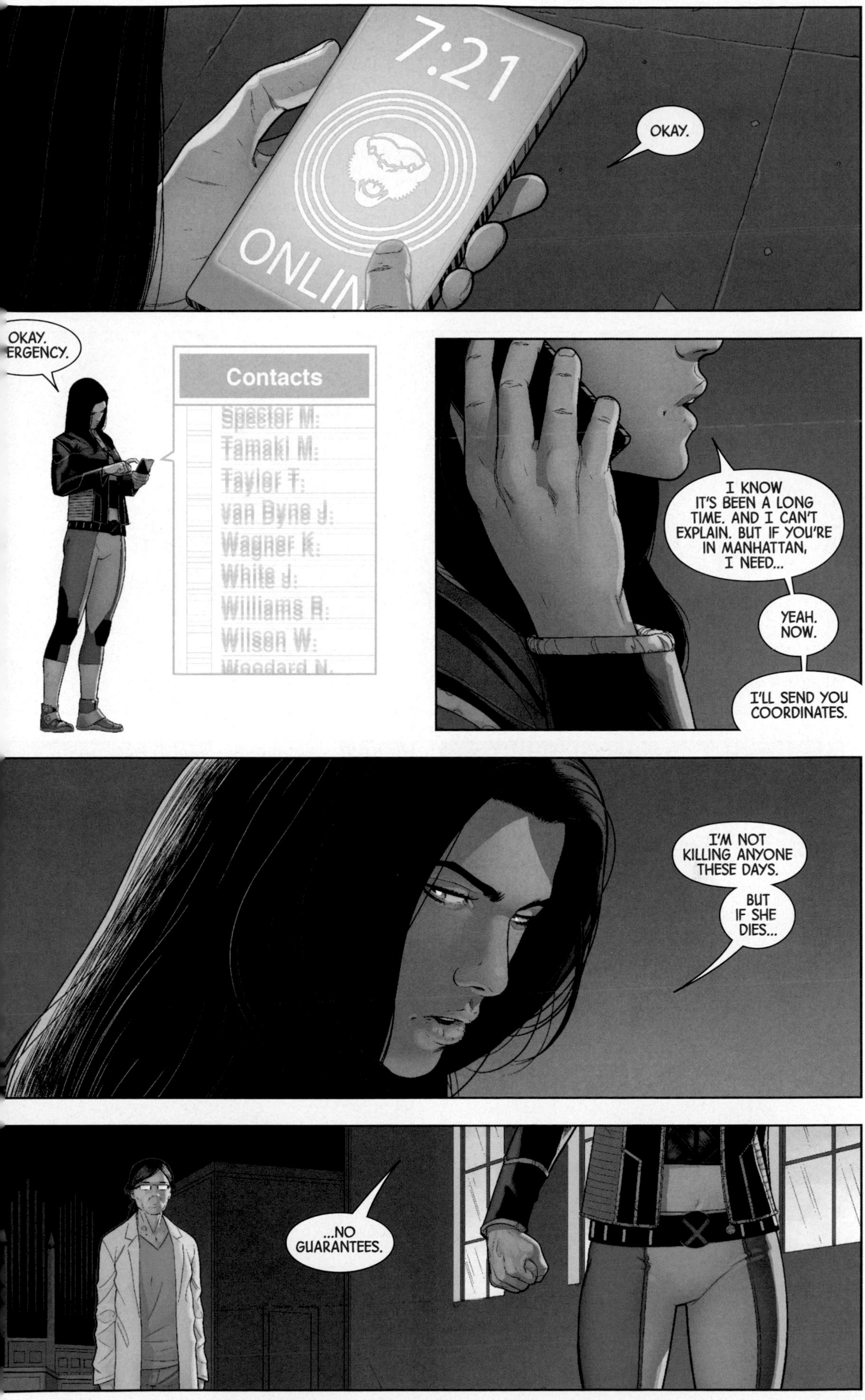
7:21
ONLIN
OKAY.
OKAY.
ERGENCY.
Contacts
Spector M:
Tamaki M:
Taylor T:
van Byne J:
Wagner K:
White J:
Williams R:
Wilson W:
Woodard N.
I KNOW IT'S BEEN A LONG TIME. AND I CAN'T EXPLAIN. BUT IF YOU'RE IN MANHATTAN, I NEED...
YEAH. NOW.
I'LL SEND YOU COORDINATES.
I'M NOT KILLING ANYONE THESE DAYS.
BUT IF SHE DIES...
...NO GUARANTEES.

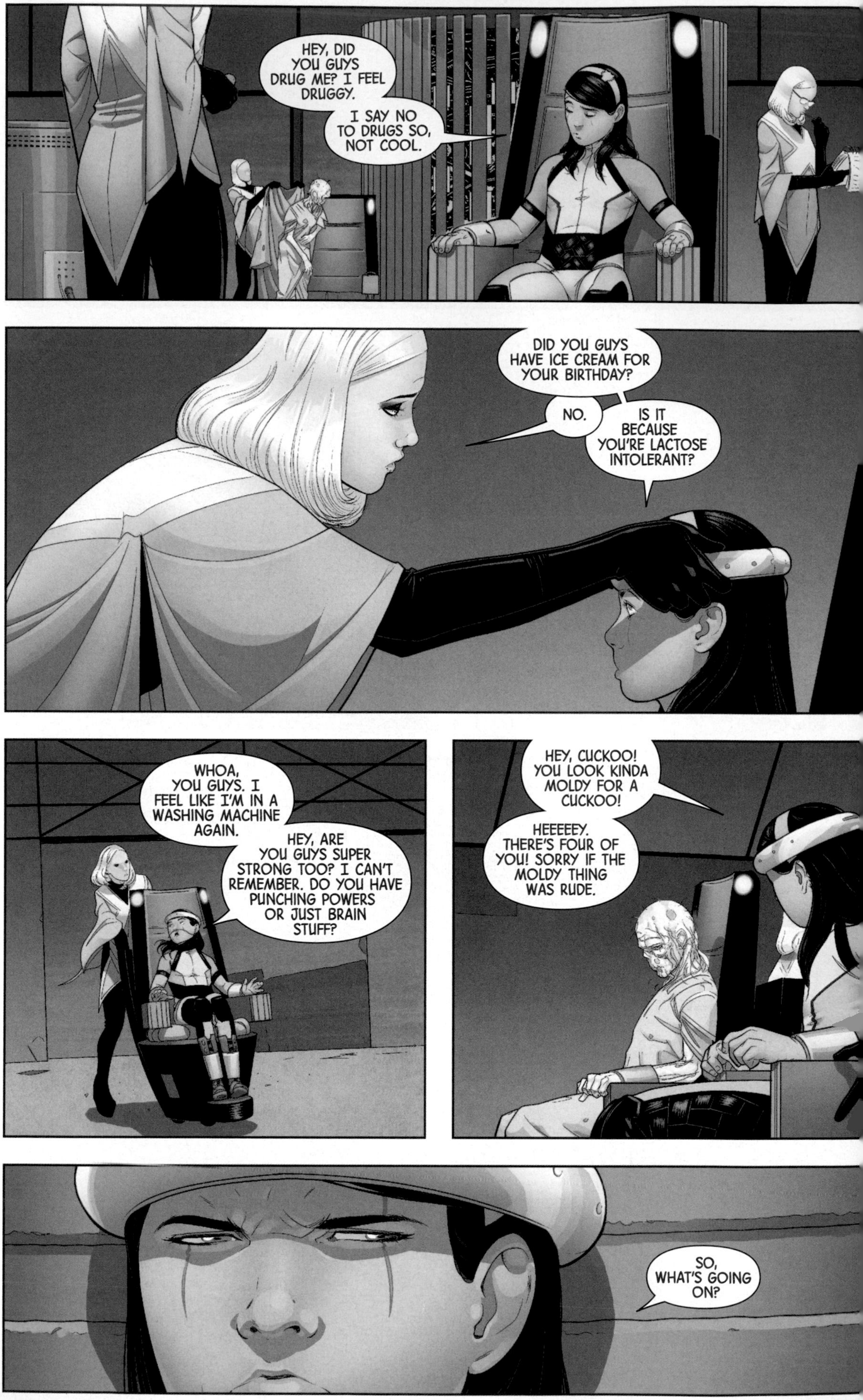
HEY, DID YOU GUYS DRUG ME? I FEEL DRUGGY.
I SAY NO TO DRUGS SO, NOT COOL.
DID YOU GUYS HAVE ICE CREAM FOR YOUR BIRTHDAY?
NO.
IS IT BECAUSE YOU'RE LACTOSE INTOLERANT?
WHOA, YOU GUYS. I FEEL LIKE I'M IN A WASHING MACHINE AGAIN.
HEY, ARE YOU GUYS SUPER STRONG TOO? I CAN'T REMEMBER. DO YOU HAVE PUNCHING POWERS OR JUST BRAIN STUFF?
HEY, CUCKOO! YOU LOOK KINDA MOLDY FOR A CUCKOO!
HEEEEEY. THERE'S FOUR OF YOU! SORRY IF THE MOLDY THING WAS RUDE.
SO, WHAT'S GOING ON?

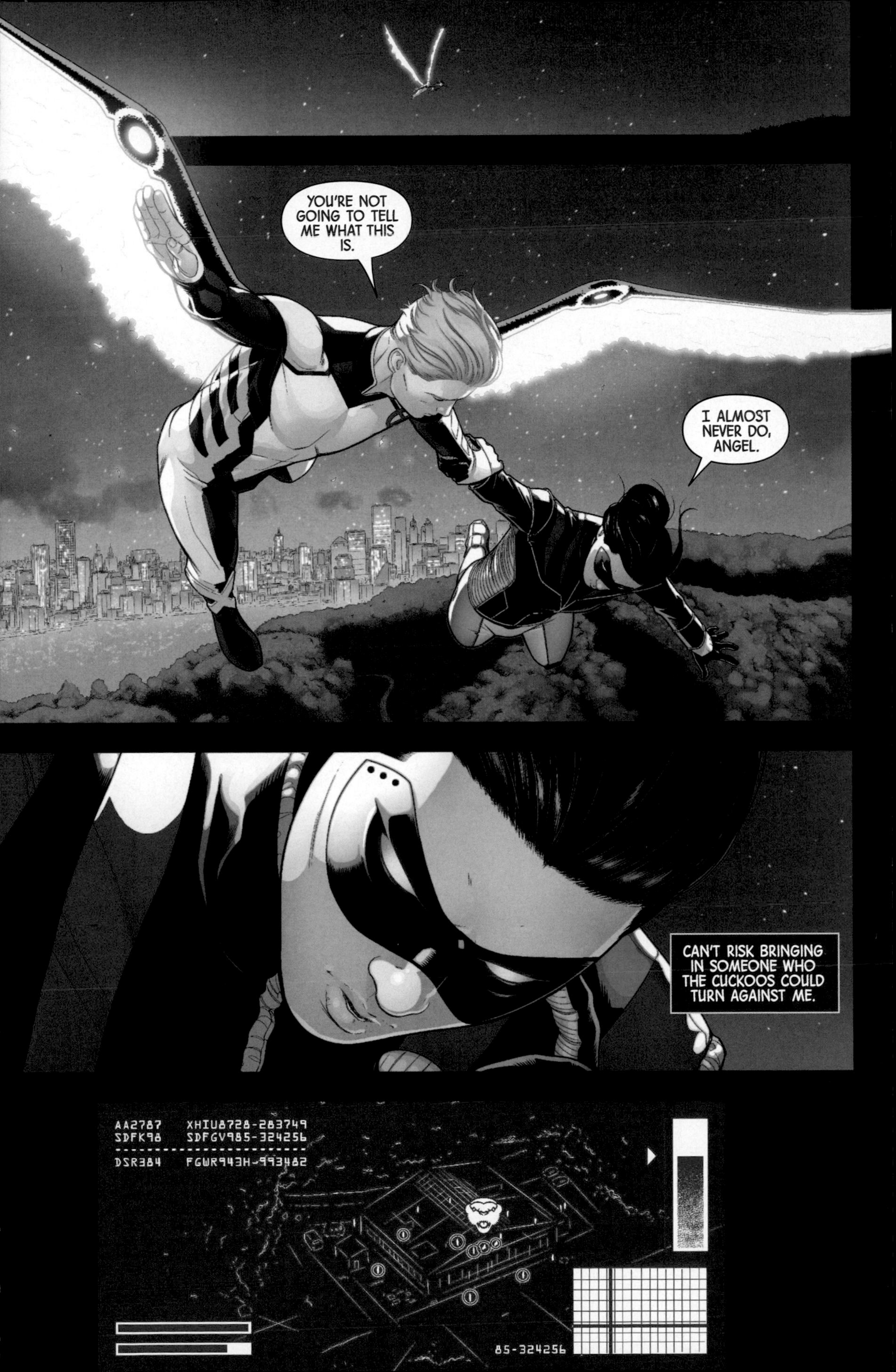
YOU'RE NOT GOING TO TELL ME WHAT THIS IS.
I ALMOST NEVER DO, ANGEL.
CAN'T RISK BRINGING IN SOMEONE WHO THE CUCKOOS COULD TURN AGAINST ME.
AA2787 XHIU8728-283749
SDFK98 SDFGV985-324256
DSR384 FGWR943H-993482
85-324256

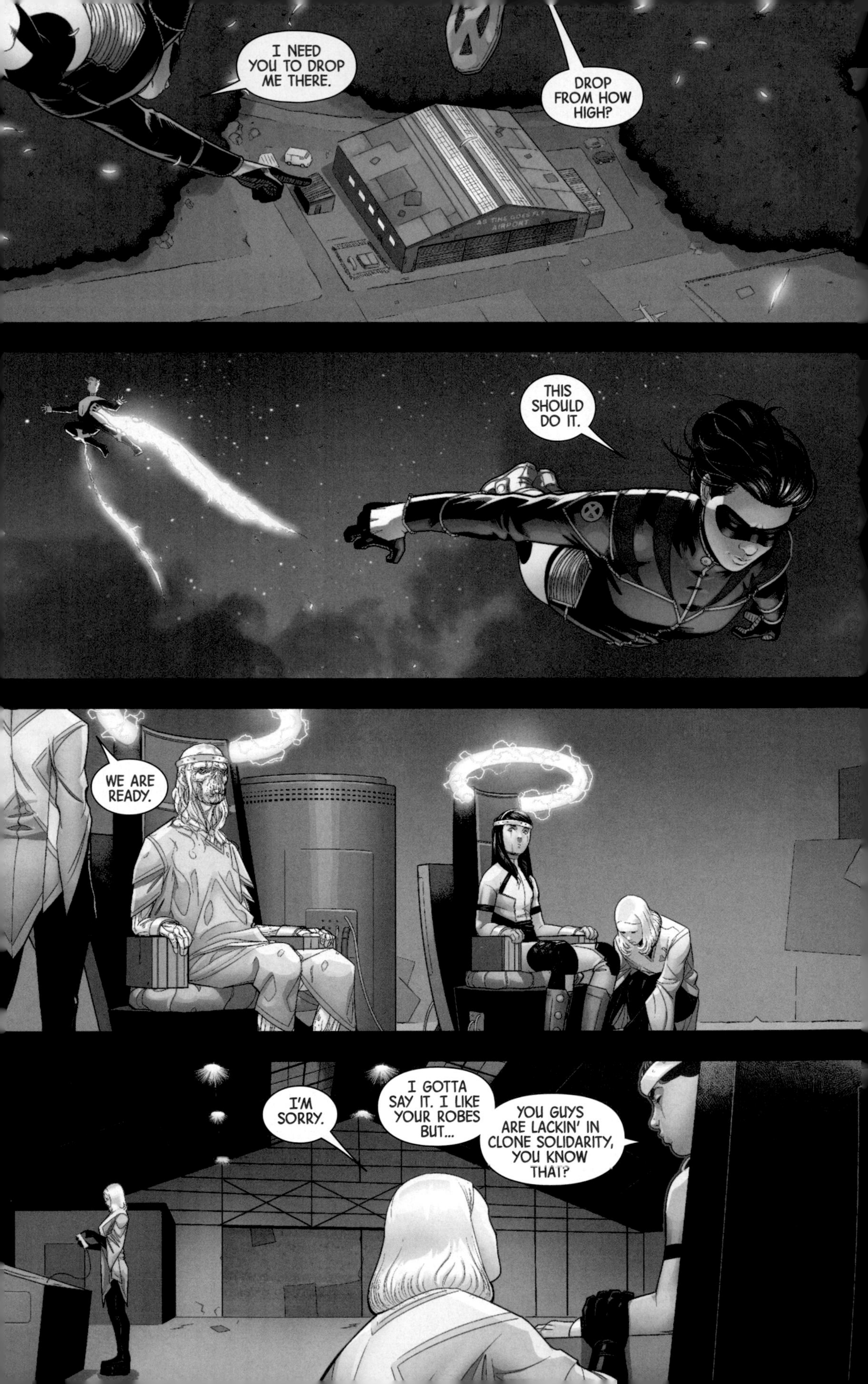
I NEED YOU TO DROP ME THERE.
DROP FROM HOW HIGH?
THIS SHOULD DO IT.
WE ARE READY.
I'M SORRY.
I GOTTA SAY IT. I LIKE YOUR ROBES BUT...
YOU GUYS ARE LACKIN' IN CLONE SOLIDARITY, YOU KNOW THAT?

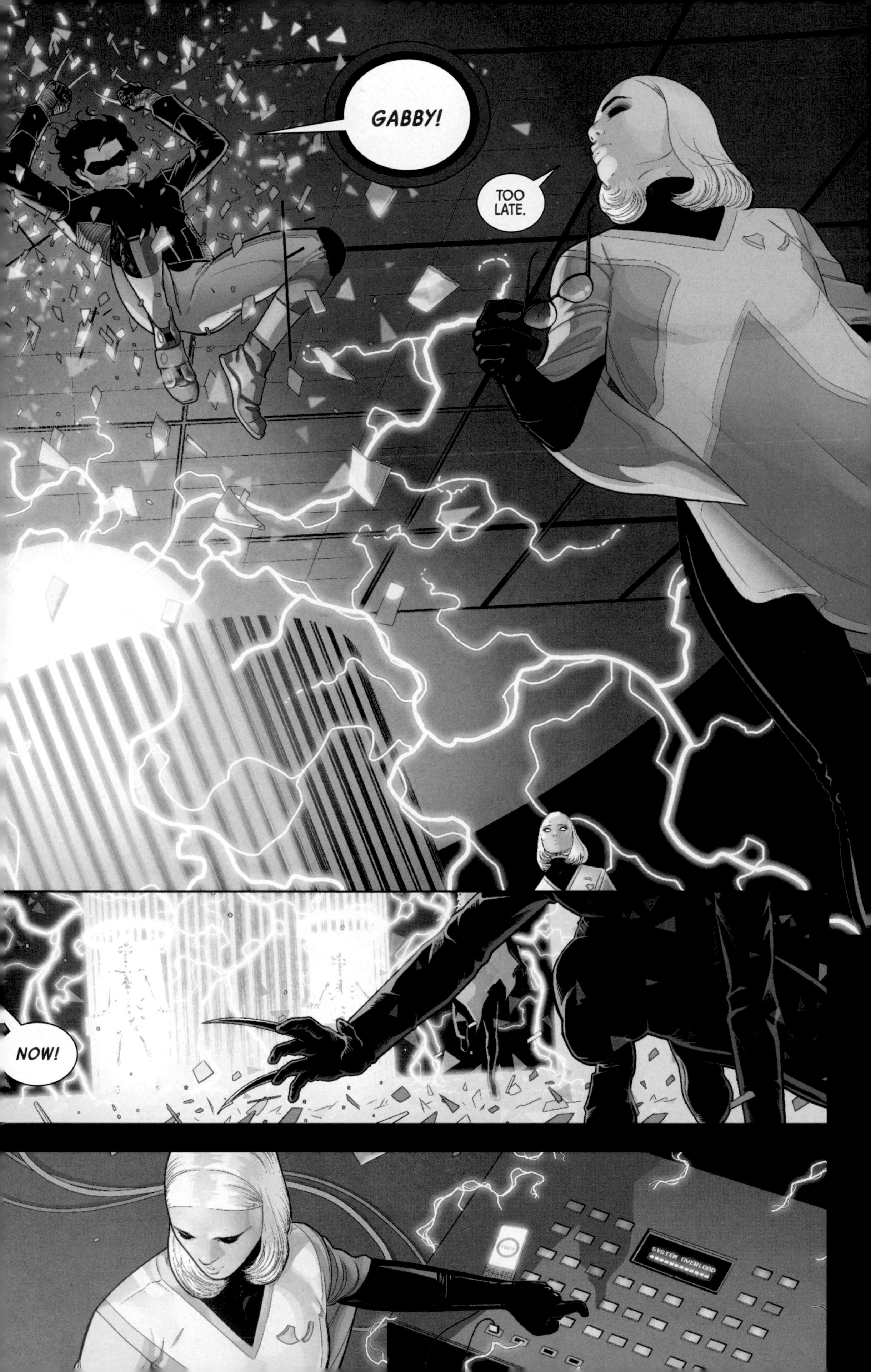
GABBY!
TOO LATE.
NOW!
SYSTEM OVERLOAD

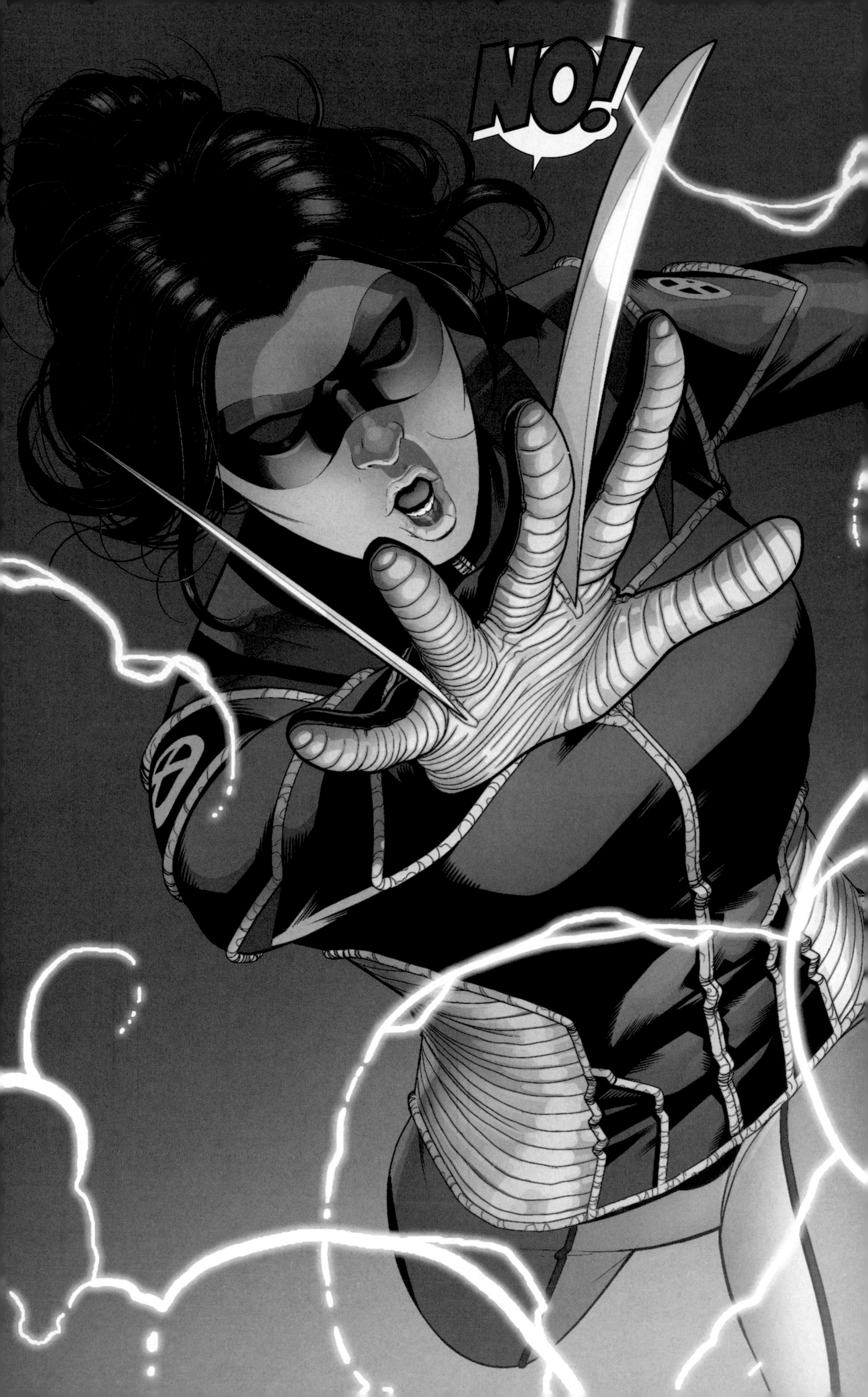
NO!

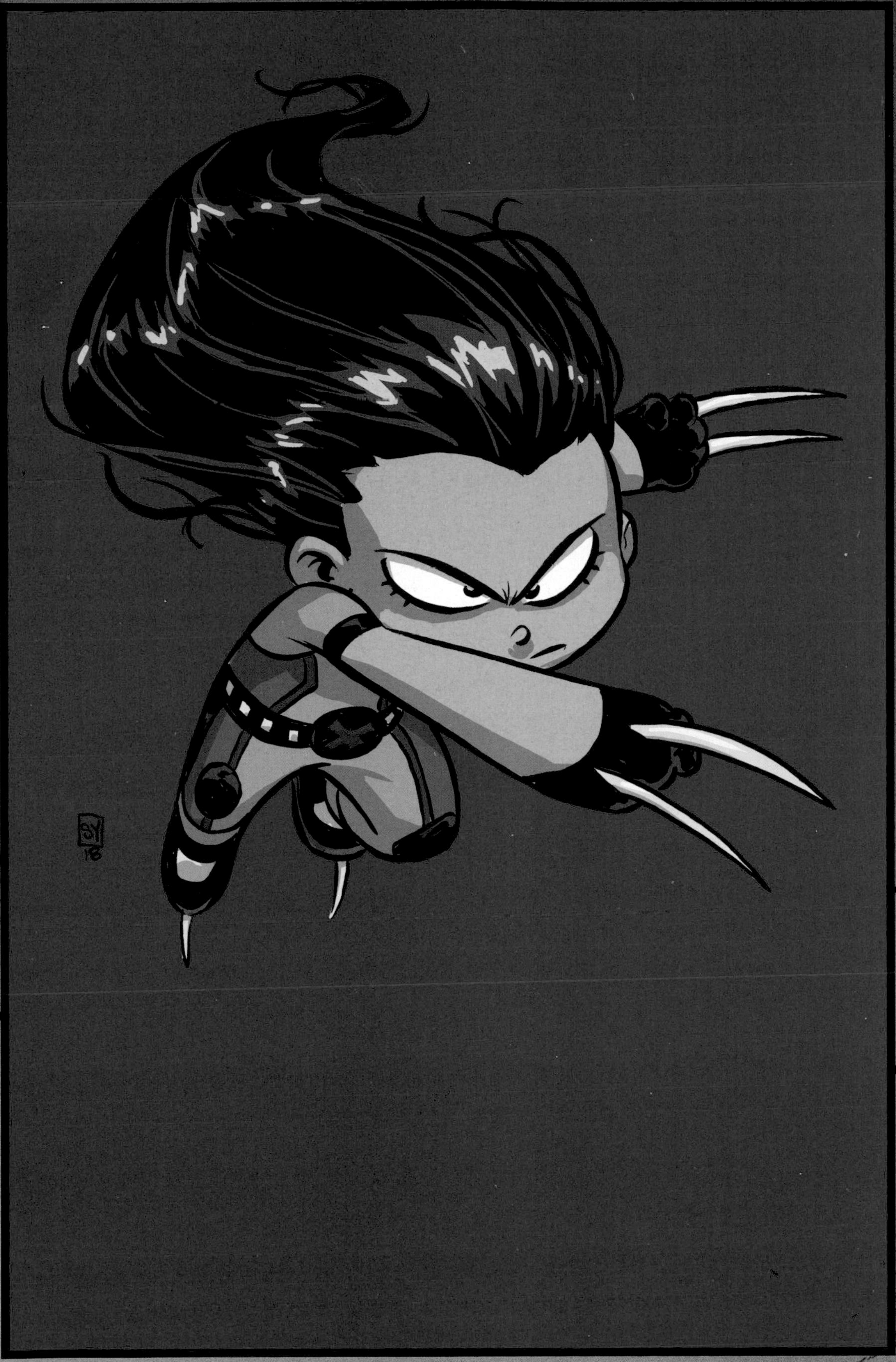
SY
18

#1 VARIANT BY SKOTTIE YOUNG

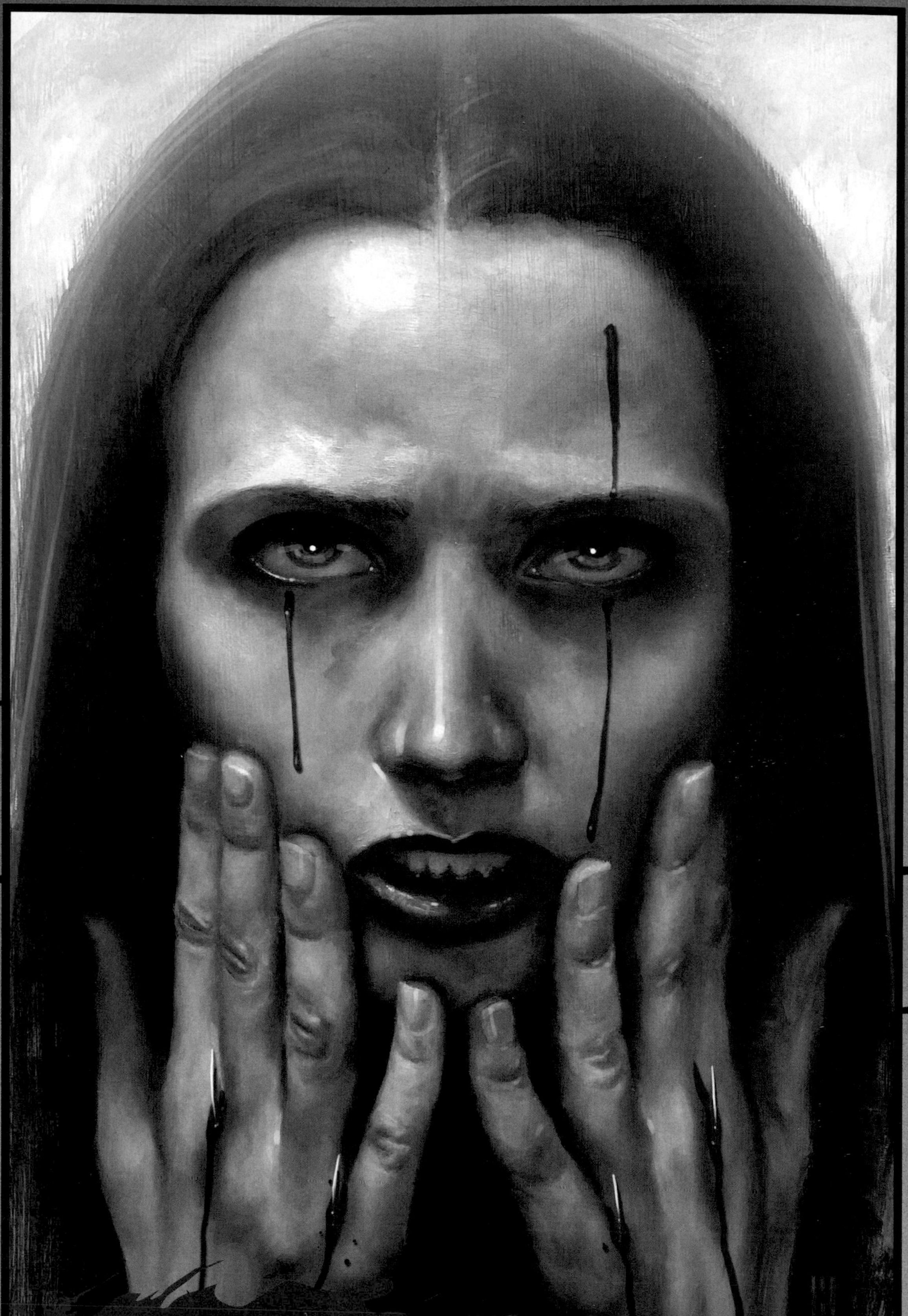

4 TWO BIRTHDAYS AND THREE FUNERALS PART 4

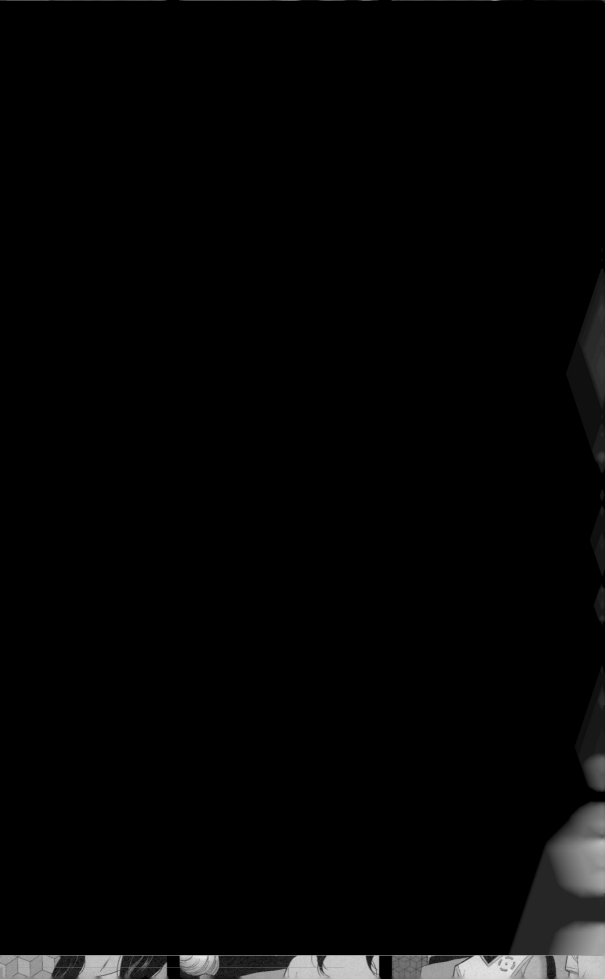

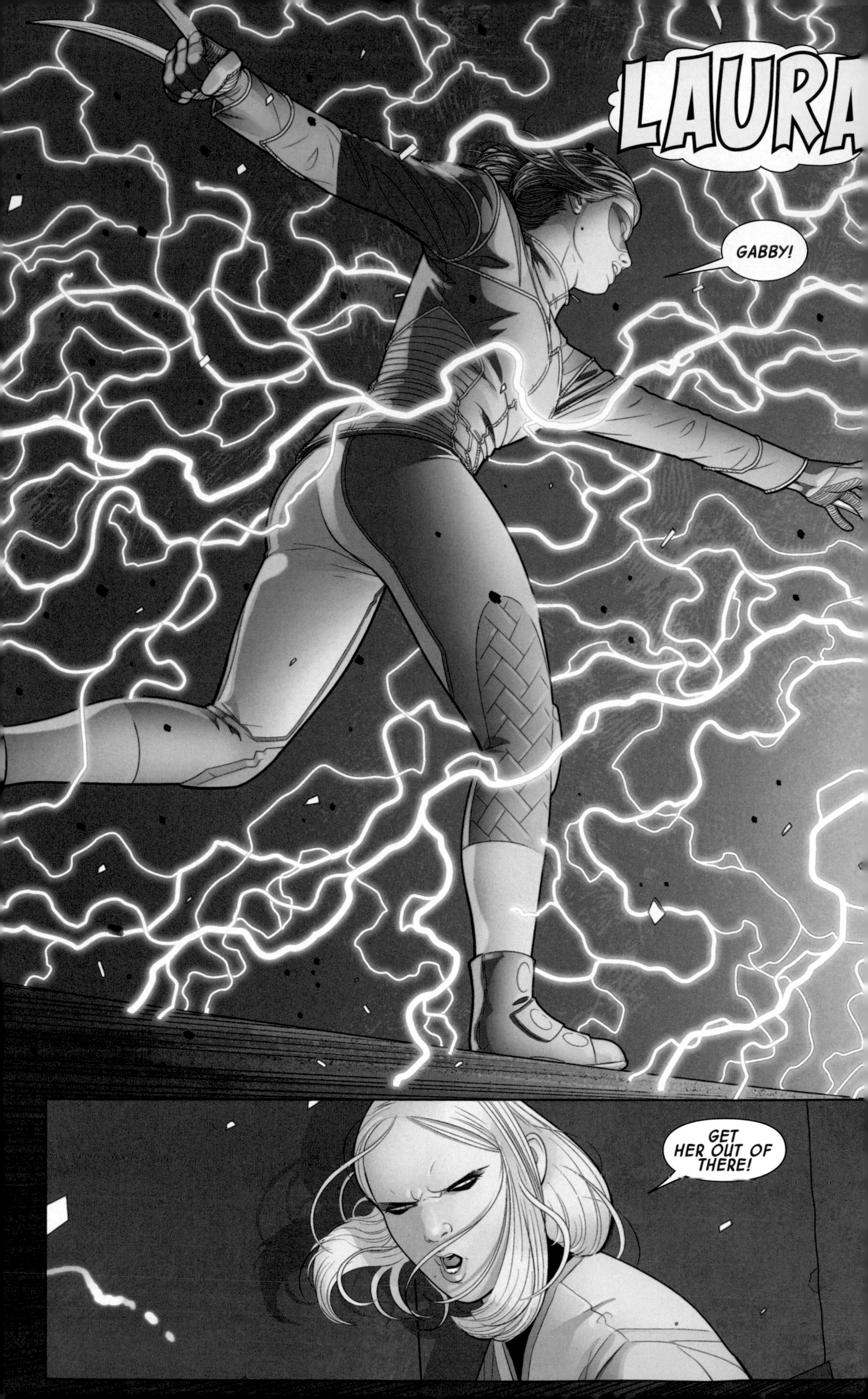
LAURA
GABBY!
GET HER OUT OF THERE!

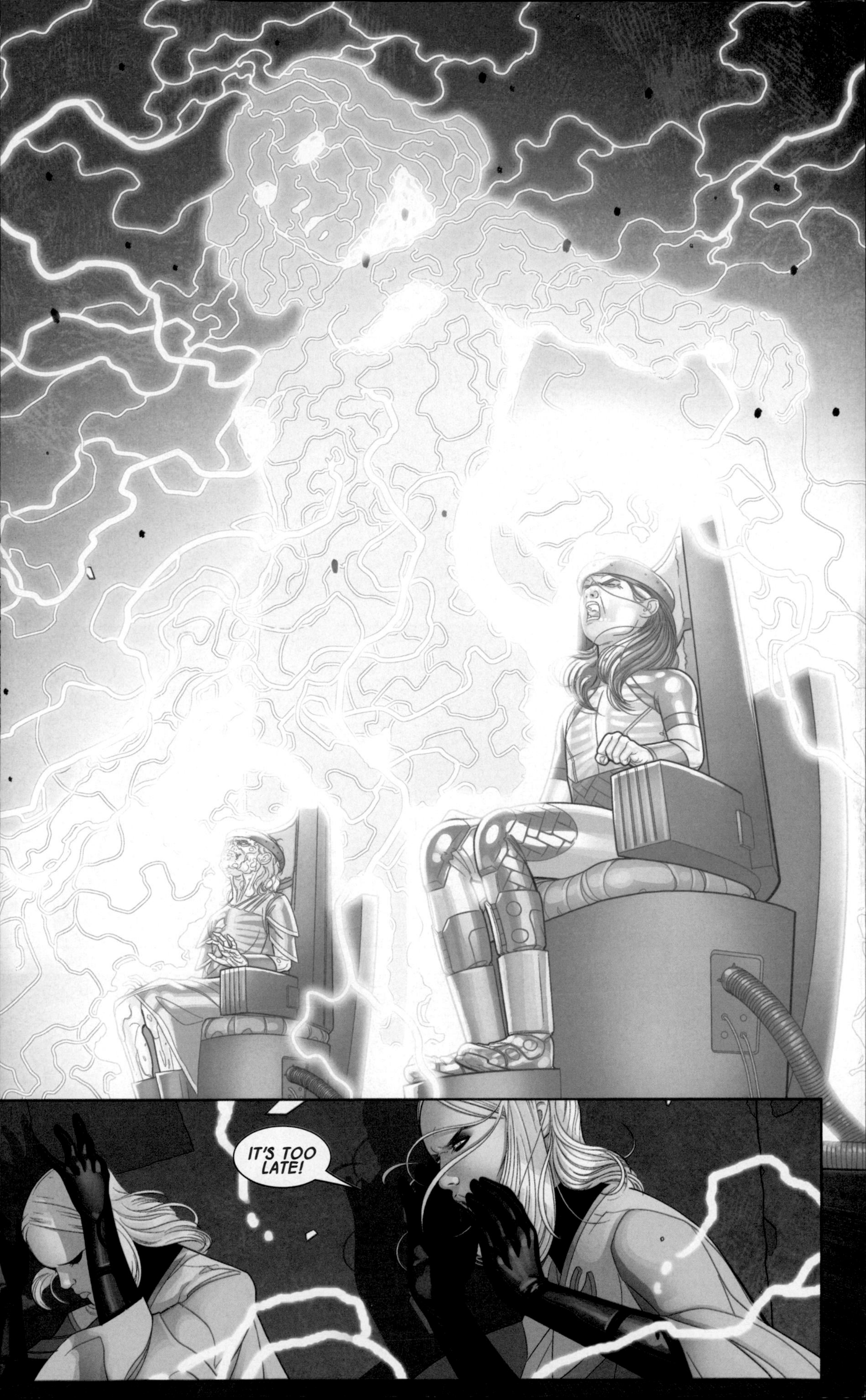
IT'S TOO LATE!

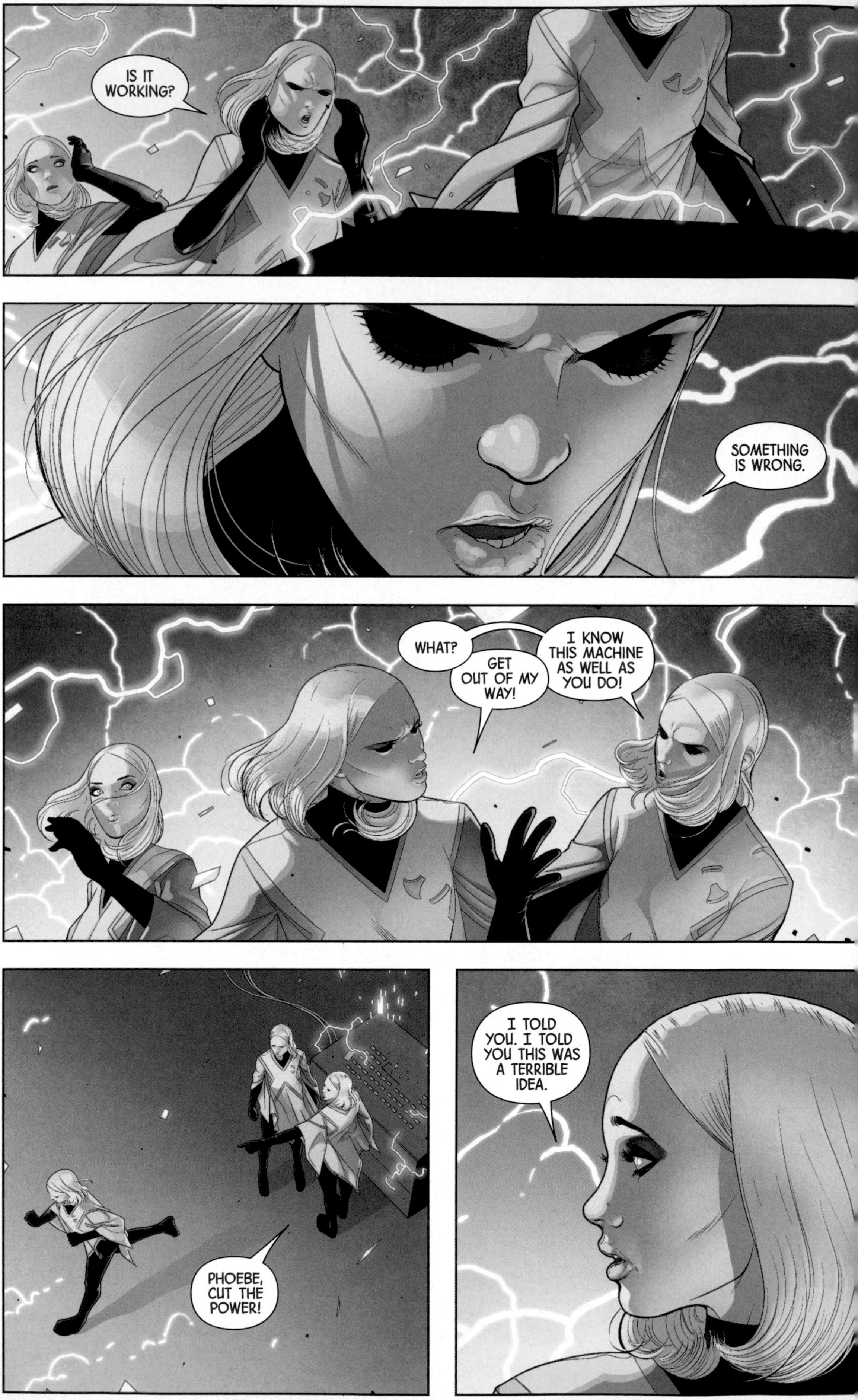
IS IT WORKING?
SOMETHING IS WRONG.
WHAT?
I KNOW THIS MACHINE AS WELL AS YOU DO!
GET OUT OF MY WAY!
PHOEBE, CUT THE POWER!
I TOLD YOU. I TOLD YOU THIS WAS A TERRIBLE IDEA.

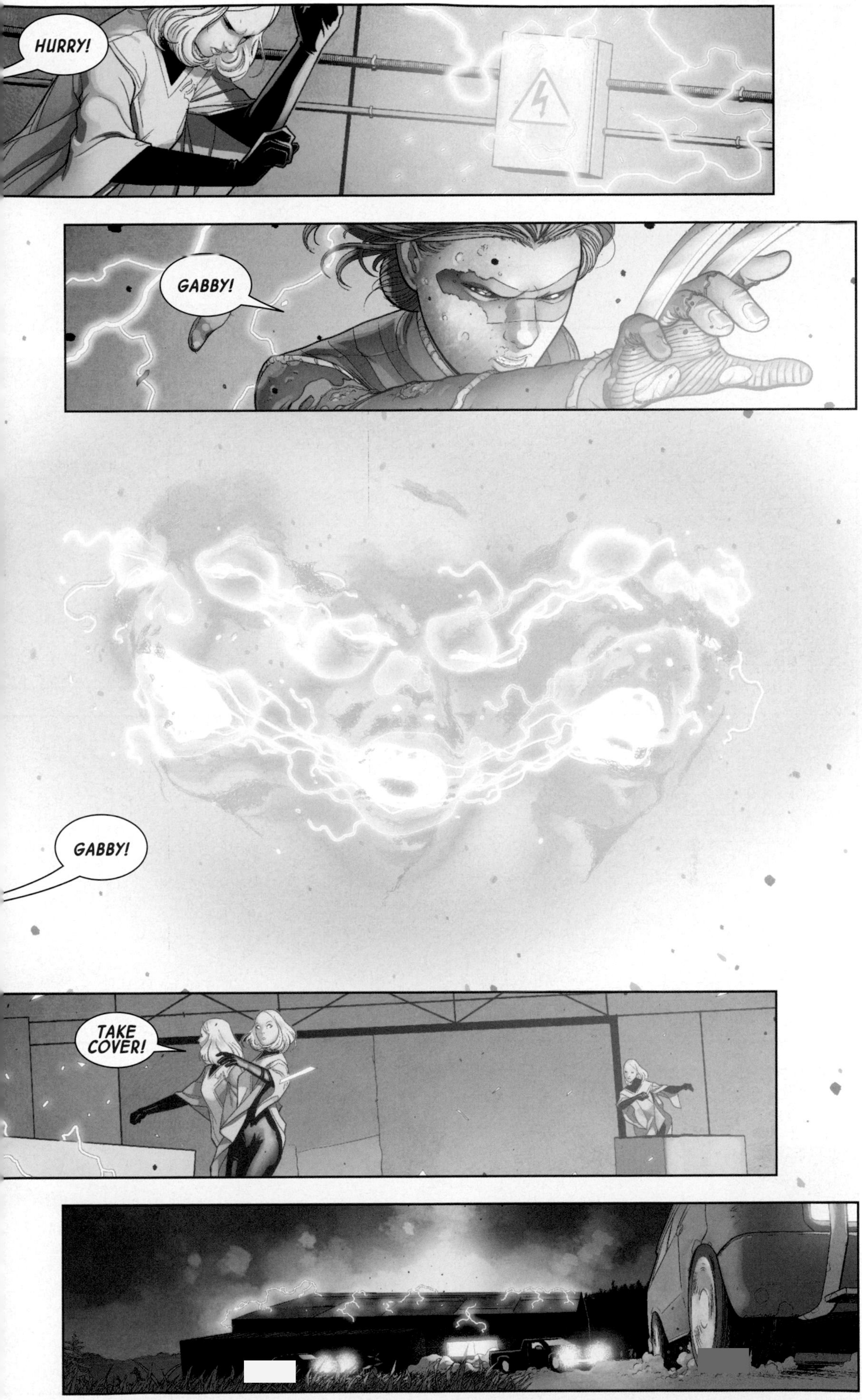
HURRY!
GABBY!
GABBY!
TAKE COVER!

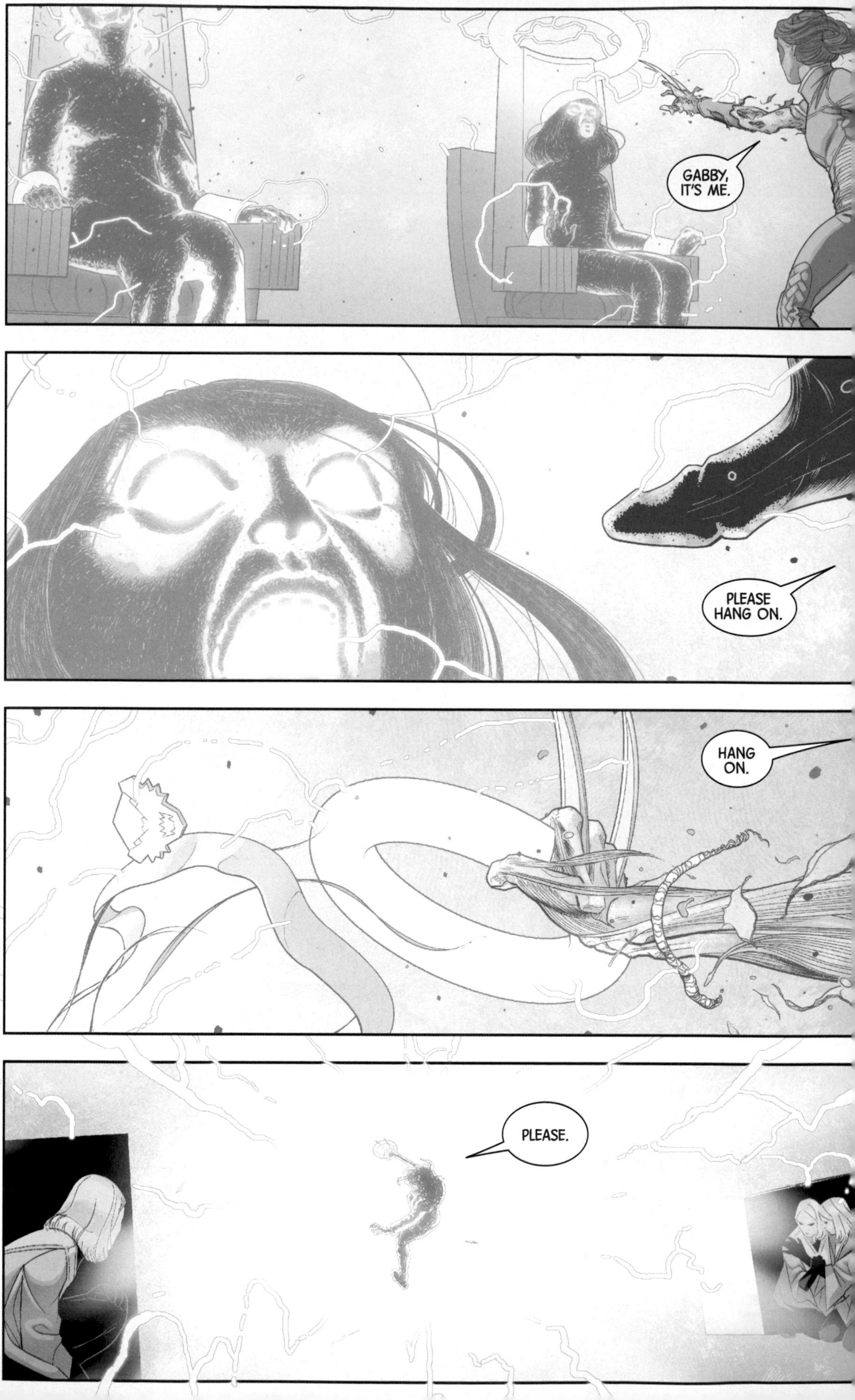
GABBY, IT'S ME.
PLEASE HANG ON.
HANG ON.
PLEASE.

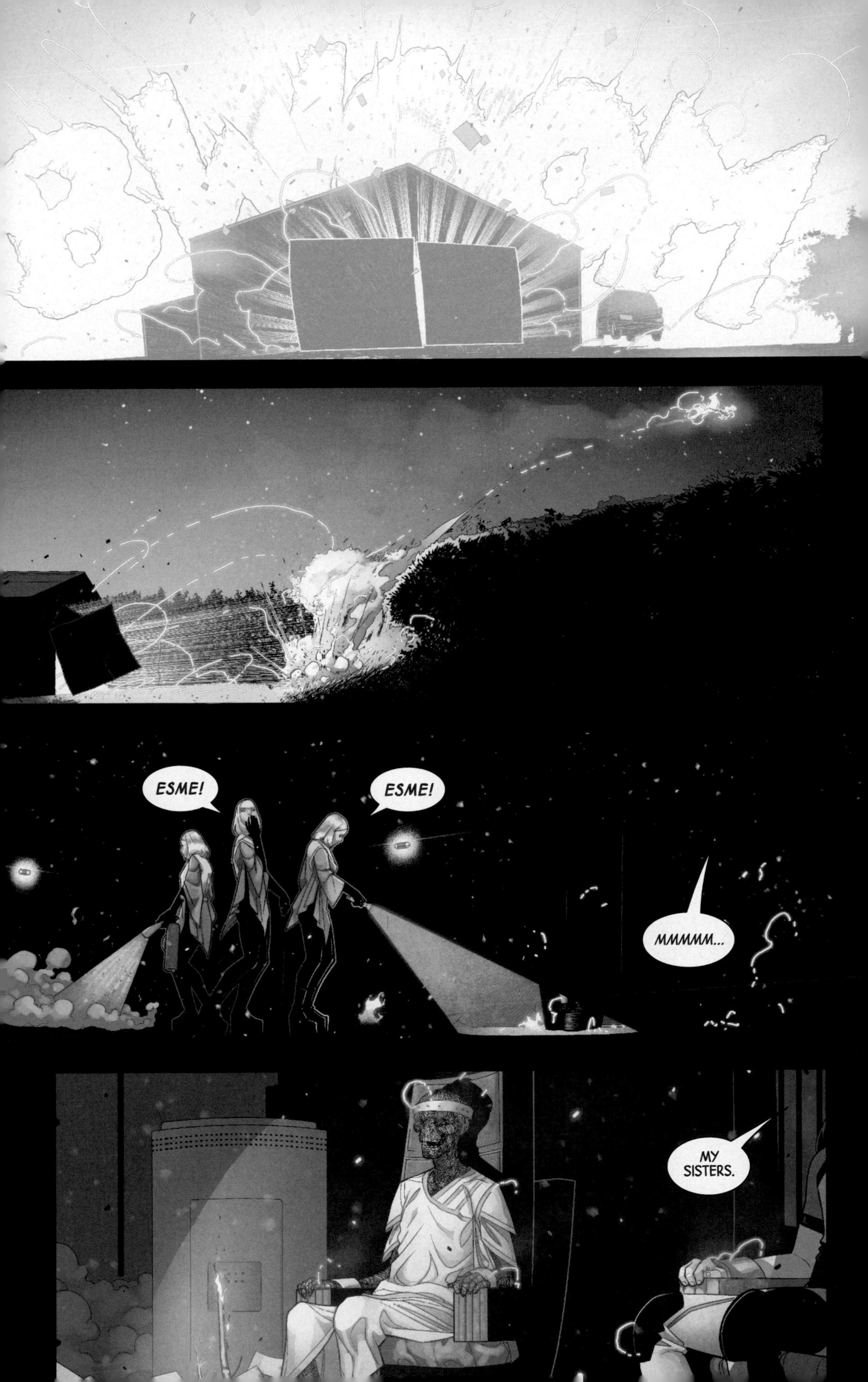
ESME!
ESME!
MMMMM...
MY SISTERS.

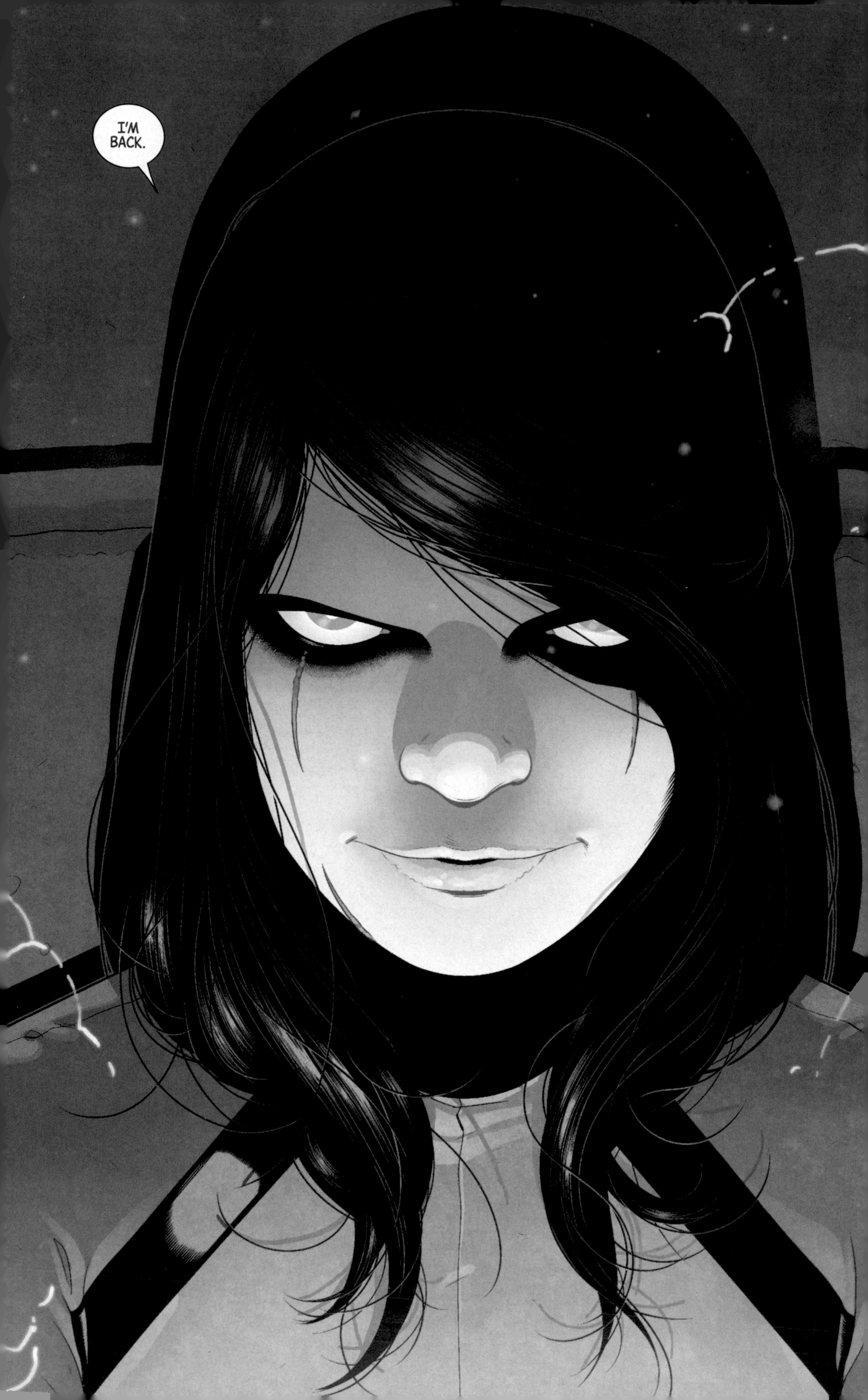
I'M BACK.

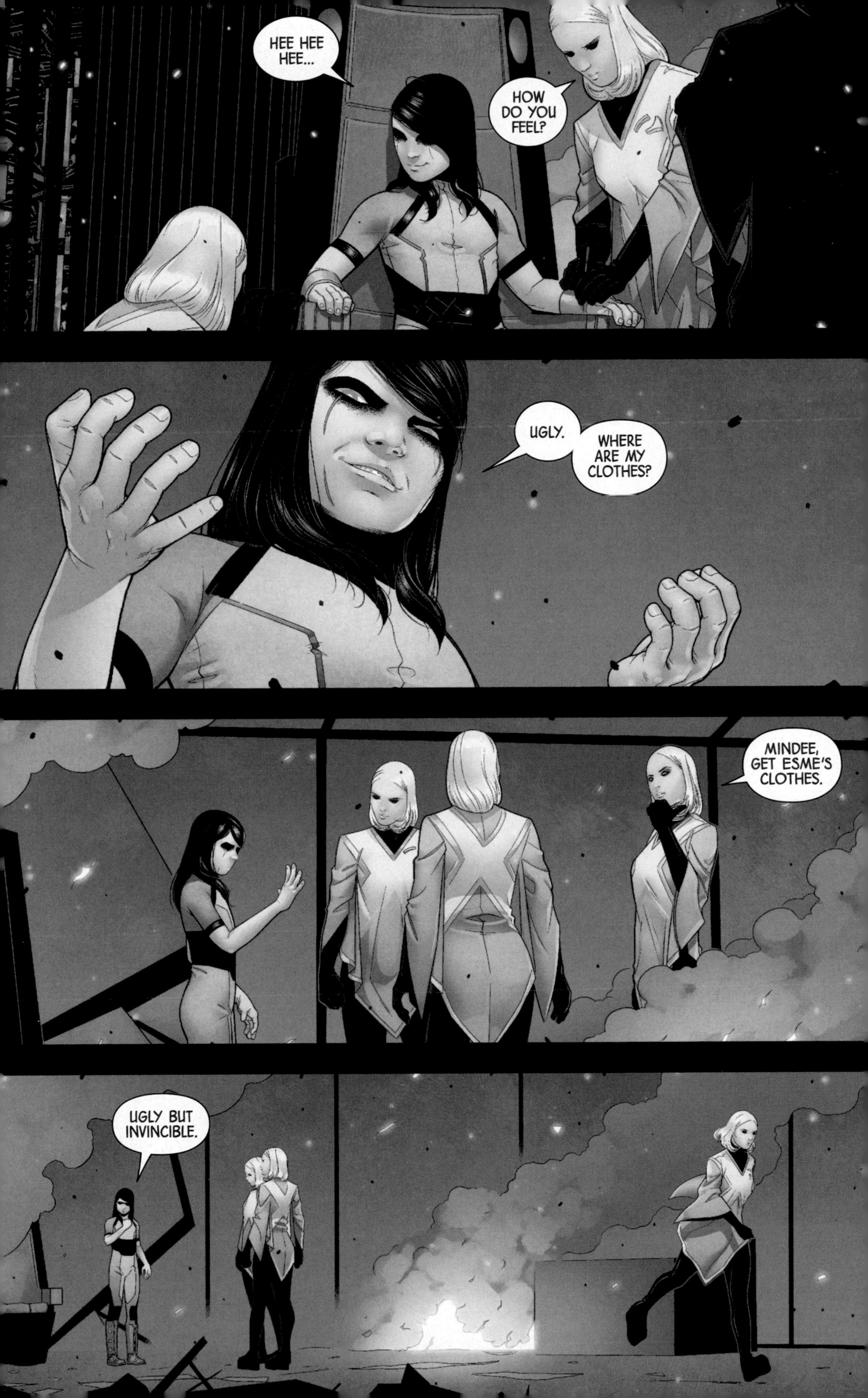
HEE HEE HEE...
HOW DO YOU FEEL?
UGLY.
WHERE ARE MY CLOTHES?
MINDEE, GET ESME'S CLOTHES.
UGLY BUT INVINCIBLE.

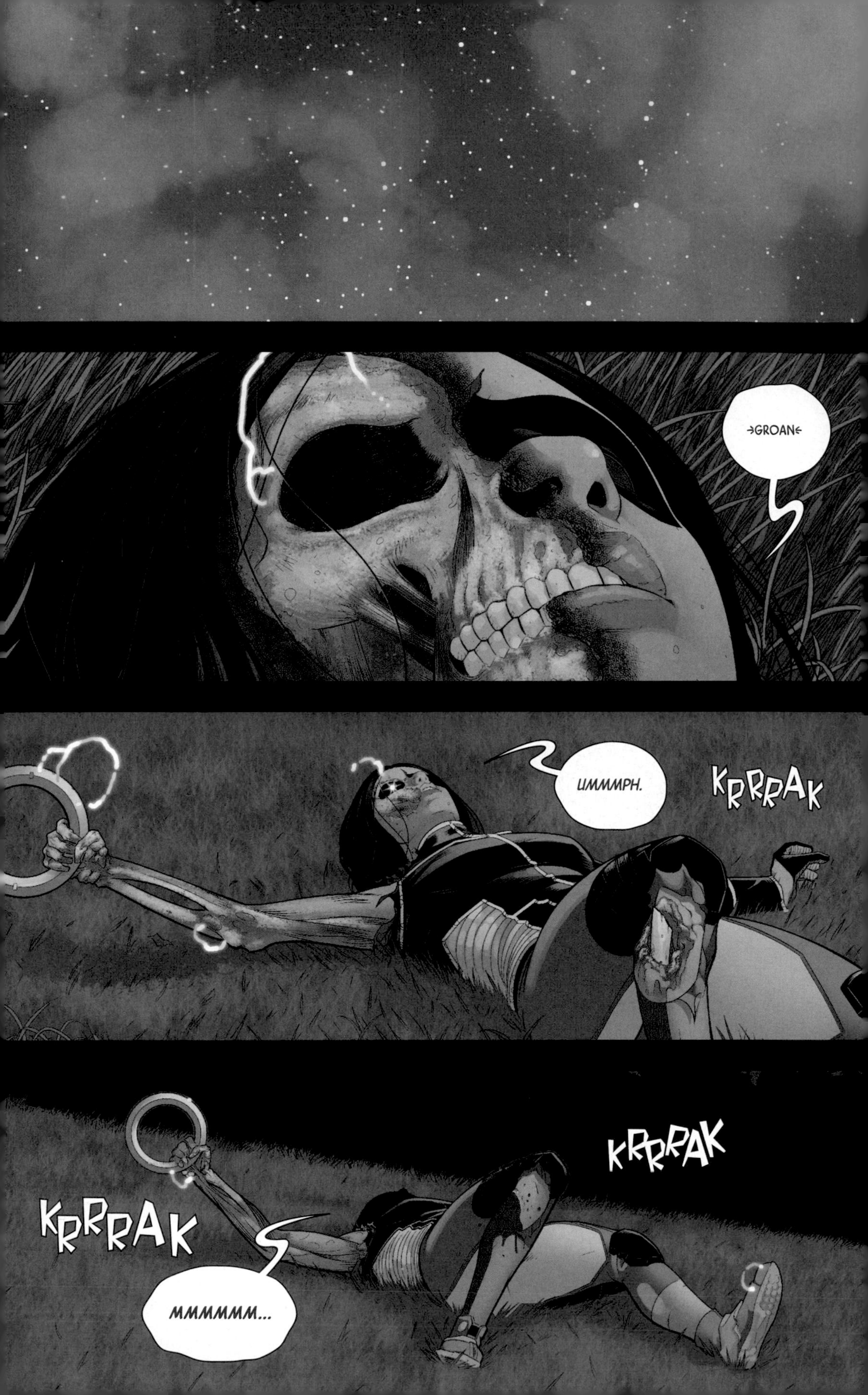

›GROAN‹
UMMMPH.
KRRRAK
KRRRAK
KRRRAK
MMMMMM...

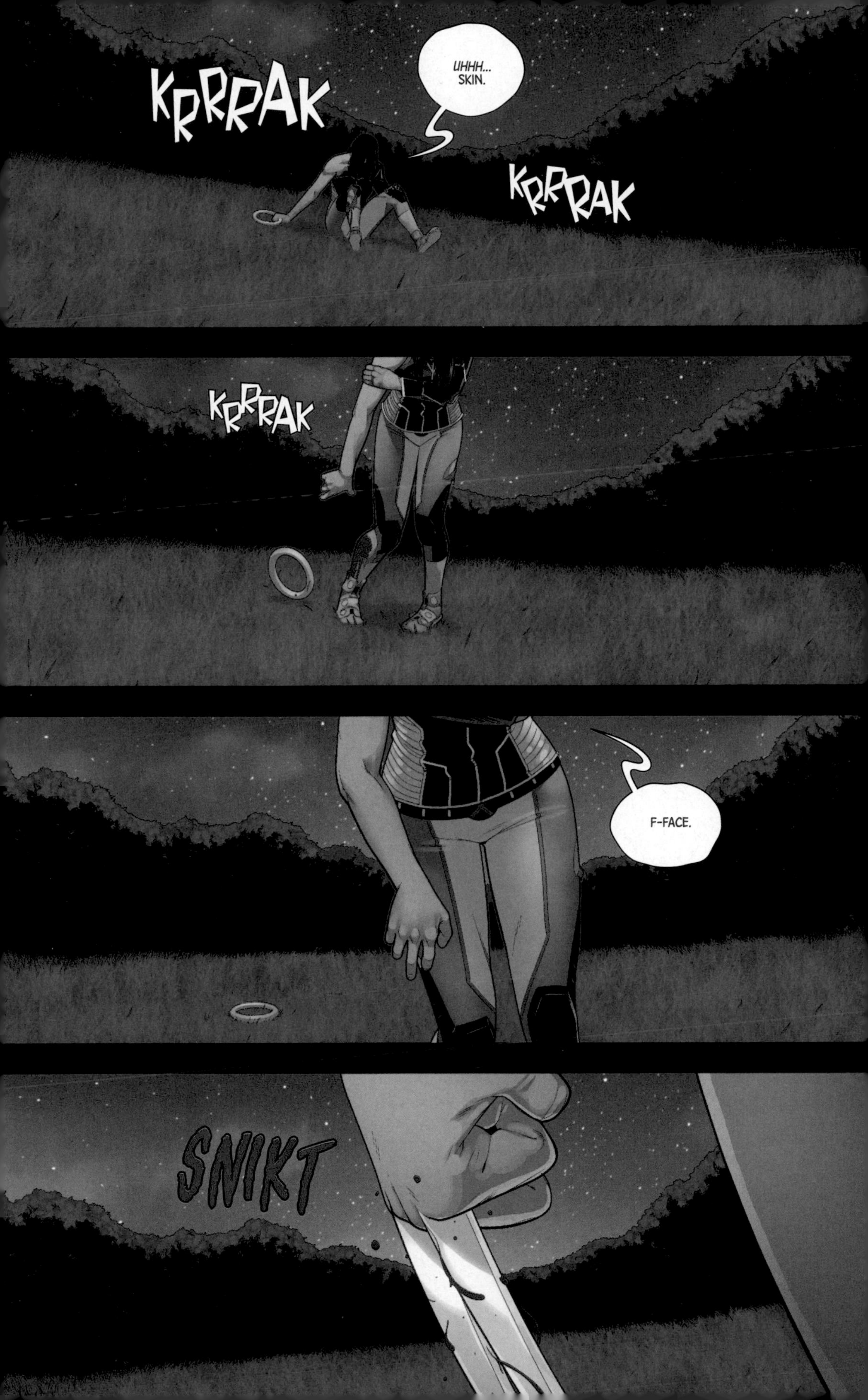
KRRRAK
UHHH... SKIN.
KRRRAK
KRRRAK
F-FACE.
SNIKT

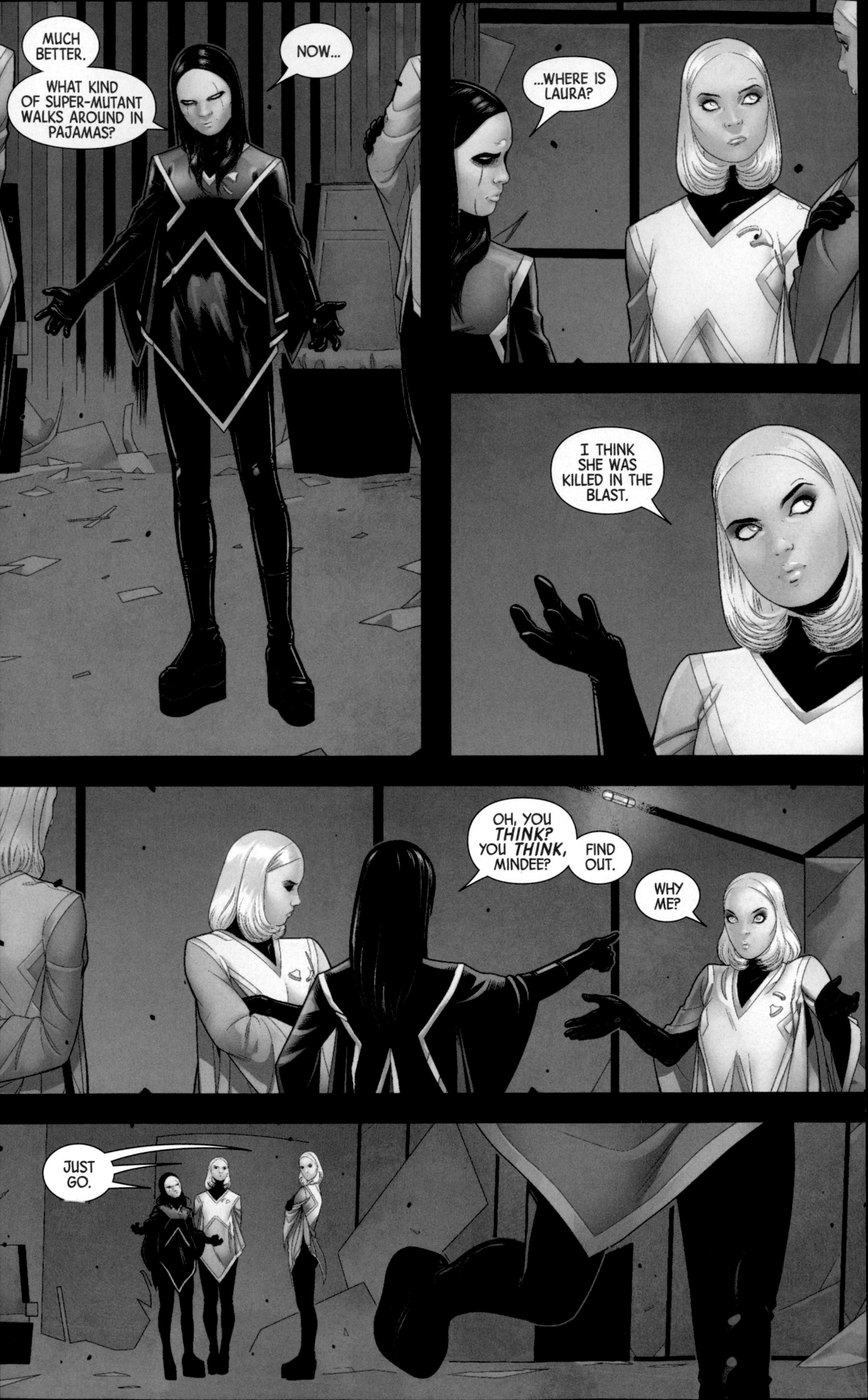
MUCH BETTER.
WHAT KIND OF SUPER-MUTANT WALKS AROUND IN PAJAMAS?
NOW...
...WHERE IS LAURA?
I THINK SHE WAS KILLED IN THE BLAST.
OH, YOU *THINK?* YOU *THINK,* MINDEE?
FIND OUT.
WHY ME?
JUST GO.

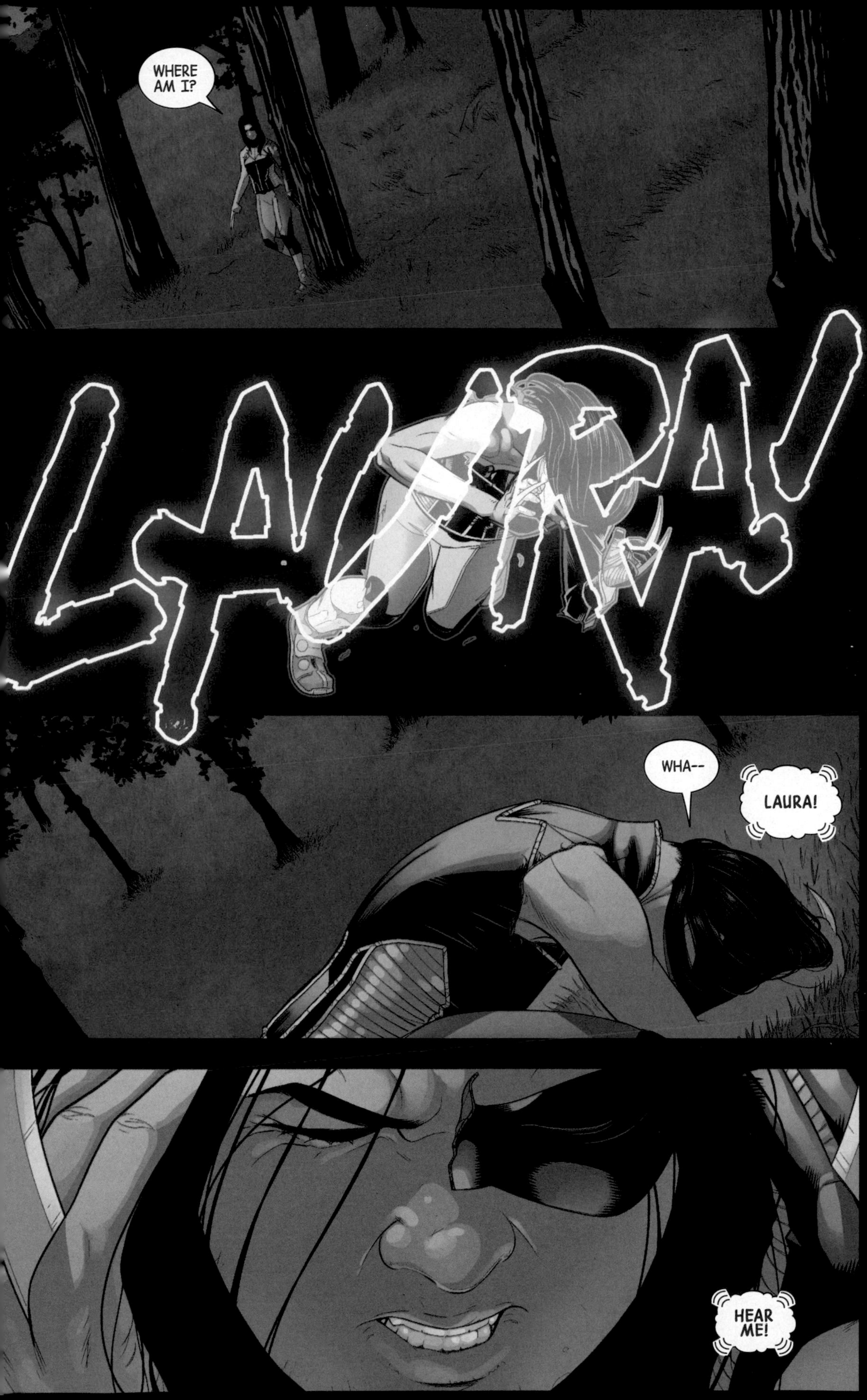
WHERE AM I?
LAURA!
WHA--
LAURA!
HEAR ME!

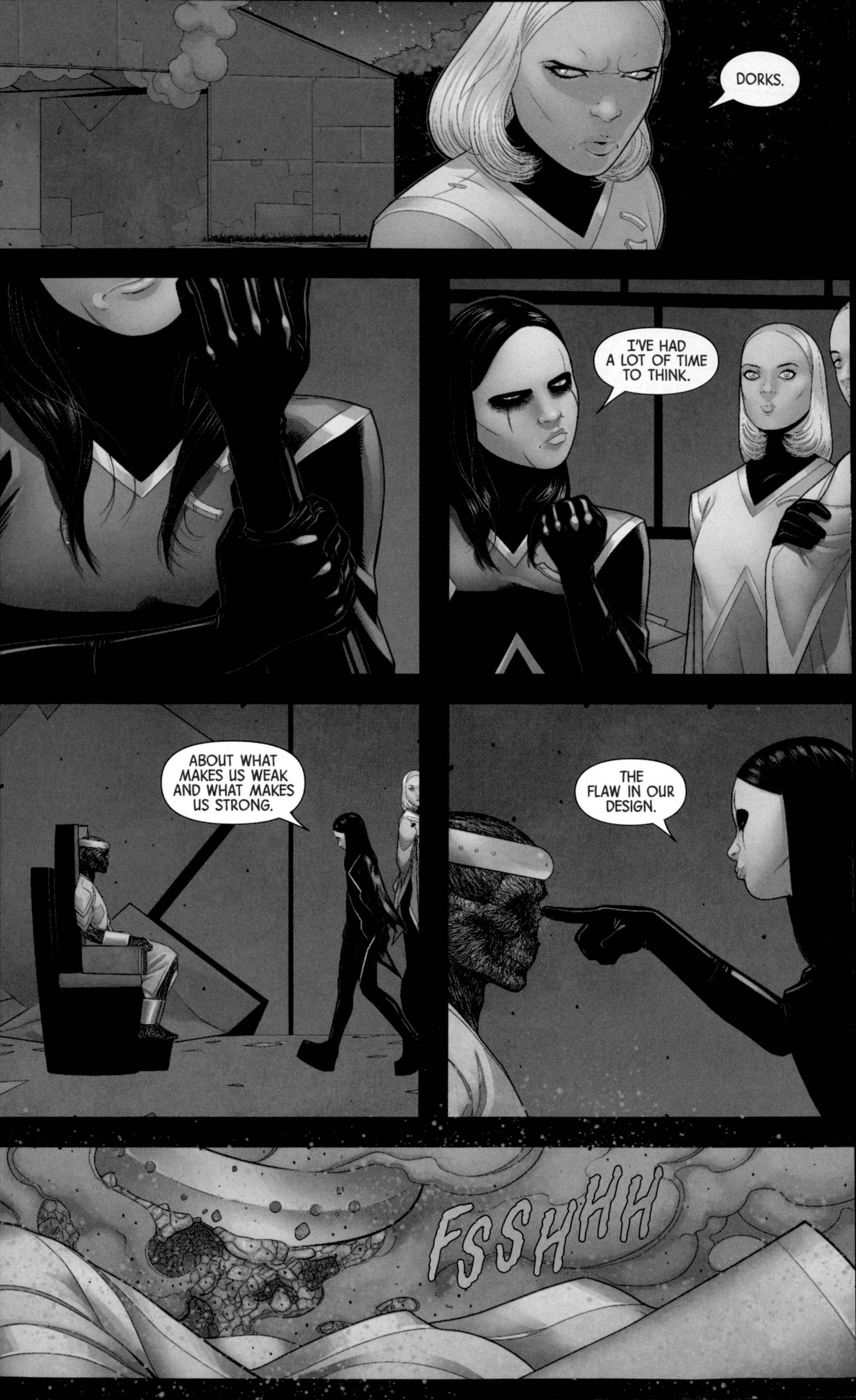
DORKS.
I'VE HAD A LOT OF TIME TO THINK.
ABOUT WHAT MAKES US WEAK AND WHAT MAKES US STRONG.
THE FLAW IN OUR DESIGN.
FSSHHH

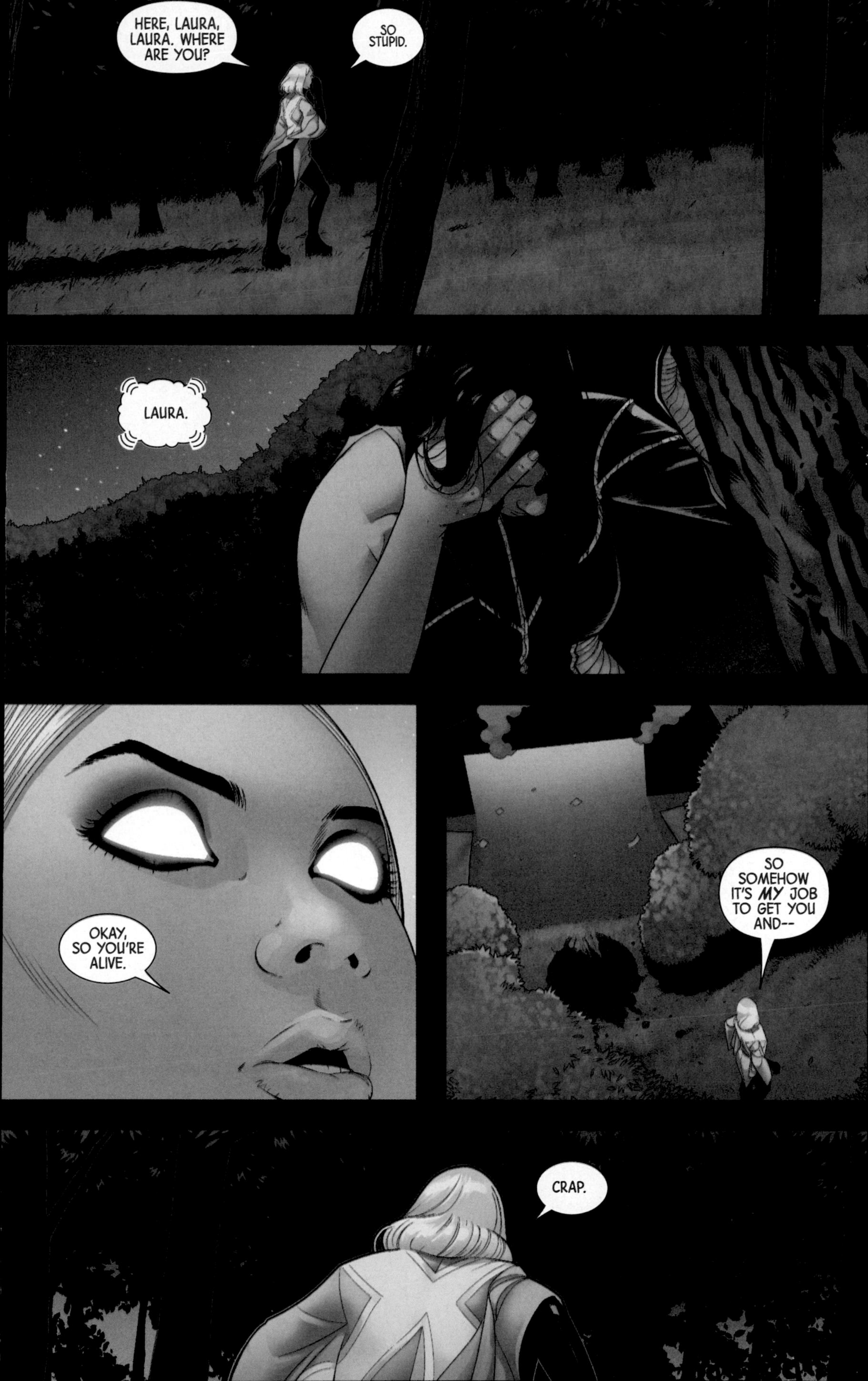

HERE, LAURA, LAURA. WHERE ARE YOU?
SO STUPID.
LAURA.
OKAY, SO YOU'RE ALIVE.
SO SOMEHOW IT'S MY JOB TO GET YOU AND--
CRAP.

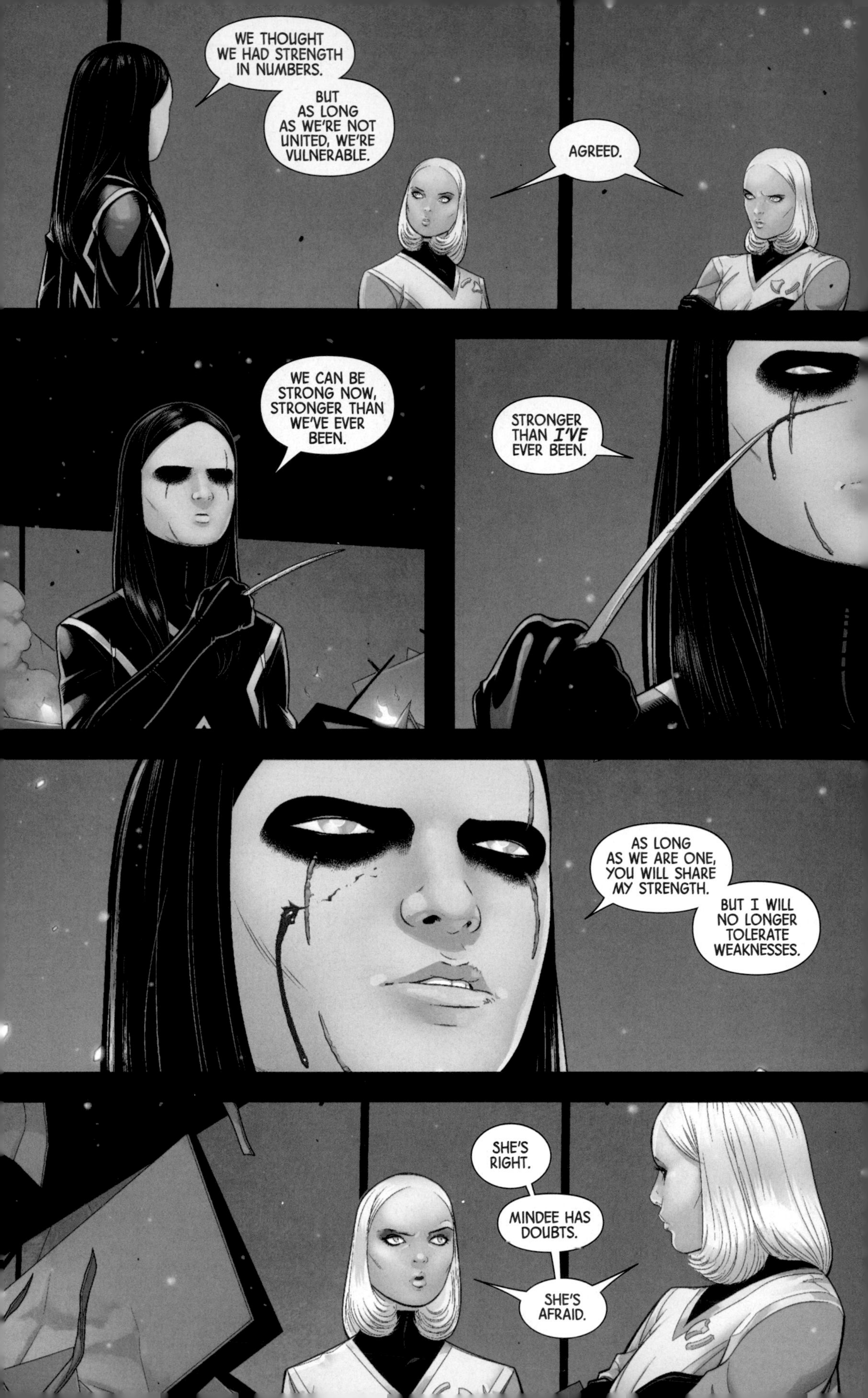
WE THOUGHT WE HAD STRENGTH IN NUMBERS.
BUT AS LONG AS WE'RE NOT UNITED, WE'RE VULNERABLE.
AGREED.
WE CAN BE STRONG NOW, STRONGER THAN WE'VE EVER BEEN.
STRONGER THAN *I'VE* EVER BEEN.
AS LONG AS WE ARE ONE, YOU WILL SHARE MY STRENGTH.
BUT I WILL NO LONGER TOLERATE WEAKNESSES.
SHE'S RIGHT.
MINDEE HAS DOUBTS.
SHE'S AFRAID.

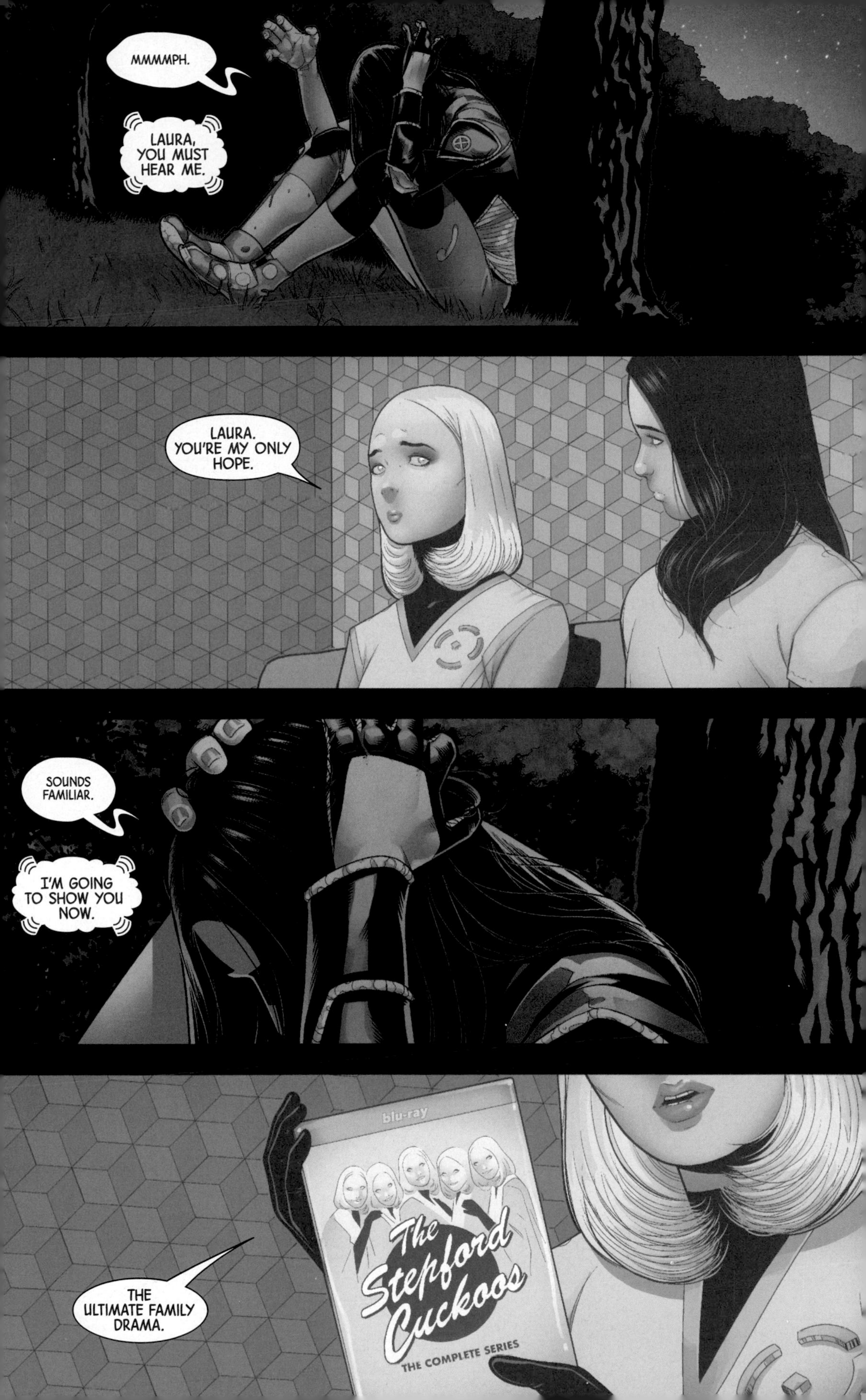
MMMMPH.
LAURA, YOU MUST HEAR ME.
LAURA. YOU'RE MY ONLY HOPE.
SOUNDS FAMILIAR.
I'M GOING TO SHOW YOU NOW.
blu-ray
The Stepford Cuckoos
THE COMPLETE SERIES
THE ULTIMATE FAMILY DRAMA.

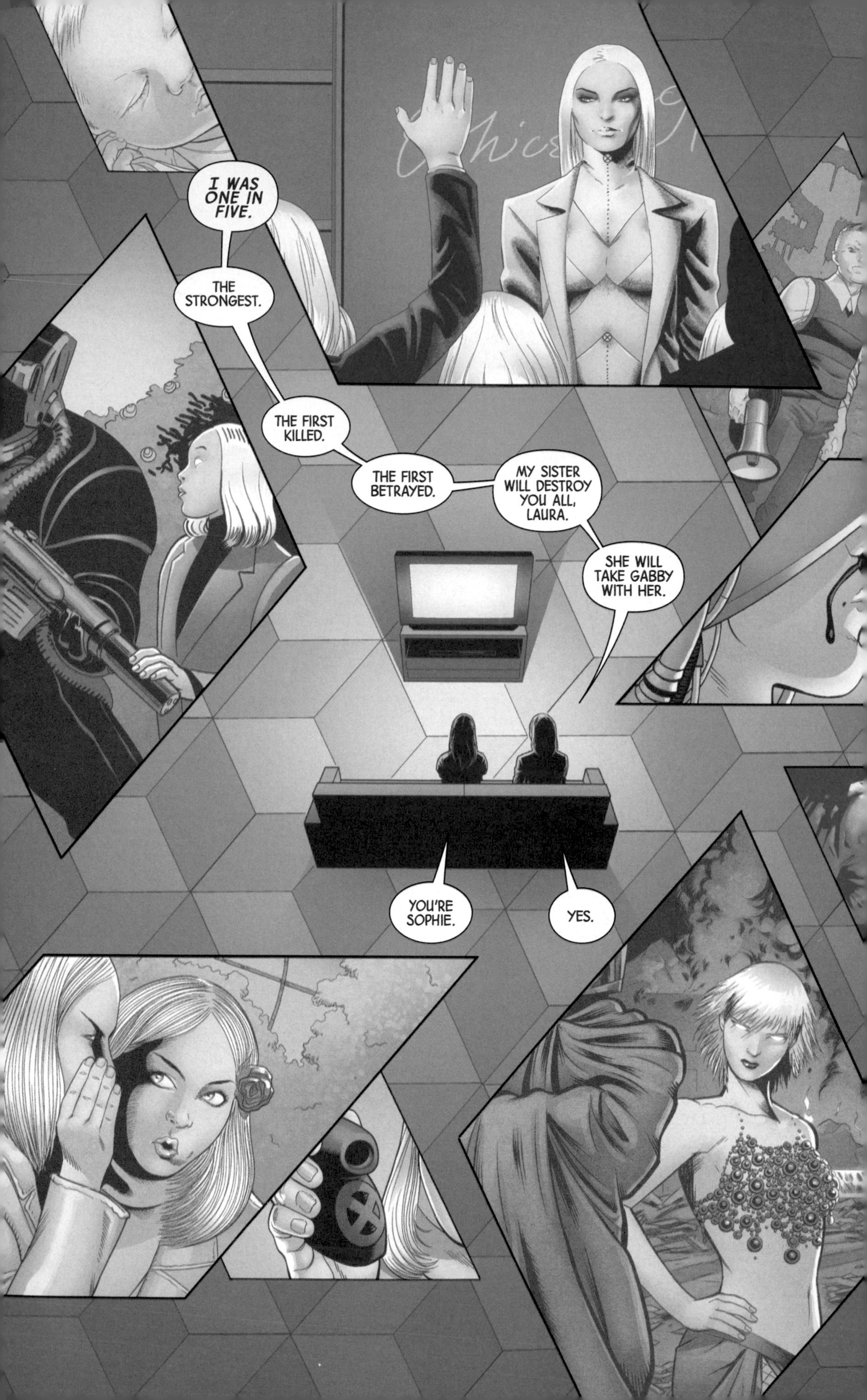
I WAS ONE IN FIVE.
THE STRONGEST.
THE FIRST KILLED.
THE FIRST BETRAYED.
MY SISTER WILL DESTROY YOU ALL, LAURA.
SHE WILL TAKE GABBY WITH HER.
YOU'RE SOPHIE.
YES.

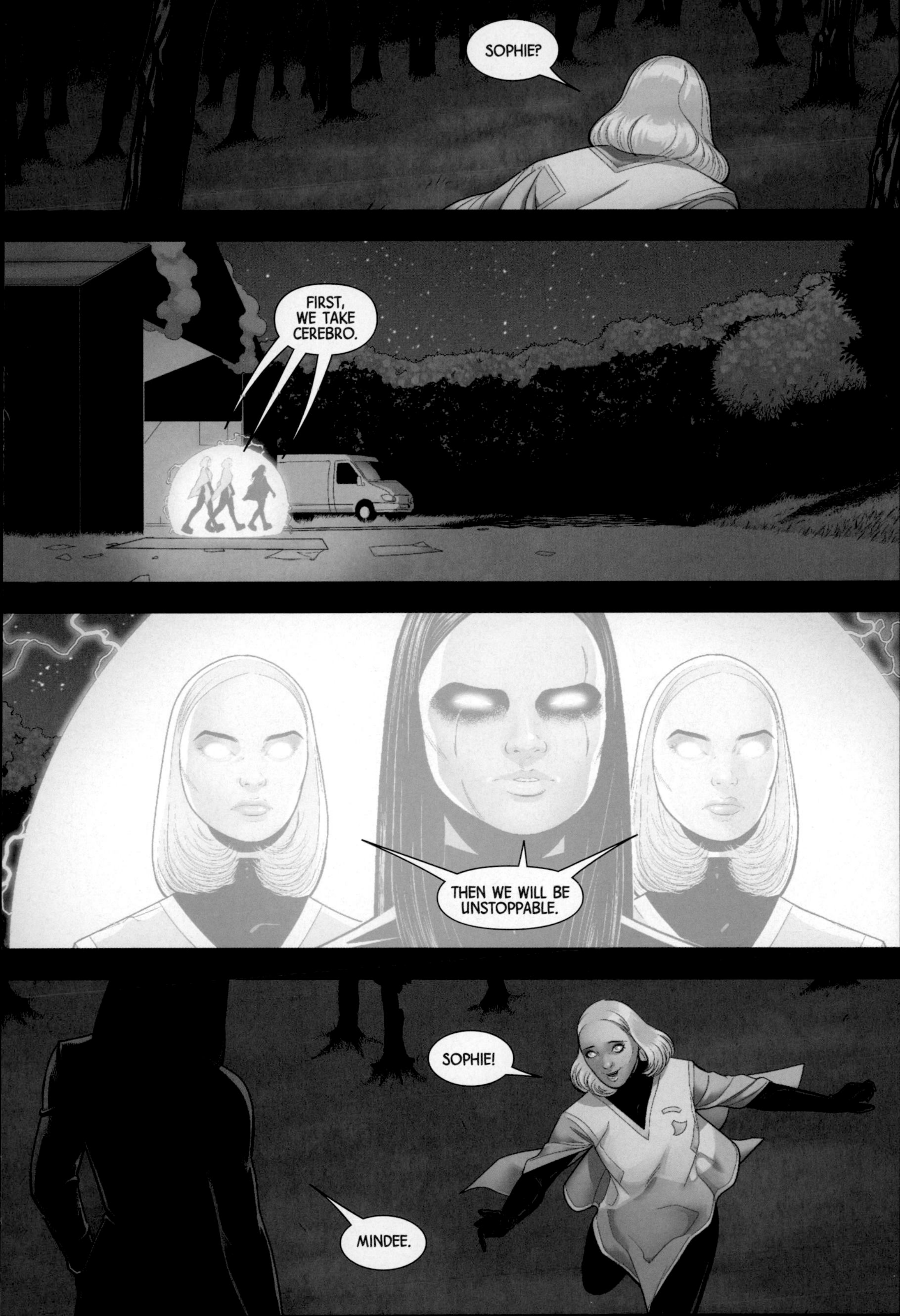
SOPHIE?
FIRST, WE TAKE CEREBRO.
THEN WE WILL BE UNSTOPPABLE.
SOPHIE!
MINDEE.

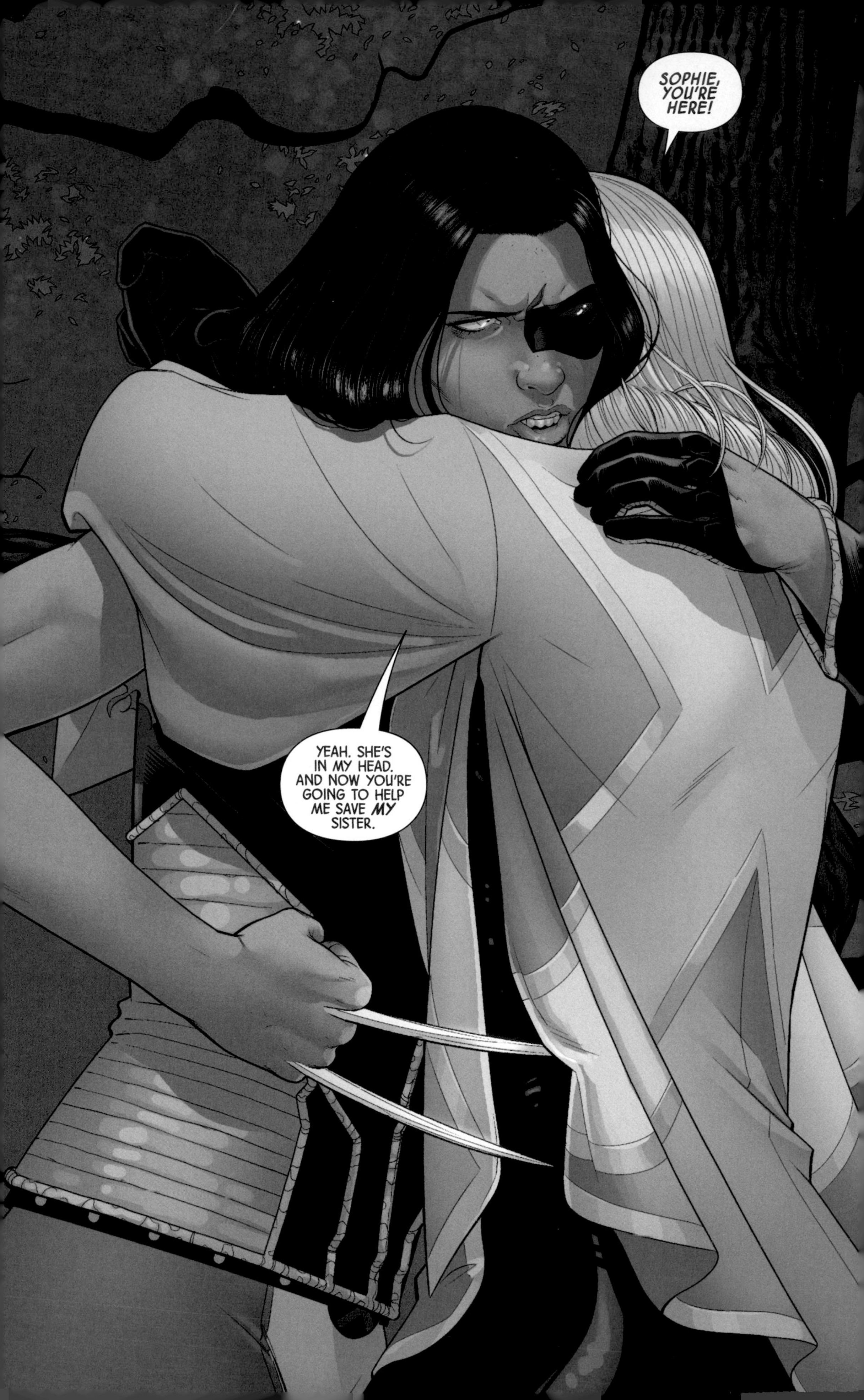
SOPHIE, YOU'RE HERE!
YEAH. SHE'S IN MY HEAD. AND NOW YOU'RE GOING TO HELP ME SAVE MY SISTER.

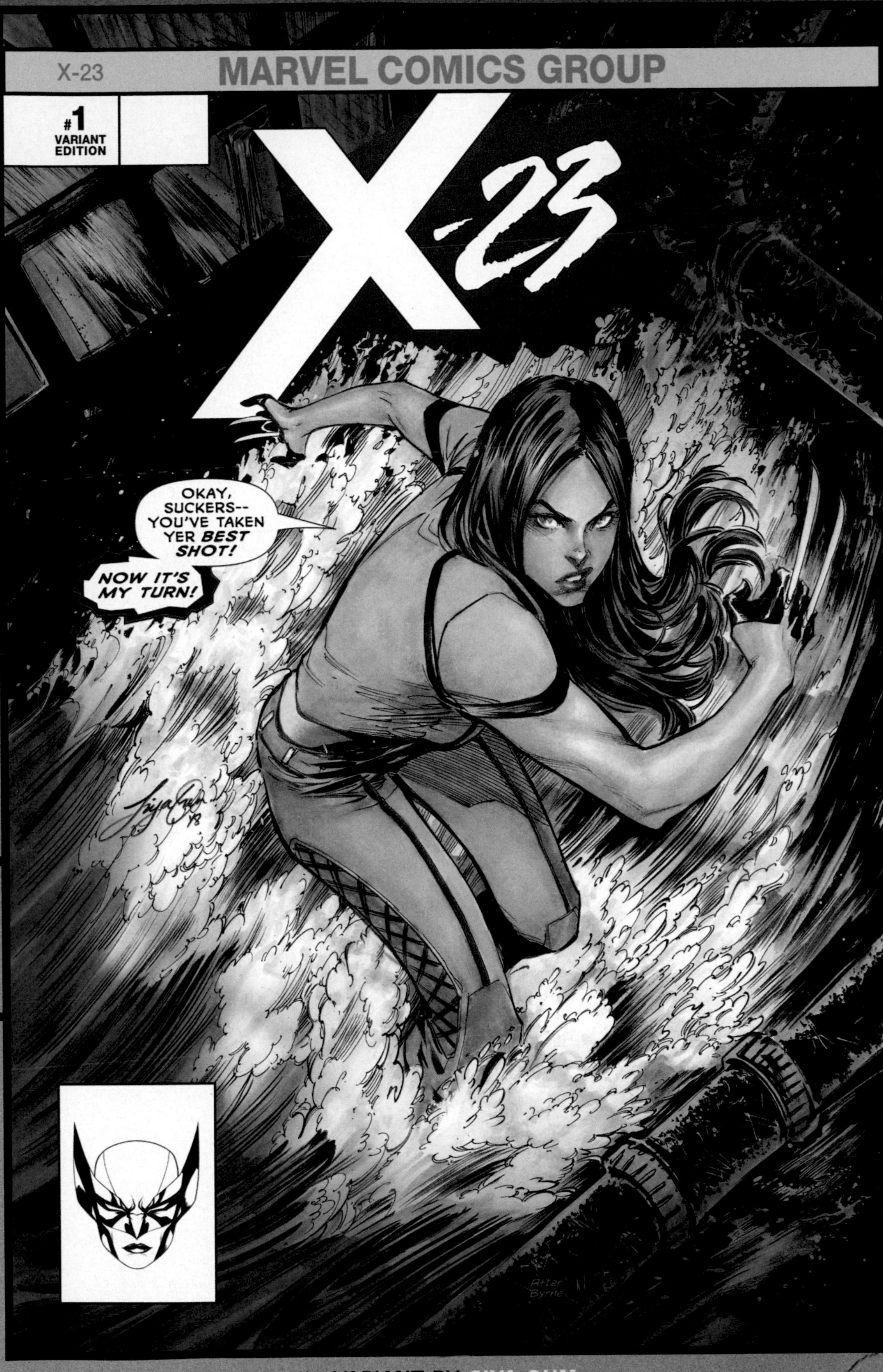
X-23
MARVEL COMICS GROUP
#1
VARIANT
EDITION
X-23
OKAY, SUCKERS-- YOU'VE TAKEN YER BEST SHOT!
NOW IT'S MY TURN!

#1 VARIANT BY SIYA OUM

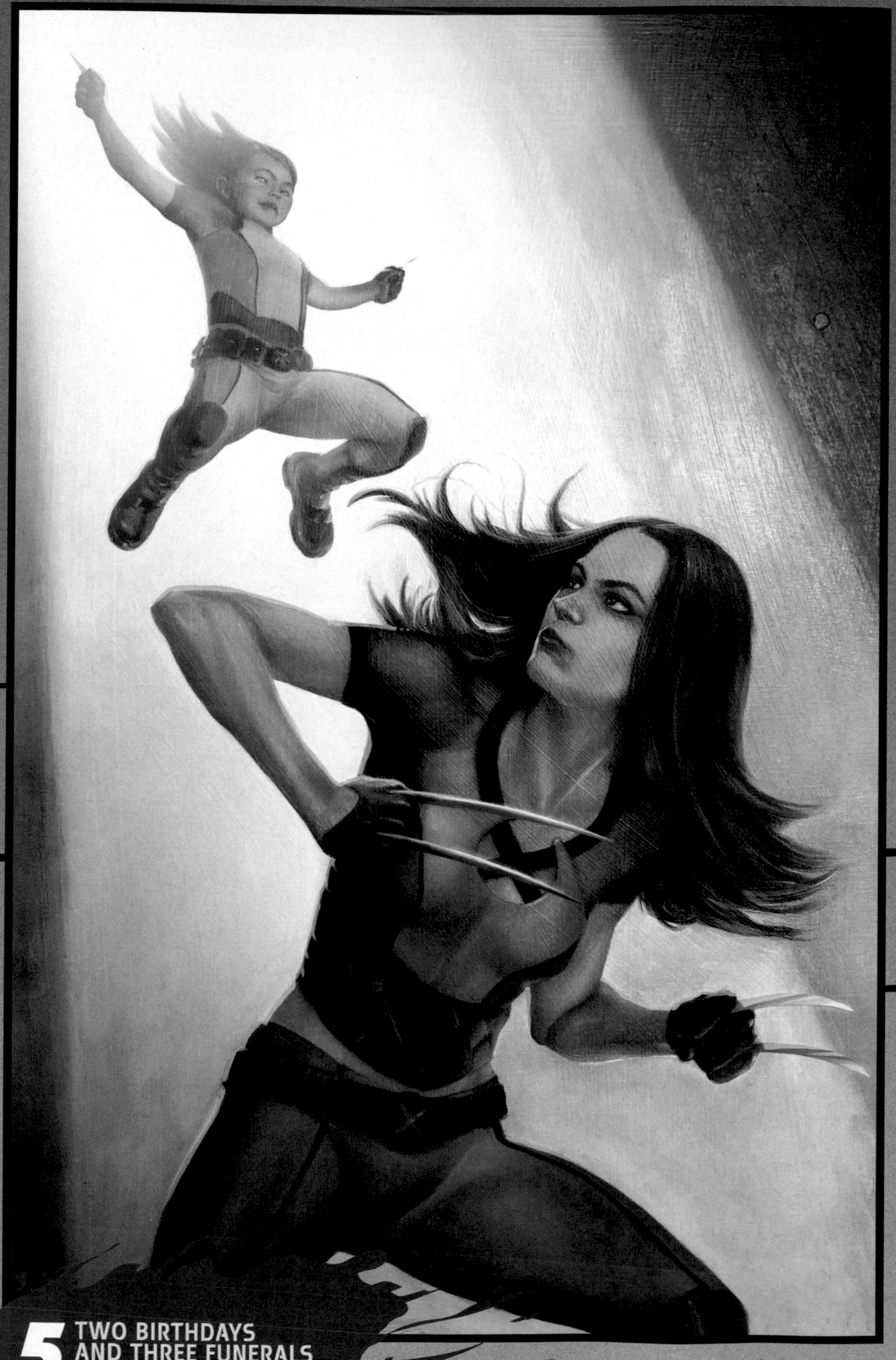

5 TWO BIRTHDAYS AND THREE FUNERALS PART 5

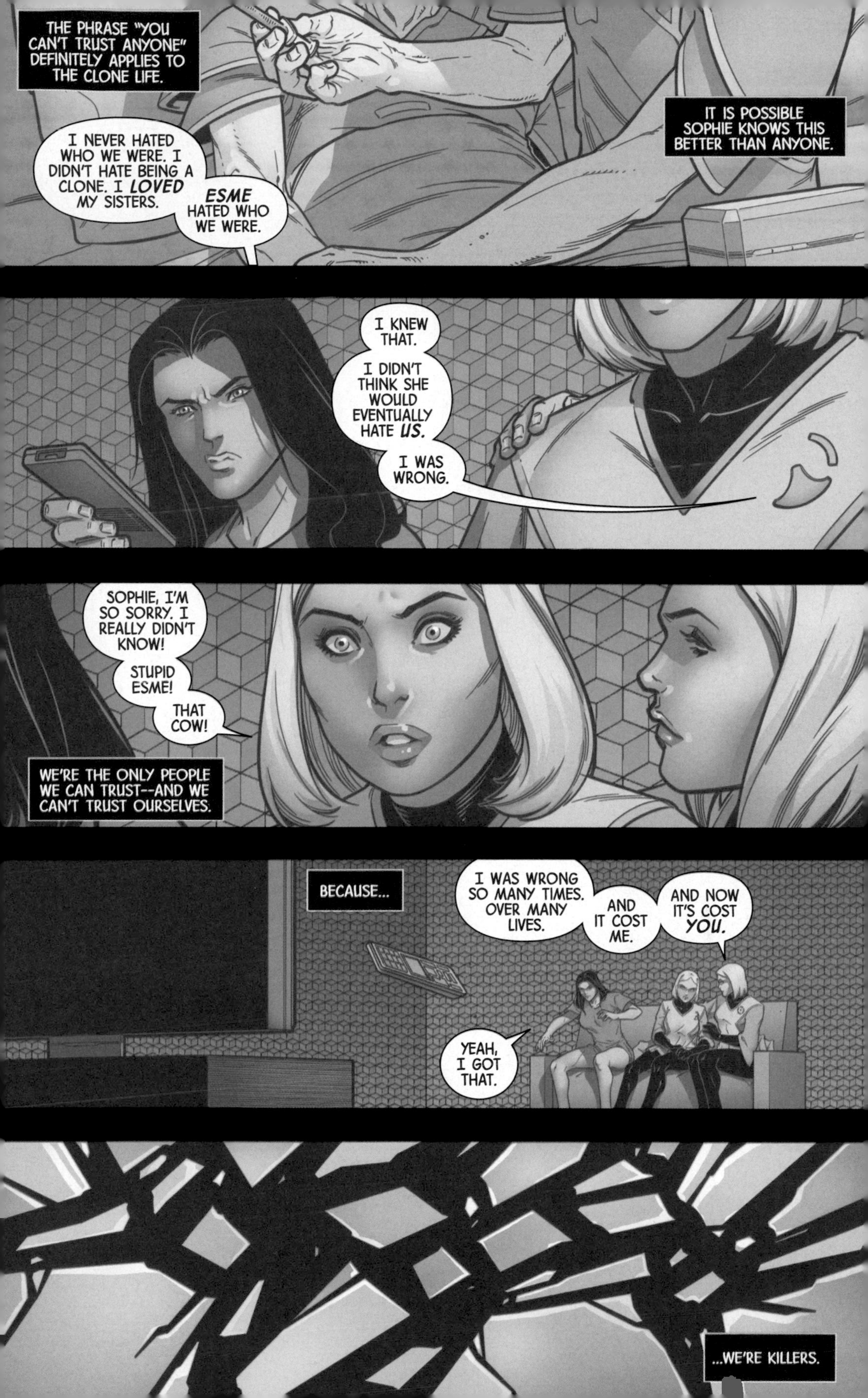
THE PHRASE "YOU CAN'T TRUST ANYONE" DEFINITELY APPLIES TO THE CLONE LIFE.
I NEVER HATED WHO WE WERE. I DIDN'T HATE BEING A CLONE. I LOVED MY SISTERS.
ESME HATED WHO WE WERE.
IT IS POSSIBLE SOPHIE KNOWS THIS BETTER THAN ANYONE.
I KNEW THAT.
I DIDN'T THINK SHE WOULD EVENTUALLY HATE US.
I WAS WRONG.
SOPHIE, I'M SO SORRY. I REALLY DIDN'T KNOW!
STUPID ESME!
THAT COW!
WE'RE THE ONLY PEOPLE WE CAN TRUST--AND WE CAN'T TRUST OURSELVES.
BECAUSE...
I WAS WRONG SO MANY TIMES. OVER MANY LIVES.
AND IT COST ME.
AND NOW IT'S COST YOU.
YEAH, I GOT THAT.
...WE'RE KILLERS.

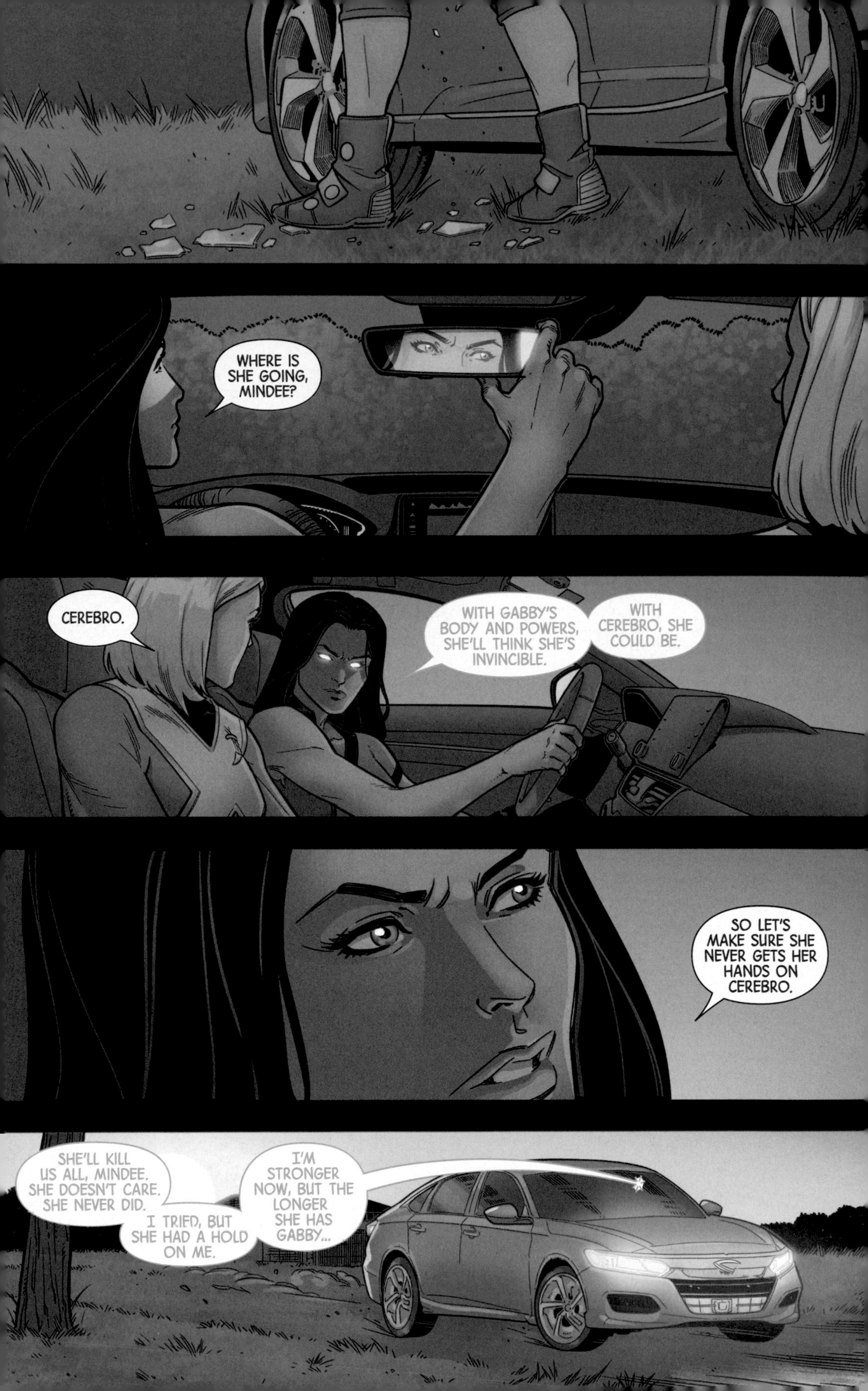
WHERE IS SHE GOING, MINDEE?
CEREBRO.
WITH GABBY'S BODY AND POWERS, SHE'LL THINK SHE'S INVINCIBLE.
WITH CEREBRO, SHE COULD BE.
SO LET'S MAKE SURE SHE NEVER GETS HER HANDS ON CEREBRO.
SHE'LL KILL US ALL, MINDEE. SHE DOESN'T CARE. SHE NEVER DID.
I TRIED, BUT SHE HAD A HOLD ON ME.
I'M STRONGER NOW, BUT THE LONGER SHE HAS GABBY...

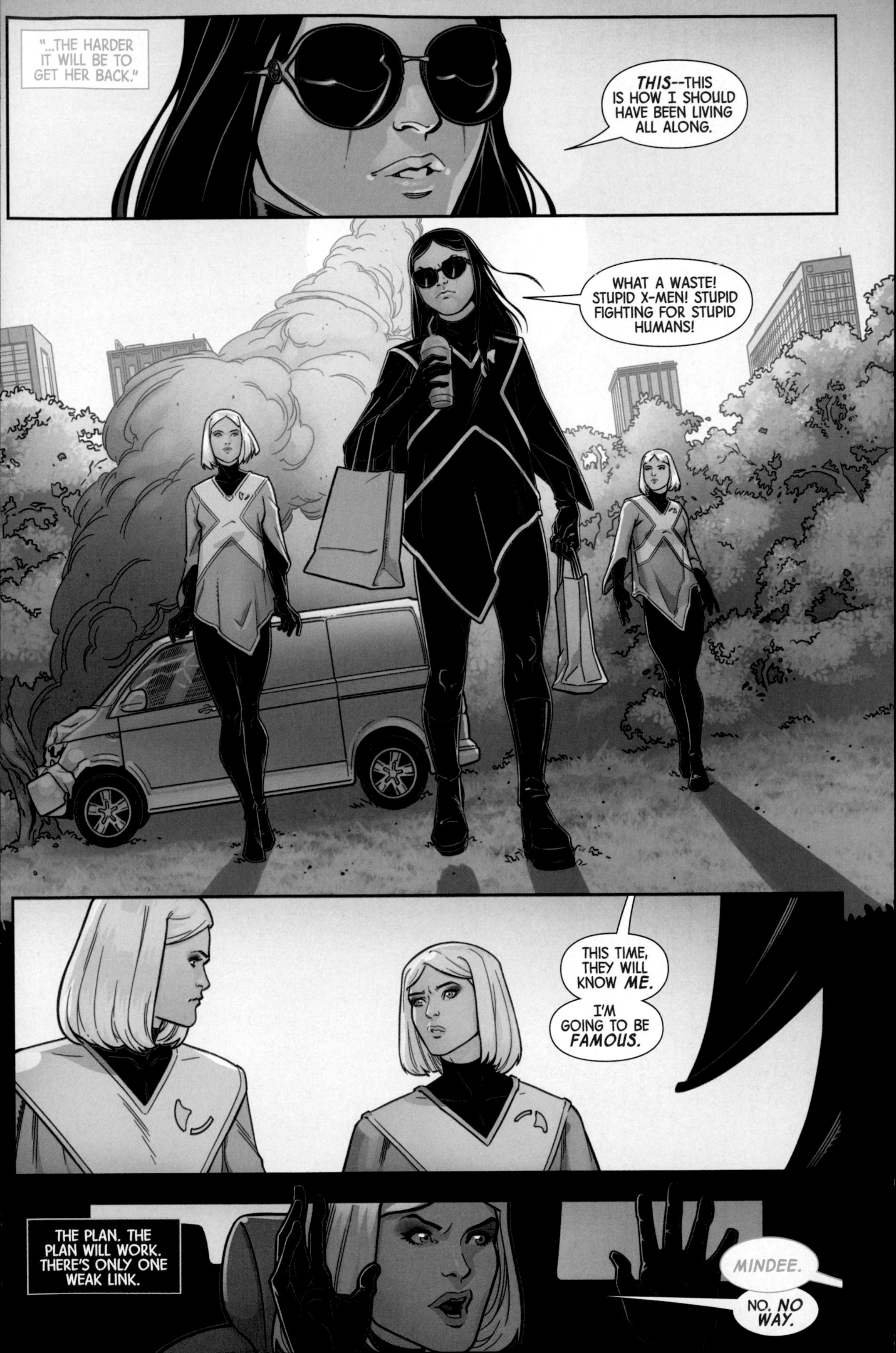
"...THE HARDER IT WILL BE TO GET HER BACK."
THIS--THIS IS HOW I SHOULD HAVE BEEN LIVING ALL ALONG.
WHAT A WASTE! STUPID X-MEN! STUPID FIGHTING FOR STUPID HUMANS!
THIS TIME, THEY WILL KNOW ME.
I'M GOING TO BE FAMOUS.
THE PLAN. THE PLAN WILL WORK. THERE'S ONLY ONE WEAK LINK.
MINDEE.
NO. NO WAY.

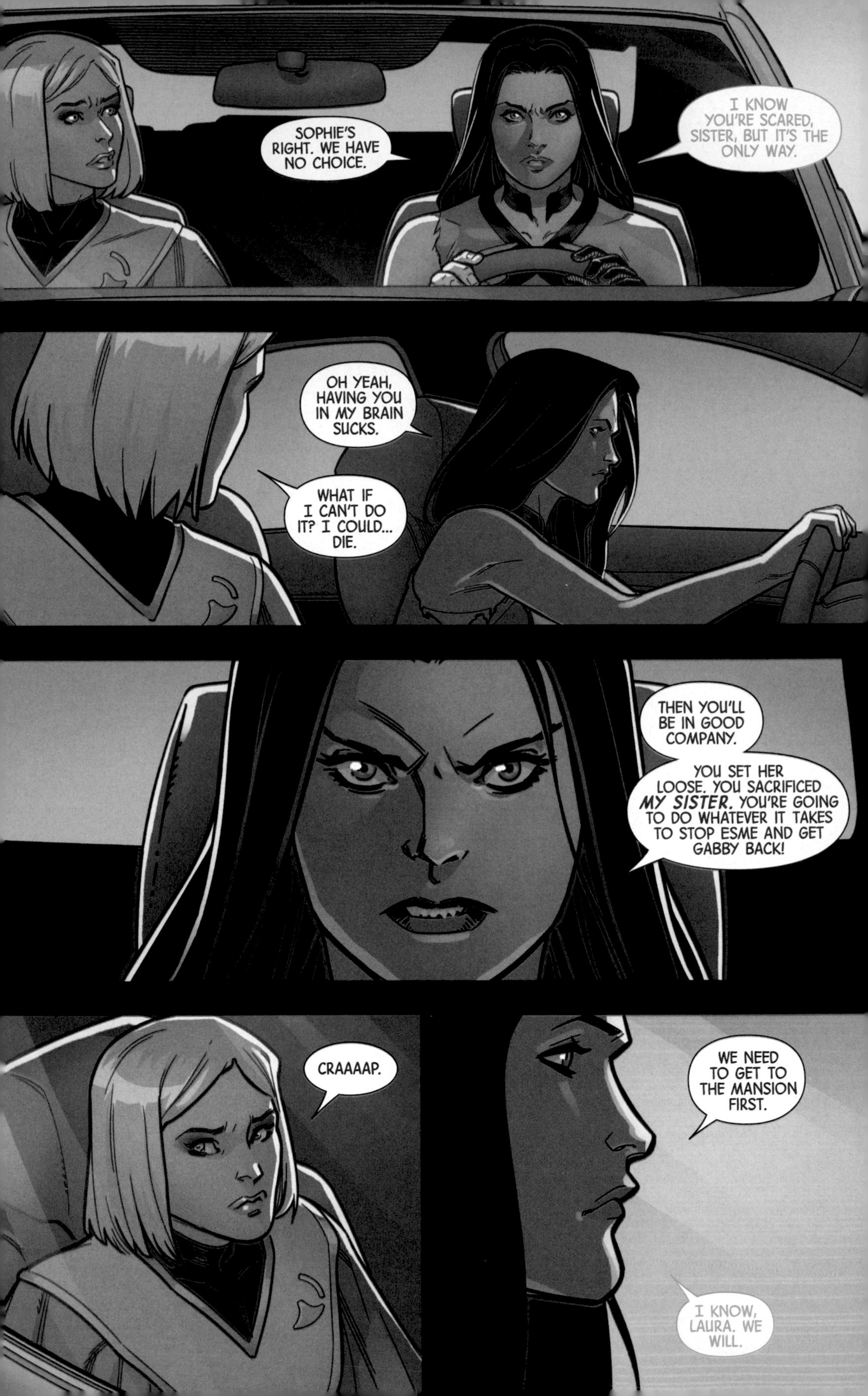
SOPHIE'S RIGHT. WE HAVE NO CHOICE.
I KNOW YOU'RE SCARED, SISTER, BUT IT'S THE ONLY WAY.
OH YEAH, HAVING YOU IN MY BRAIN SUCKS.
WHAT IF I CAN'T DO IT? I COULD... DIE.
THEN YOU'LL BE IN GOOD COMPANY.
YOU SET HER LOOSE. YOU SACRIFICED MY SISTER. YOU'RE GOING TO DO WHATEVER IT TAKES TO STOP ESME AND GET GABBY BACK!
CRAAAAP.
WE NEED TO GET TO THE MANSION FIRST.
I KNOW, LAURA. WE WILL.

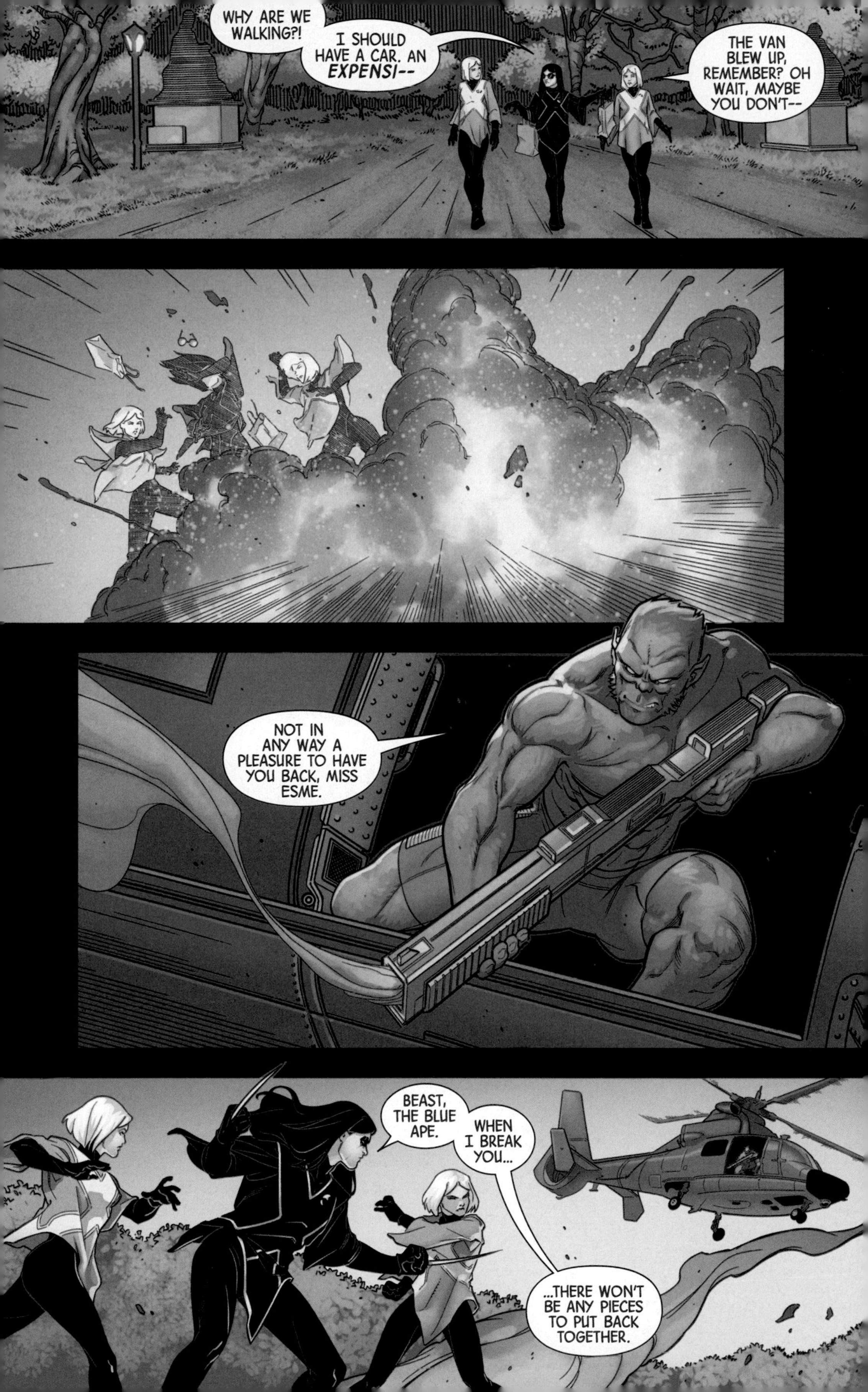
WHY ARE WE WALKING?!
I SHOULD HAVE A CAR. AN EXPENSI--
THE VAN BLEW UP, REMEMBER? OH WAIT, MAYBE YOU DON'T--
NOT IN ANY WAY A PLEASURE TO HAVE YOU BACK, MISS ESME.
BEAST, THE BLUE APE.
WHEN I BREAK YOU...
...THERE WON'T BE ANY PIECES TO PUT BACK TOGETHER.

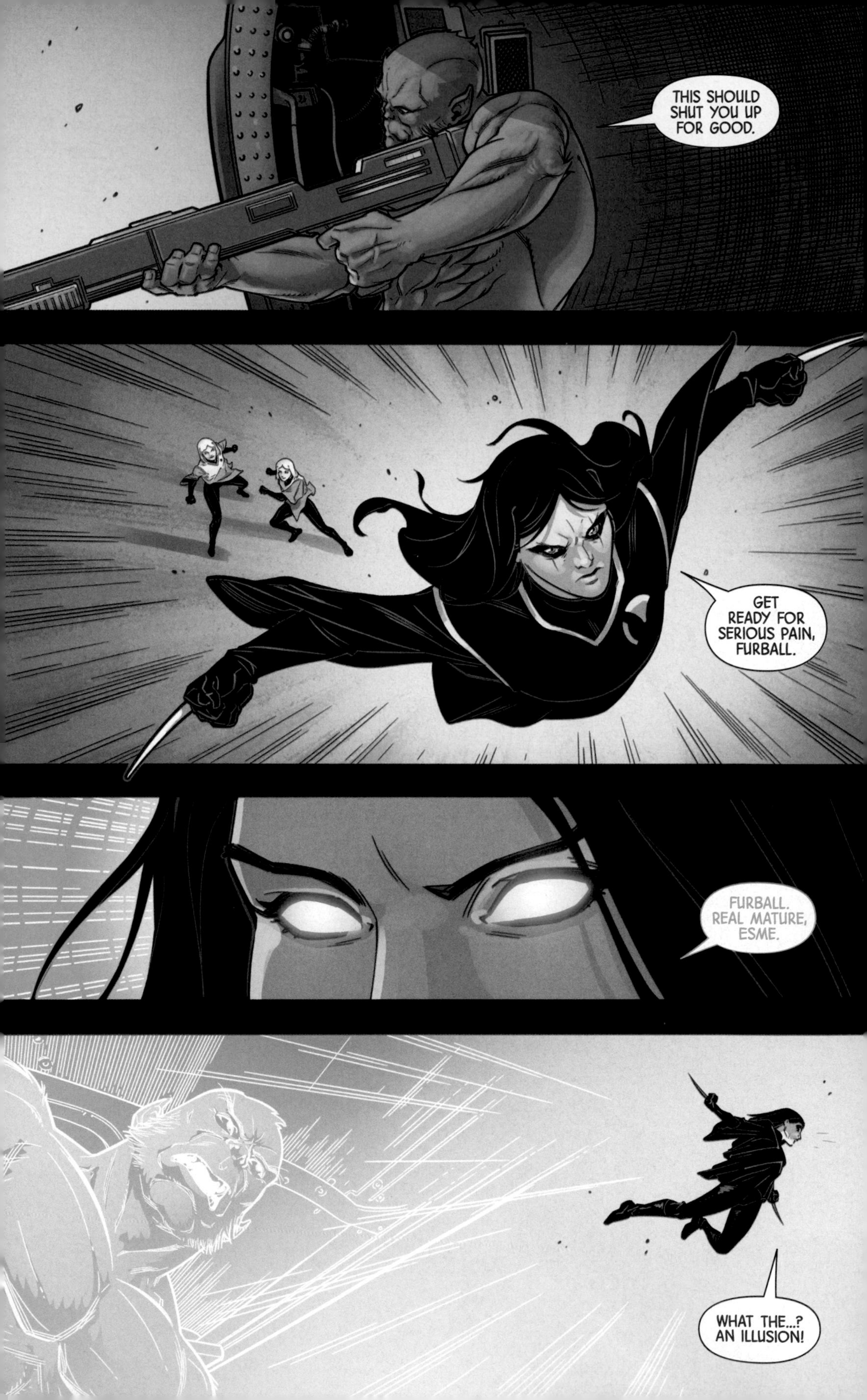
THIS SHOULD SHUT YOU UP FOR GOOD.
GET READY FOR SERIOUS PAIN, FURBALL.
FURBALL. REAL MATURE, ESME.
WHAT THE...? AN ILLUSION!

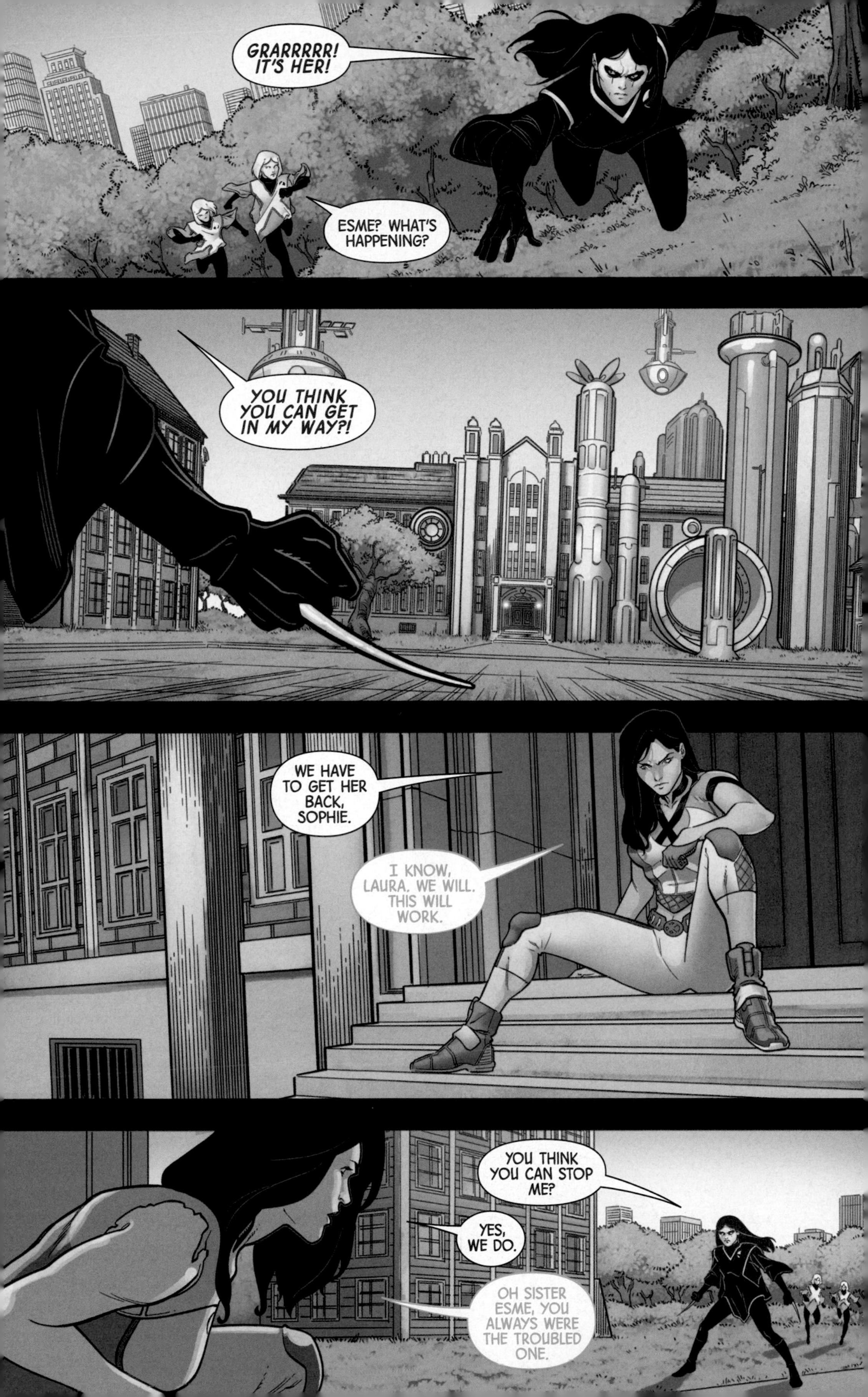
GRARRRRR! IT'S HER!
ESME? WHAT'S HAPPENING?
YOU THINK YOU CAN GET IN MY WAY?!
WE HAVE TO GET HER BACK, SOPHIE.
I KNOW, LAURA. WE WILL. THIS WILL WORK.
YOU THINK YOU CAN STOP ME?
YES, WE DO.
OH SISTER ESME, YOU ALWAYS WERE THE TROUBLED ONE.

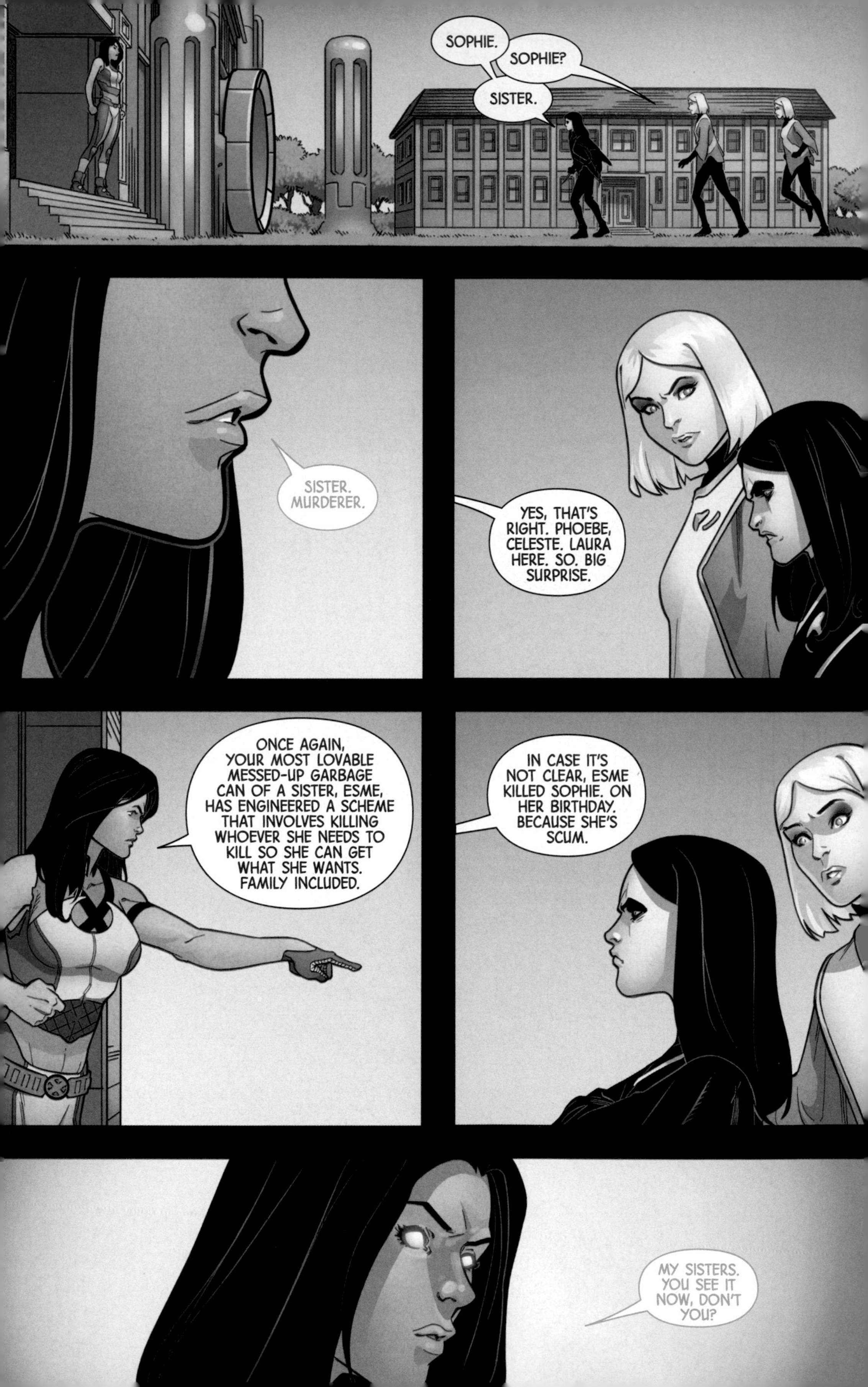
SOPHIE.
SOPHIE?
SISTER.
SISTER. MURDERER.
YES, THAT'S RIGHT. PHOEBE, CELESTE. LAURA HERE. SO. BIG SURPRISE.
ONCE AGAIN, YOUR MOST LOVABLE MESSED-UP GARBAGE CAN OF A SISTER, ESME, HAS ENGINEERED A SCHEME THAT INVOLVES KILLING WHOEVER SHE NEEDS TO KILL SO SHE CAN GET WHAT SHE WANTS. FAMILY INCLUDED.
IN CASE IT'S NOT CLEAR, ESME KILLED SOPHIE. ON HER BIRTHDAY. BECAUSE SHE'S SCUM.
MY SISTERS. YOU SEE IT NOW, DON'T YOU?

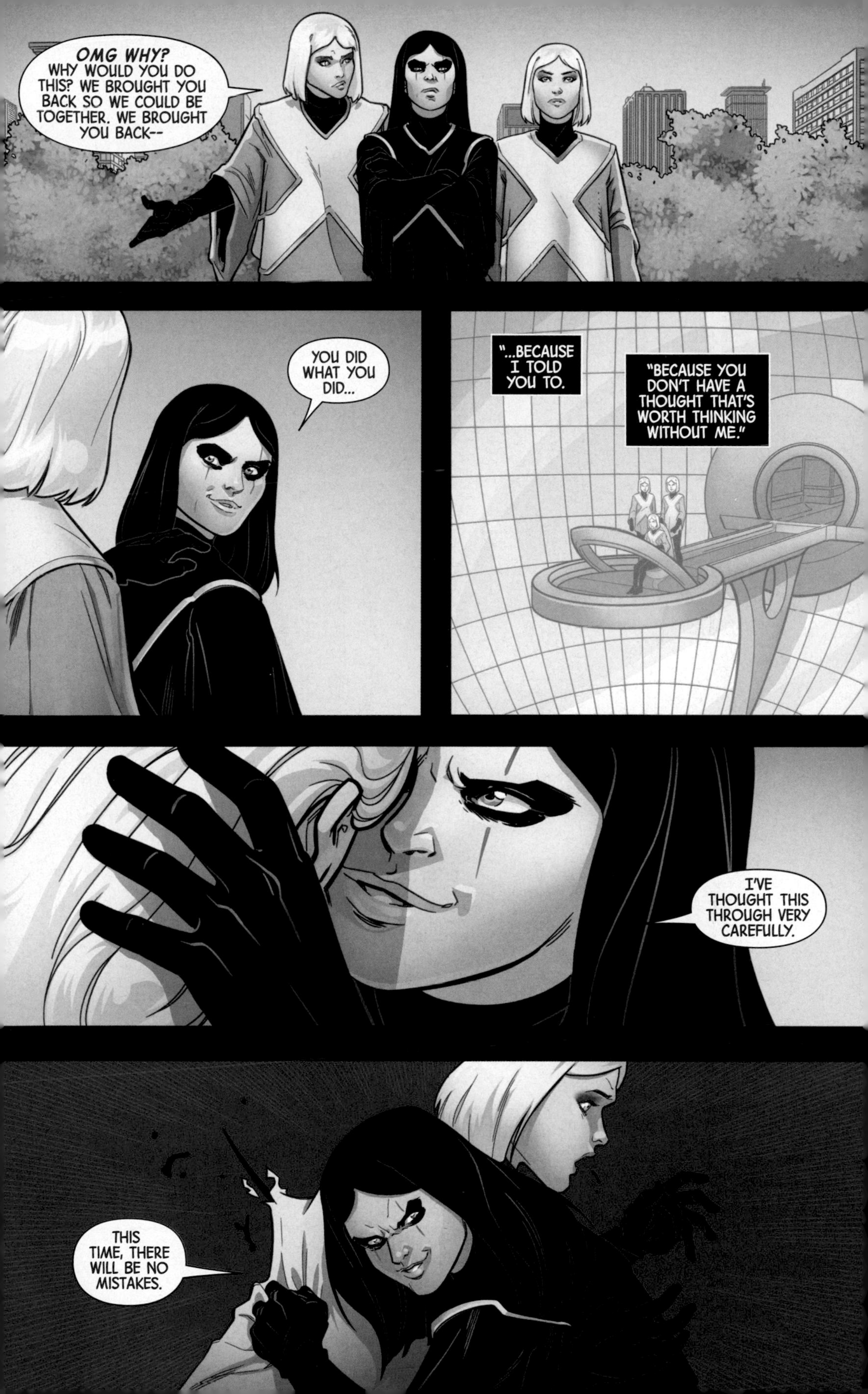
OMG WHY? WHY WOULD YOU DO THIS? WE BROUGHT YOU BACK SO WE COULD BE TOGETHER. WE BROUGHT YOU BACK--
YOU DID WHAT YOU DID...
"...BECAUSE I TOLD YOU TO.
"BECAUSE YOU DON'T HAVE A THOUGHT THAT'S WORTH THINKING WITHOUT ME."
I'VE THOUGHT THIS THROUGH VERY CAREFULLY.
THIS TIME, THERE WILL BE NO MISTAKES.

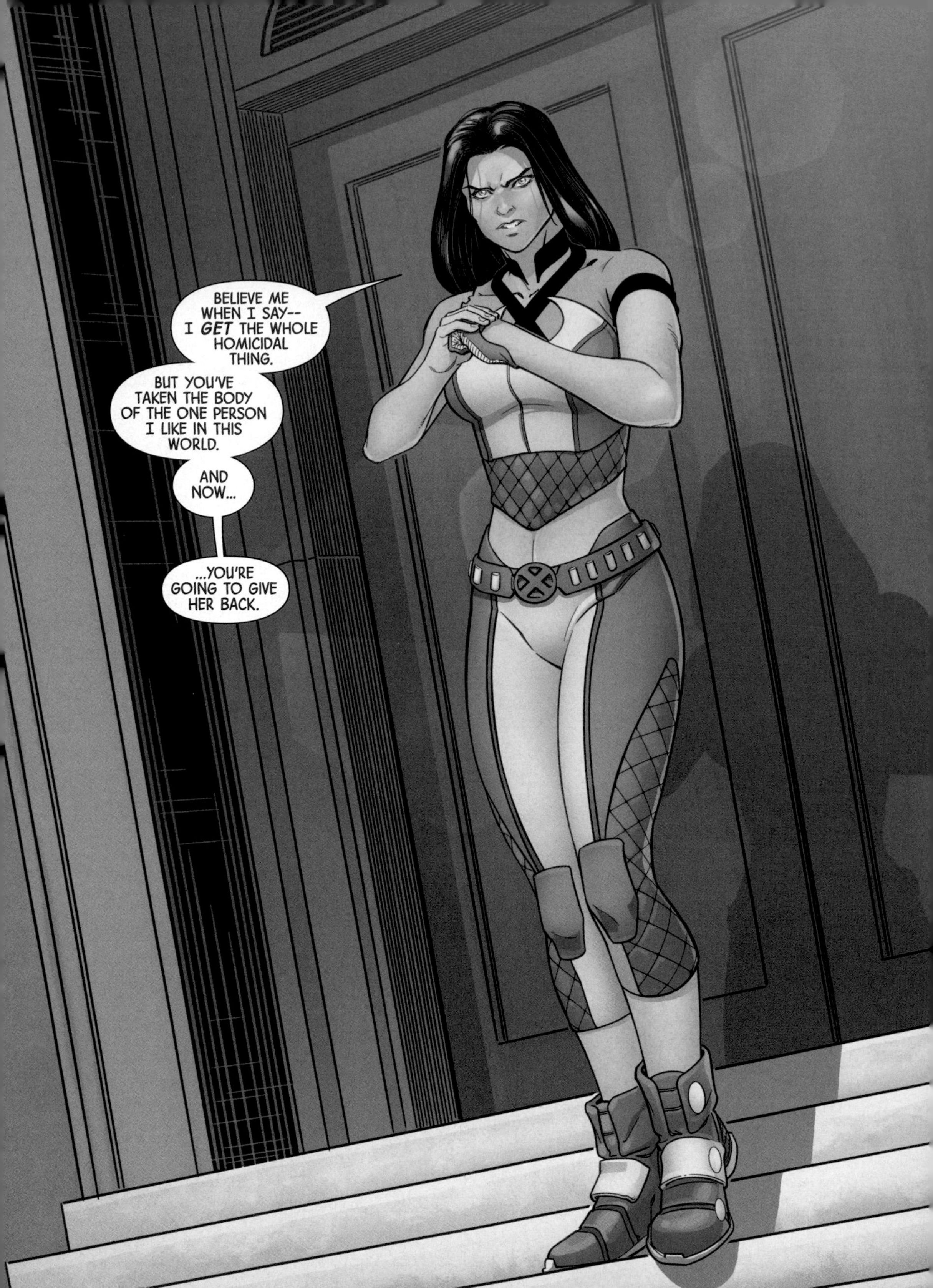
BELIEVE ME WHEN I SAY-- I GET THE WHOLE HOMICIDAL THING.
BUT YOU'VE TAKEN THE BODY OF THE ONE PERSON I LIKE IN THIS WORLD.
AND NOW...
...YOU'RE GOING TO GIVE HER BACK.

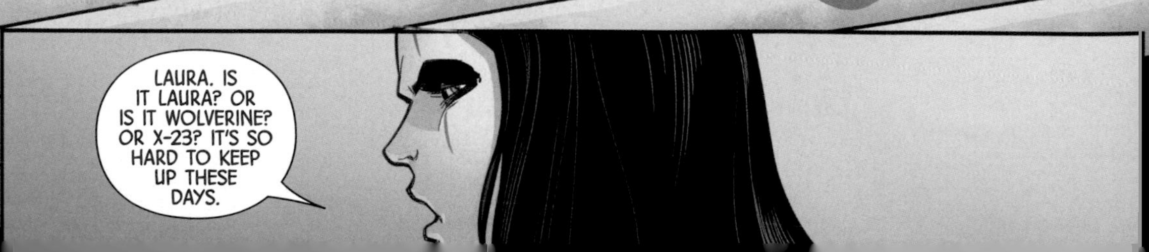
LAURA. IS IT LAURA? OR IS IT WOLVERINE? OR X-23? IT'S SO HARD TO KEEP UP THESE DAYS.

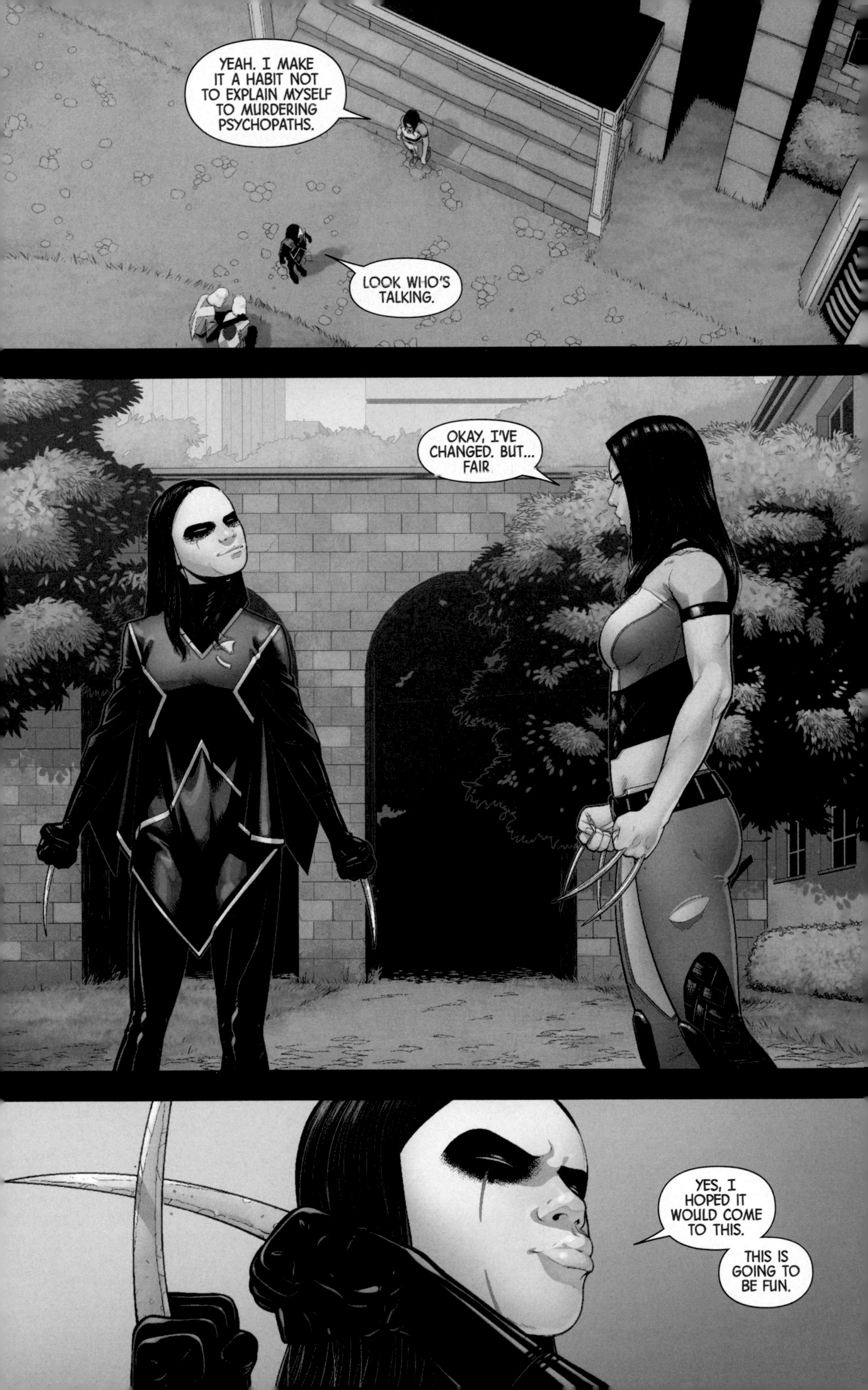
YEAH. I MAKE IT A HABIT NOT TO EXPLAIN MYSELF TO MURDERING PSYCHOPATHS.
LOOK WHO'S TALKING.
OKAY, I'VE CHANGED. BUT... FAIR.
YES, I HOPED IT WOULD COME TO THIS.
THIS IS GOING TO BE FUN.

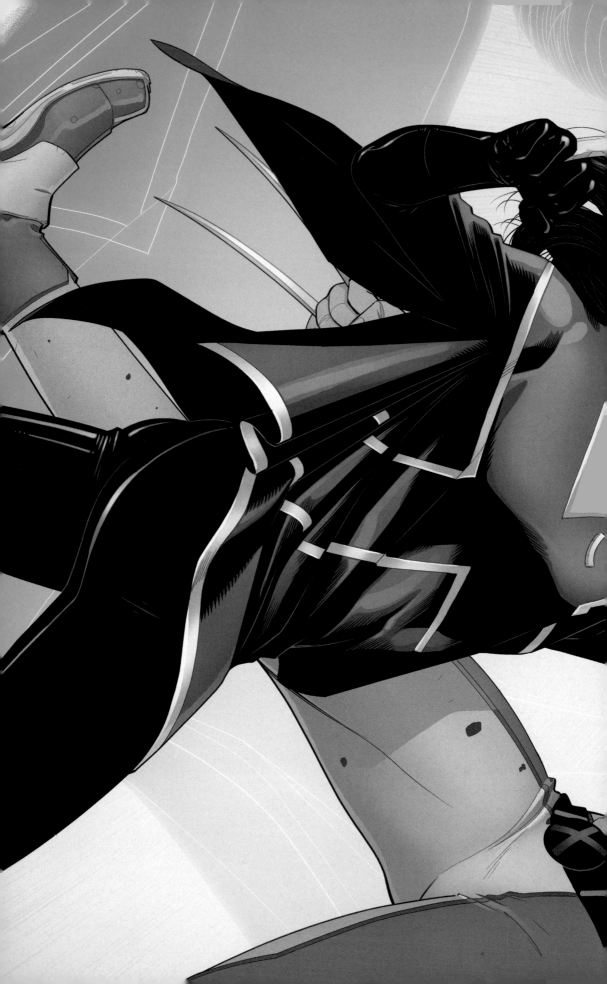

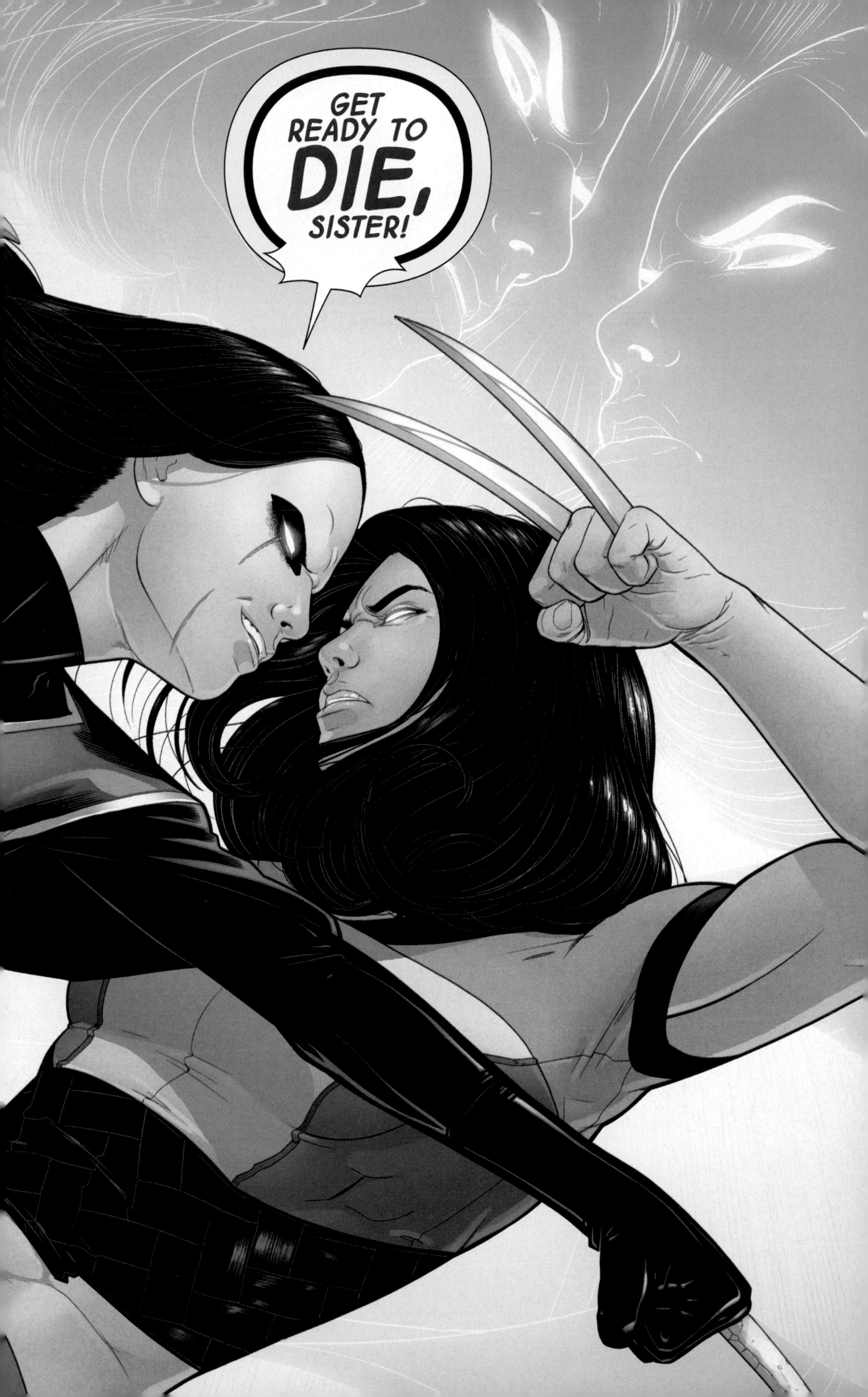
GET READY TO DIE, SISTER!

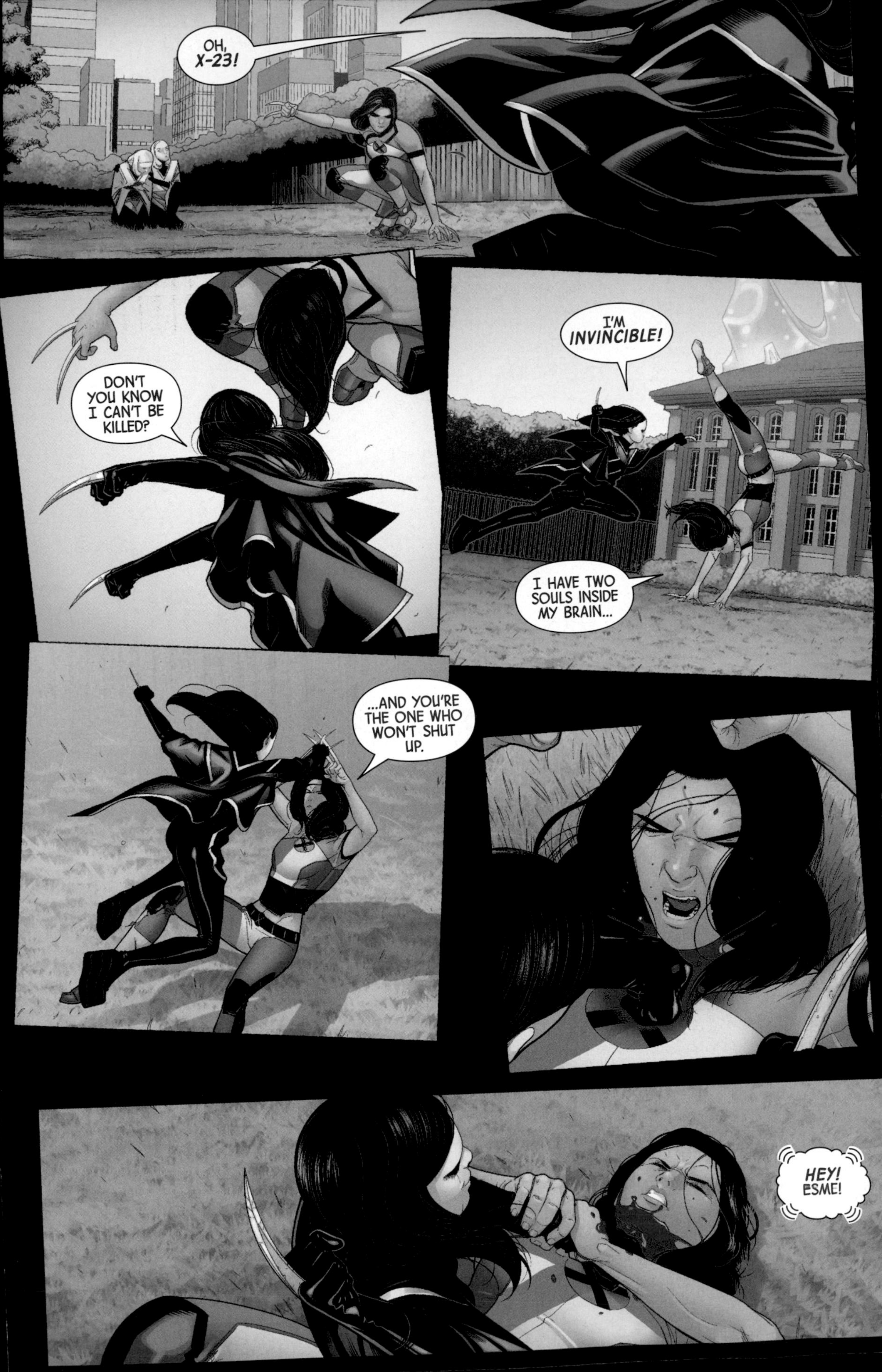

OH, X-23!
DON'T YOU KNOW I CAN'T BE KILLED?
I'M INVINCIBLE!
I HAVE TWO SOULS INSIDE MY BRAIN...
...AND YOU'RE THE ONE WHO WON'T SHUT UP.
HEY! ESME!

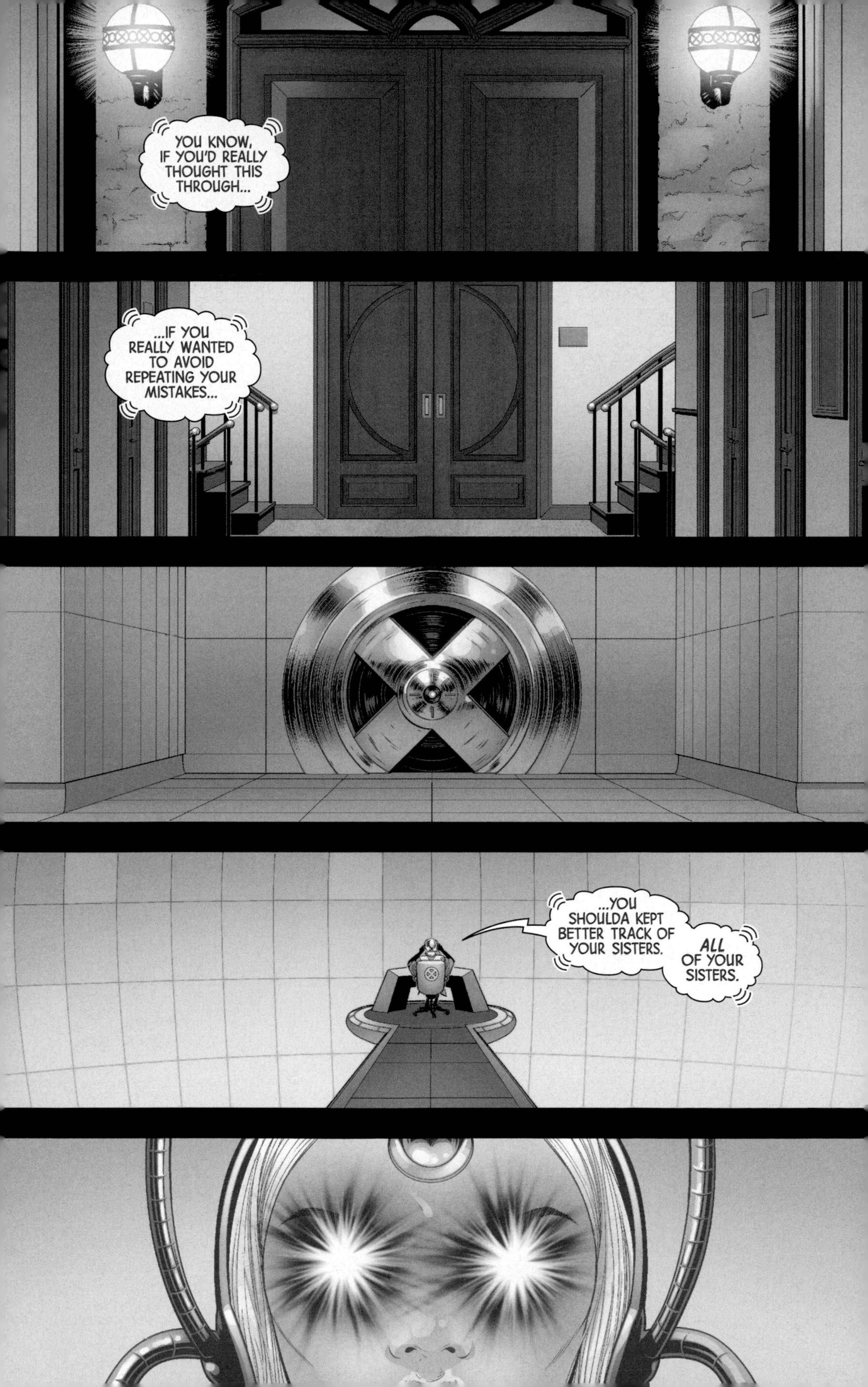
YOU KNOW, IF YOU'D REALLY THOUGHT THIS THROUGH...
...IF YOU REALLY WANTED TO AVOID REPEATING YOUR MISTAKES...
...YOU SHOULDA KEPT BETTER TRACK OF YOUR SISTERS.
ALL OF YOUR SISTERS.

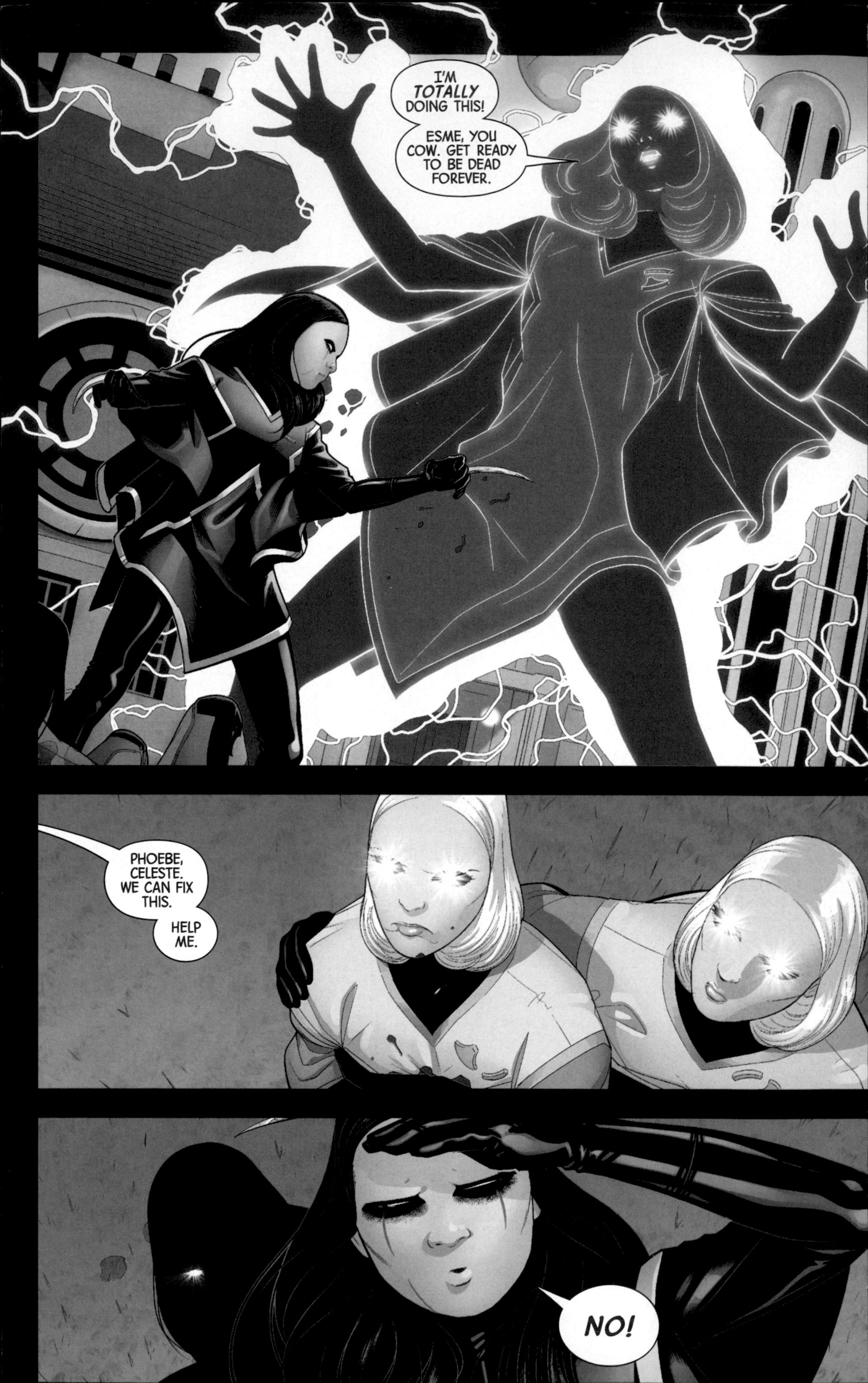
I'M *TOTALLY* DOING THIS!
ESME, YOU COW. GET READY TO BE DEAD FOREVER.
PHOEBE, CELESTE. WE CAN FIX THIS.
HELP ME.
NO!

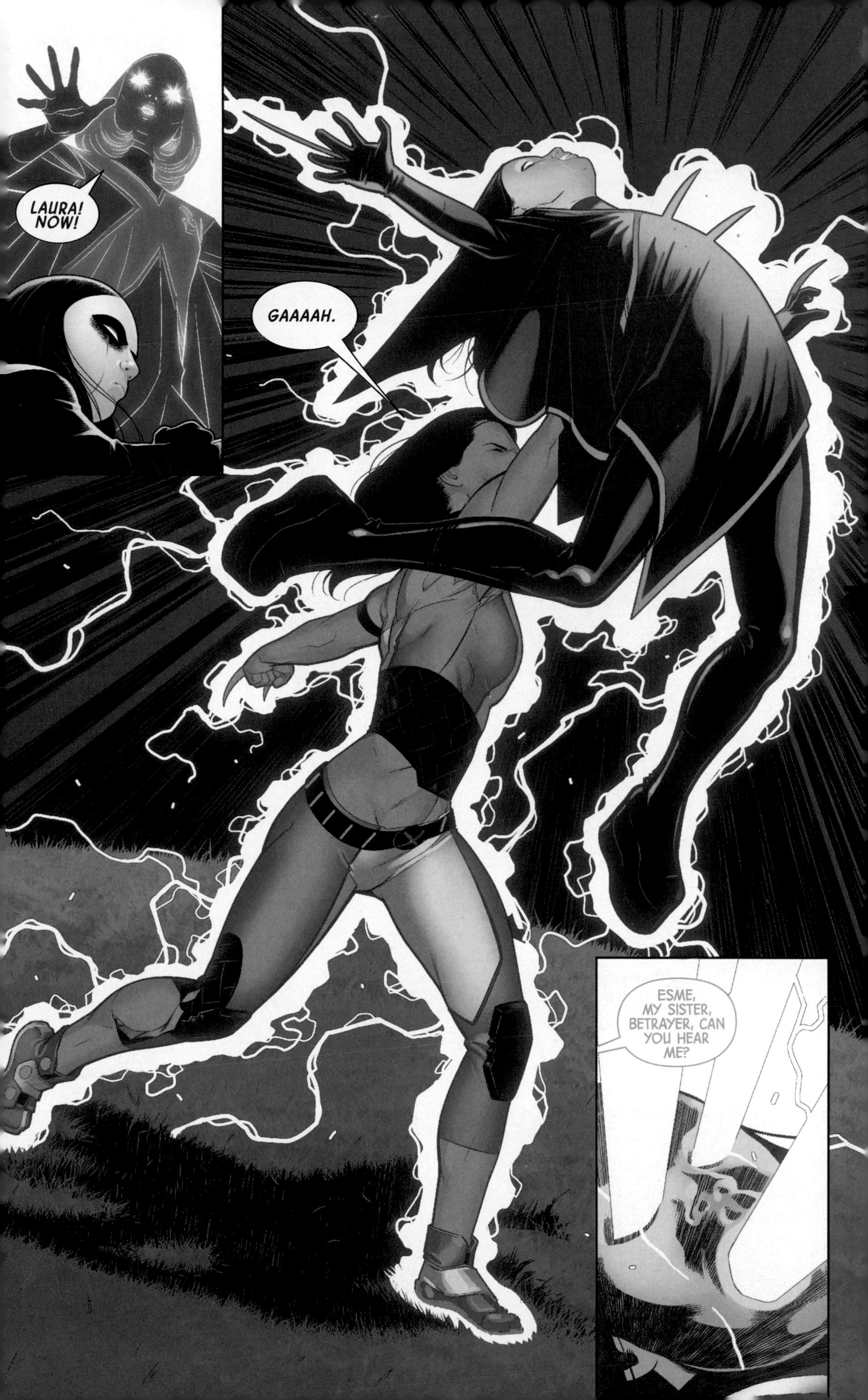
LAURA! NOW!
GAAAAH.
ESME, MY SISTER, BETRAYER, CAN YOU HEAR ME?

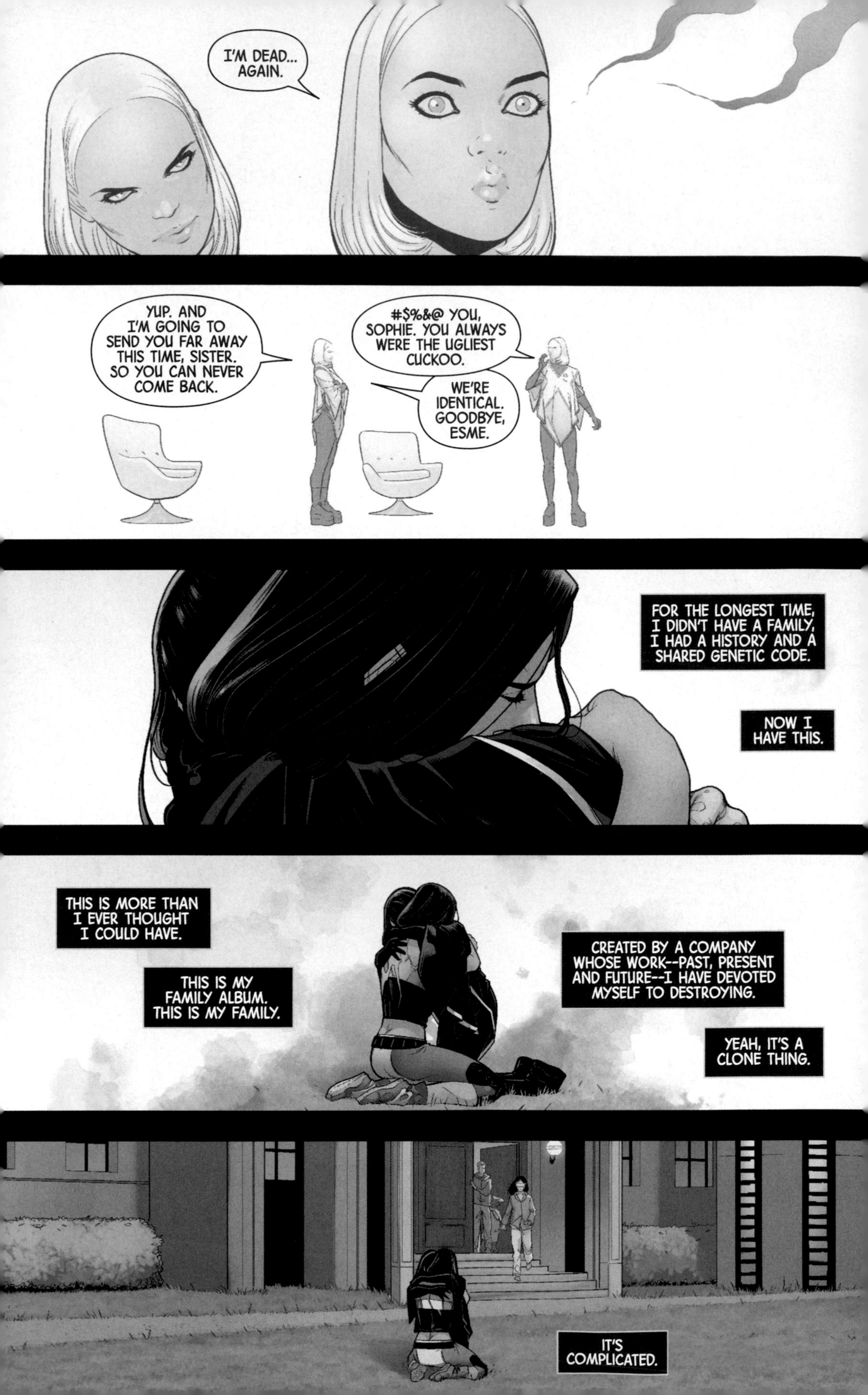
I'M DEAD... AGAIN.
YUP. AND I'M GOING TO SEND YOU FAR AWAY THIS TIME, SISTER. SO YOU CAN NEVER COME BACK.
#$%&@ YOU, SOPHIE. YOU ALWAYS WERE THE UGLIEST CUCKOO.
WE'RE IDENTICAL. GOODBYE, ESME.
FOR THE LONGEST TIME, I DIDN'T HAVE A FAMILY, I HAD A HISTORY AND A SHARED GENETIC CODE.
NOW I HAVE THIS.
THIS IS MORE THAN I EVER THOUGHT I COULD HAVE.
THIS IS MY FAMILY ALBUM. THIS IS MY FAMILY.
CREATED BY A COMPANY WHOSE WORK--PAST, PRESENT AND FUTURE--I HAVE DEVOTED MYSELF TO DESTROYING.
YEAH, IT'S A CLONE THING.
IT'S COMPLICATED.

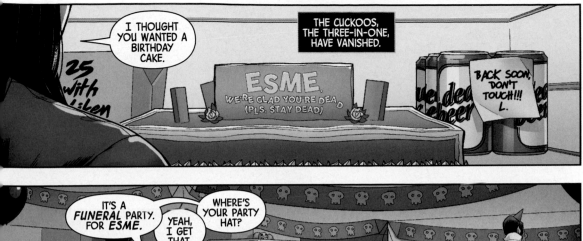

I THOUGHT YOU WANTED A BIRTHDAY CAKE.

THE CUCKOOS, THE THREE-IN-ONE, HAVE VANISHED.

ESME. WE'RE GLAD YOU'RE DEAD (PLS. STAY DEAD)

BACK SOON, DON'T TOUCH!!! L.

IT'S A *FUNERAL* PARTY. FOR *ESME.*

YEAH, I GET THAT.

WHERE'S YOUR PARTY HAT?

SOMETIMES I THINK I FEEL A PRESENCE, LIKE A GRAIN OF SAND IN MY BRAIN, BUT I'M PRETTY SURE SOPHIE IS GONE. I MEAN, Y'KNOW, I HOPE.

IT WAS SCARY BEING INSIDE ESME. LIKE A REALLY ANGRY SLEEPING BAG.

BUT I UNDERSTAND WHY SHE WAS ANGRY. BECAUSE SHE WANTED TO BE SOMETHING, BECAUSE SOME PEOPLE DON'T FEEL CLONE POWER, THEY FEEL CLONE RAGE.

YEAH, THEY DO.

LIKE YOU DO SOMETIMES. ME TOO.

YEAH.

LAST I HEARD, THEY WERE SPOTTED IN PARIS, WHICH I KNOW SOPHIE WOULD LIKE.

WHEN WE CELEBRATE OUR BIRTHDAY, WE'RE GONNA DO IT TOGETHER.

'CAUSE *SOMEDAY* YOU'RE GONNA TELL ME YOUR BIRTHDAY.

OUR BIRTHDAY.

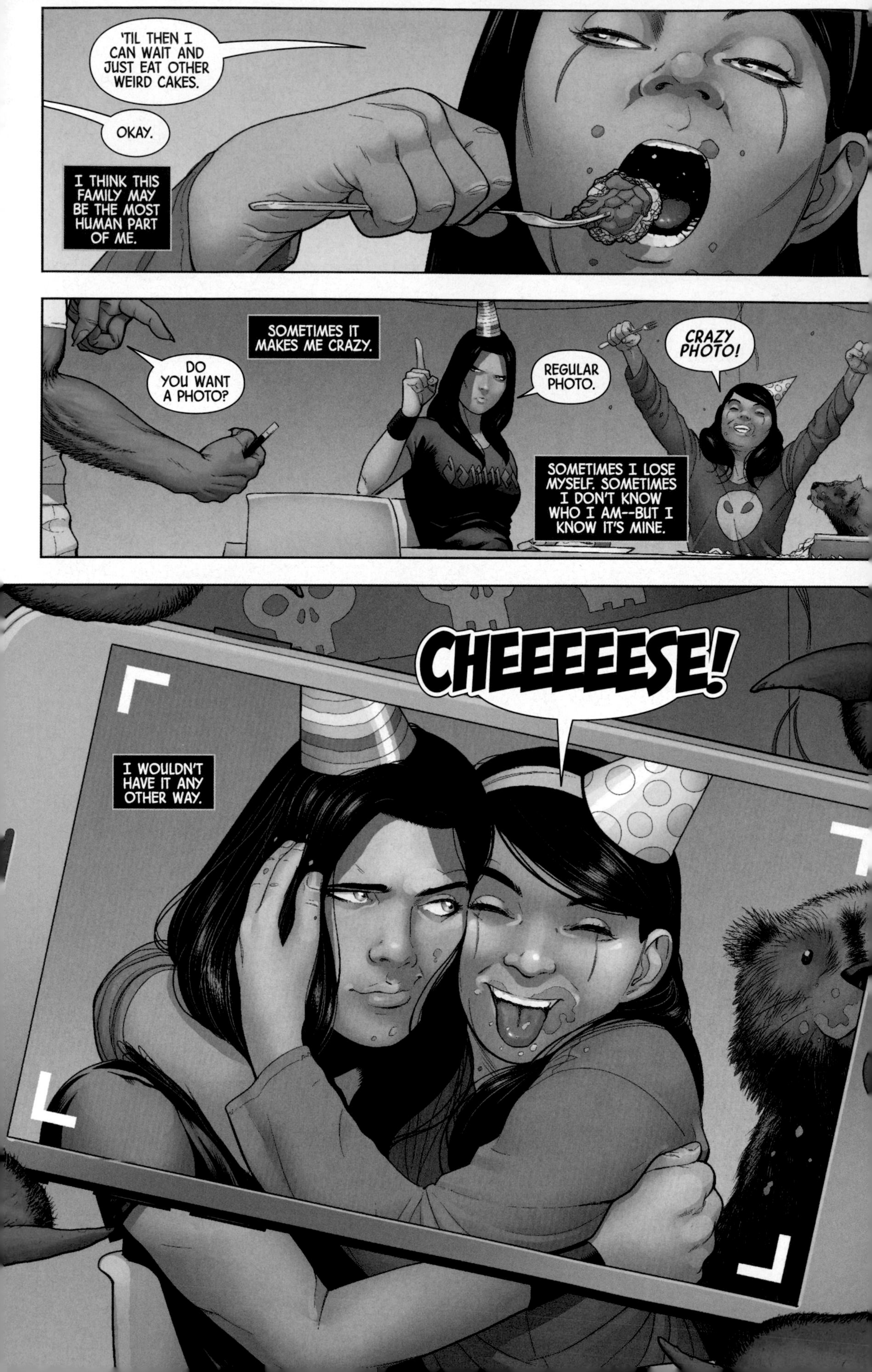
'TIL THEN I CAN WAIT AND JUST EAT OTHER WEIRD CAKES.
OKAY.
I THINK THIS FAMILY MAY BE THE MOST HUMAN PART OF ME.
SOMETIMES IT MAKES ME CRAZY.
DO YOU WANT A PHOTO?
REGULAR PHOTO.
CRAZY PHOTO!
SOMETIMES I LOSE MYSELF. SOMETIMES I DON'T KNOW WHO I AM--BUT I KNOW IT'S MINE.
CHEEEEEESE!
I WOULDN'T HAVE IT ANY OTHER WAY.

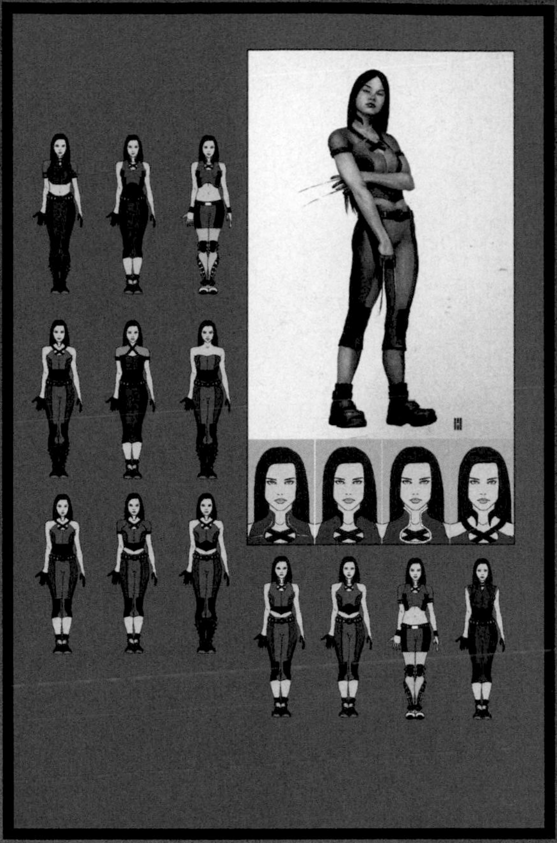

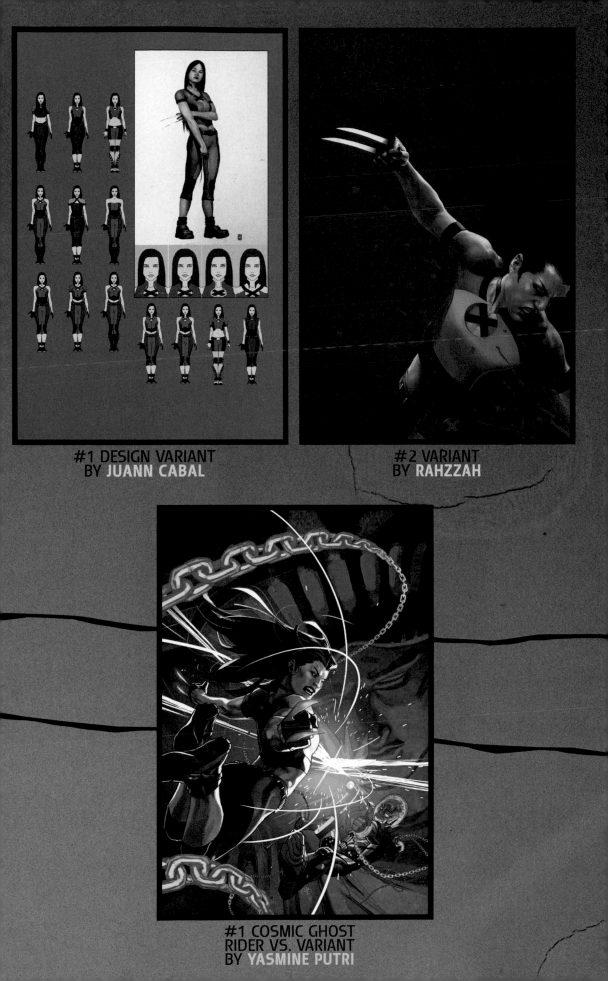

#1 DESIGN VARIANT
BY JUANN CABAL

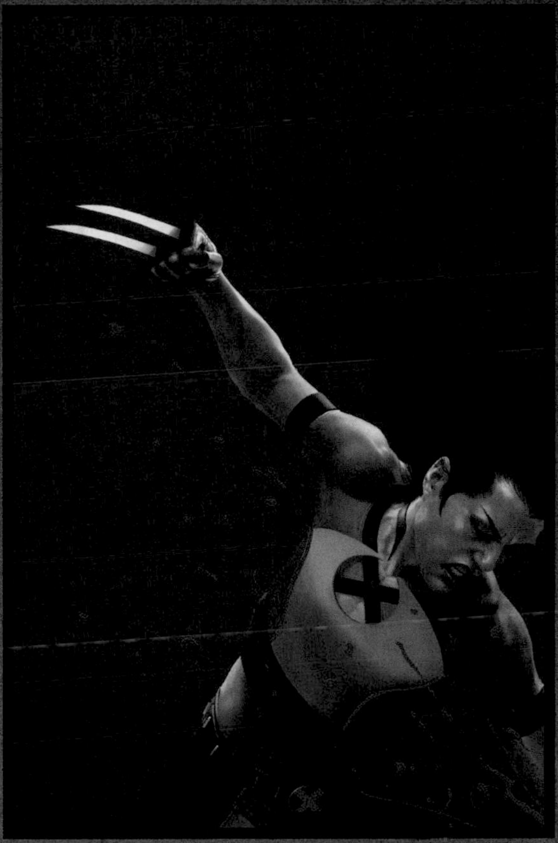

#2 VARIANT
BY RAHZZAH

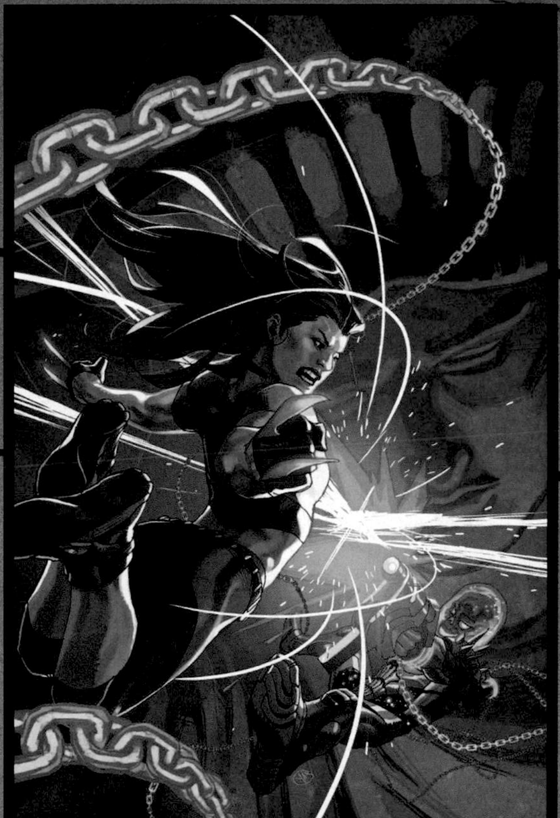

#1 COSMIC GHOST
RIDER VS. VARIANT
BY YASMINE PUTRI

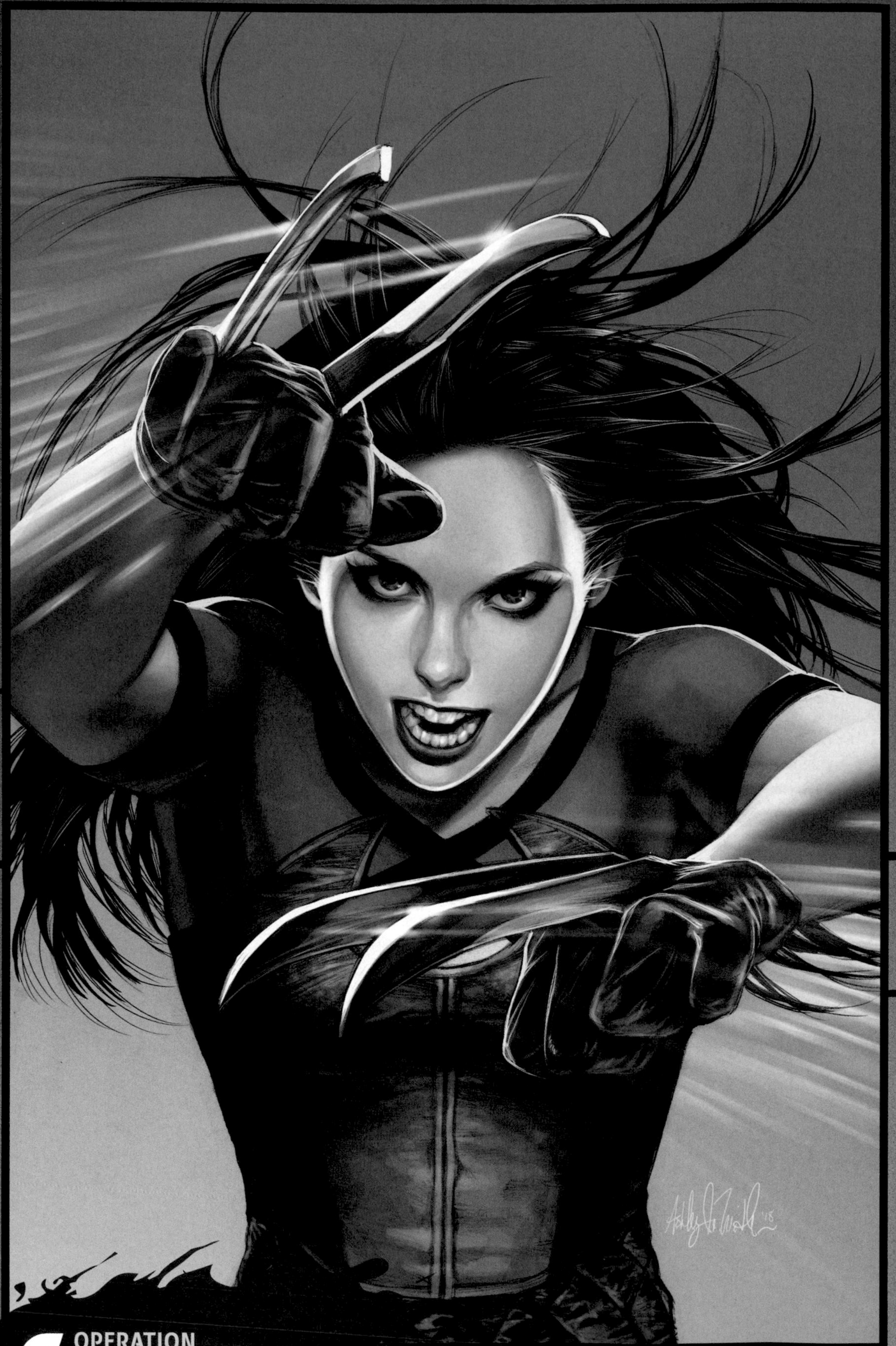

6 OPERATION KINDERGARTEN CLONE

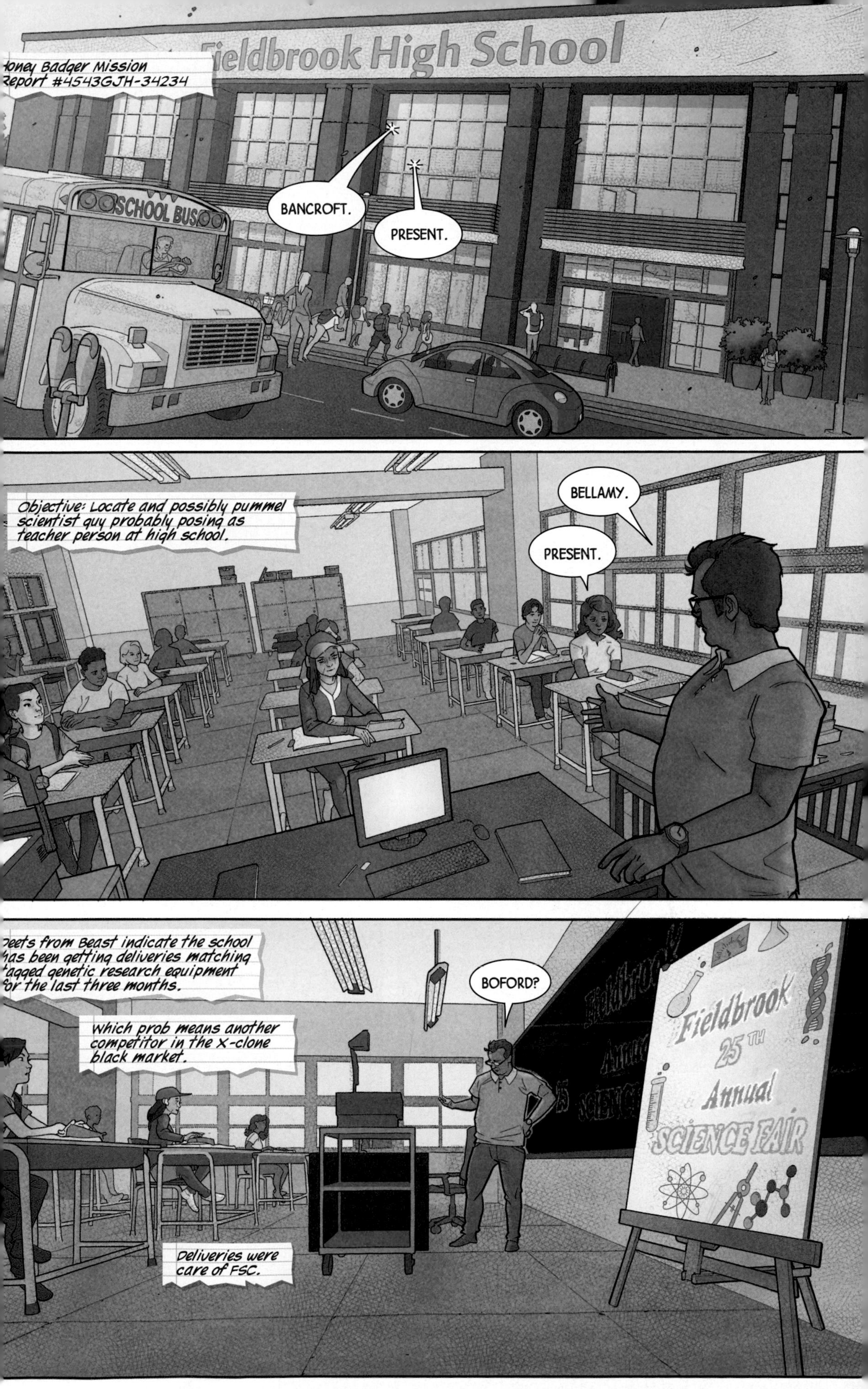
Fieldbrook High School
Honey Badger Mission Report #4543GJH-34234
SCHOOL BUS
BANCROFT.
PRESENT.
Objective: Locate and possibly pummel scientist guy probably posing as teacher person at high school.
BELLAMY.
PRESENT.
Deets from Beast indicate the school has been getting deliveries matching tagged genetic research equipment for the last three months.
Which prob means another competitor in the X-clone black market.
BOFORD?
Deliveries were care of FSC.
Fieldbrook 25TH Annual SCIENCE FAIR

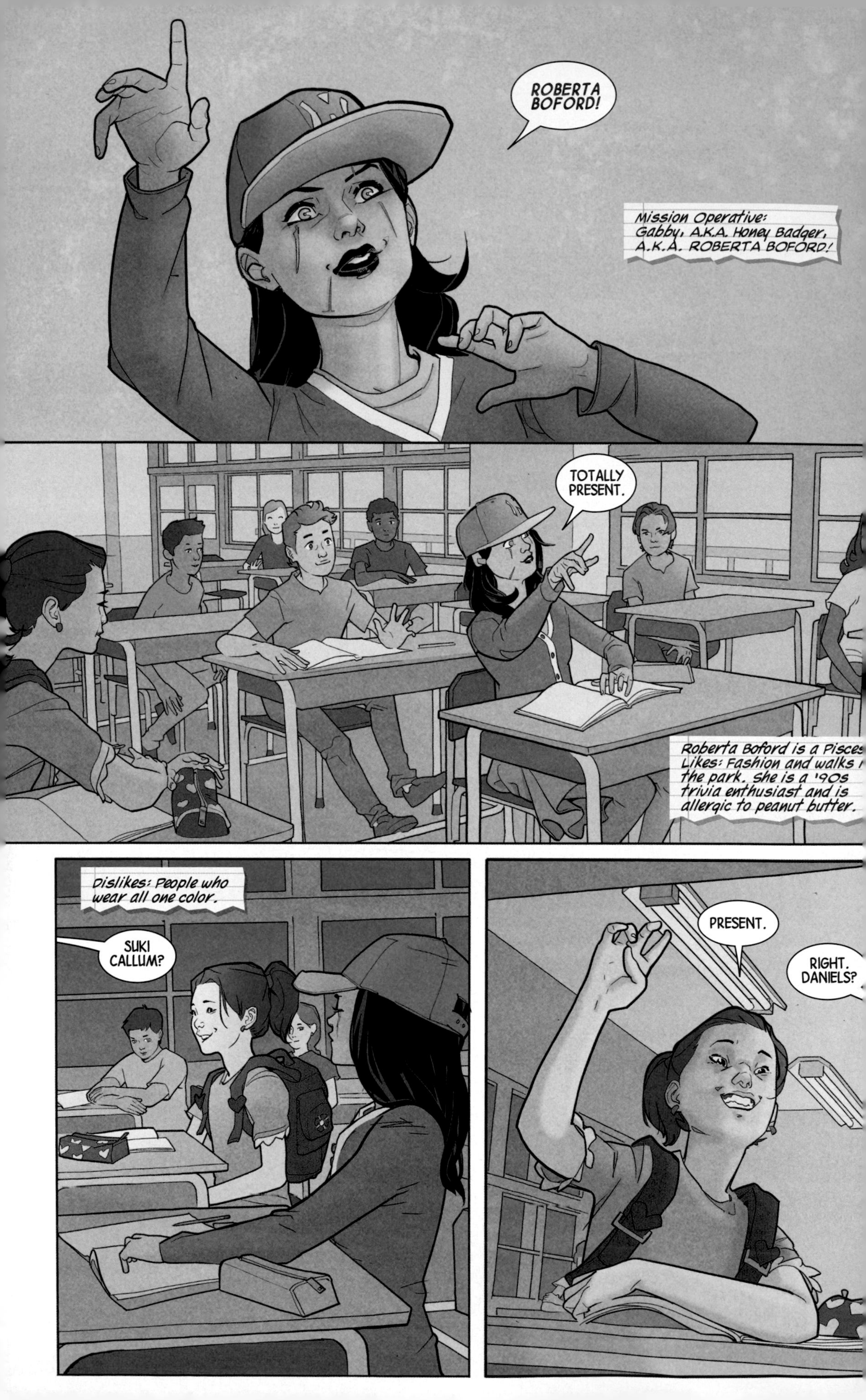
ROBERTA BOFORD!
Mission Operative: Gabby, A.K.A. Honey Badger, A.K.A. ROBERTA BOFORD!
TOTALLY PRESENT.
Roberta Boford is a Pisces Likes: Fashion and walks the park. she is a '90s trivia enthusiast and is allergic to peanut butter.
Dislikes: People who wear all one color.
SUKI CALLUM?
PRESENT.
RIGHT. DANIELS?

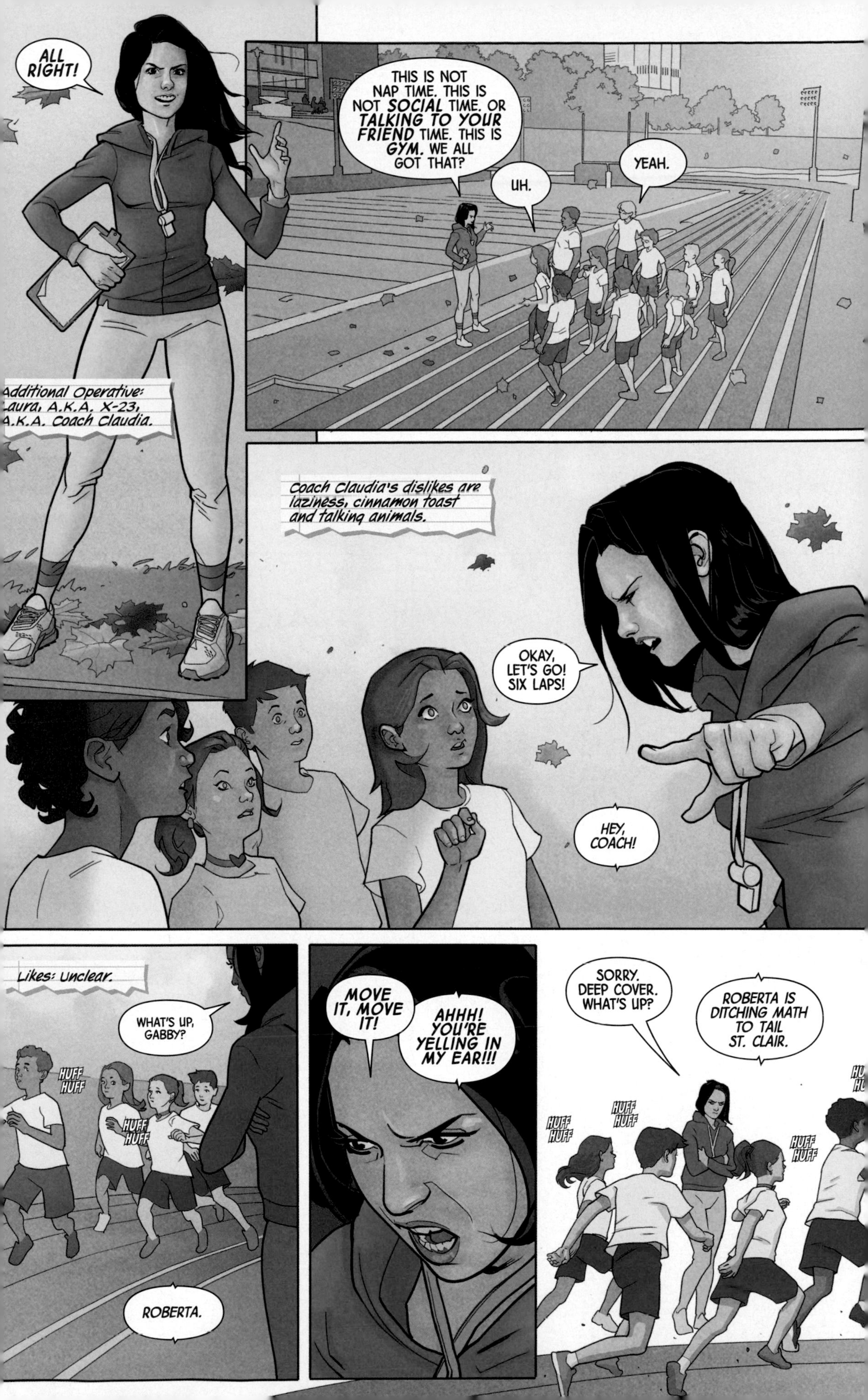
ALL RIGHT!
THIS IS NOT NAP TIME. THIS IS NOT SOCIAL TIME. OR TALKING TO YOUR FRIEND TIME. THIS IS GYM. WE ALL GOT THAT?
UH.
YEAH.
Additional Operative: Laura, A.K.A. X-23, A.K.A. Coach Claudia.
Coach Claudia's dislikes are laziness, cinnamon toast and talking animals.
OKAY, LET'S GO! SIX LAPS!
HEY, COACH!
Likes: Unclear.
WHAT'S UP, GABBY?
HUFF HUFF
HUFF HUFF
ROBERTA.
MOVE IT, MOVE IT!
AHHH! YOU'RE YELLING IN MY EAR!!!
SORRY. DEEP COVER. WHAT'S UP?
ROBERTA IS DITCHING MATH TO TAIL ST. CLAIR.
HUFF HUFF
HUFF HUFF
HUFF HUFF

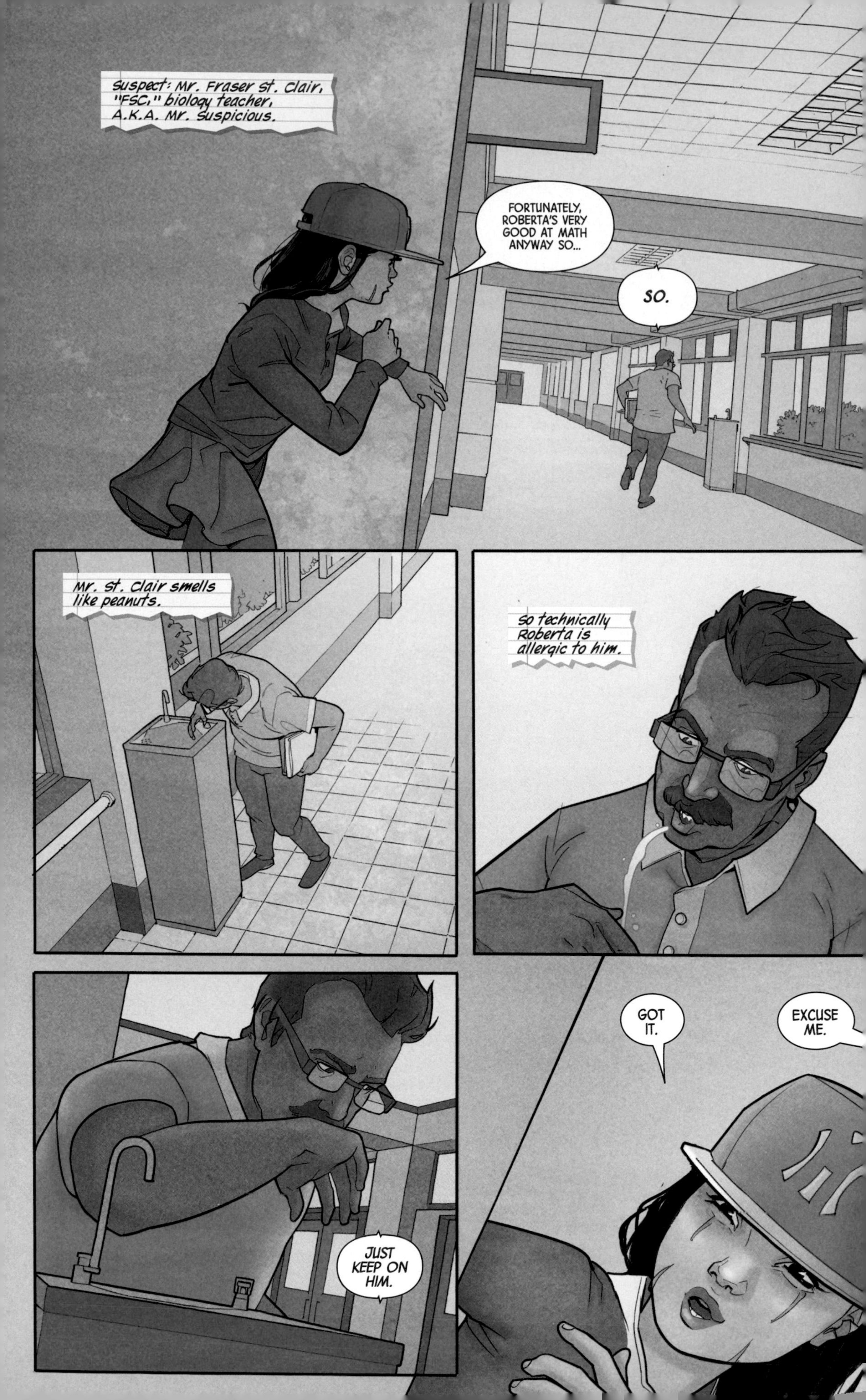
Suspect: Mr. Fraser St. Clair, "FSC," biology teacher, A.K.A. Mr. Suspicious.
FORTUNATELY, ROBERTA'S VERY GOOD AT MATH ANYWAY SO...
SO.
Mr. St. Clair smells like peanuts.
So technically Roberta is allergic to him.
JUST KEEP ON HIM.
GOT IT.
EXCUSE ME.

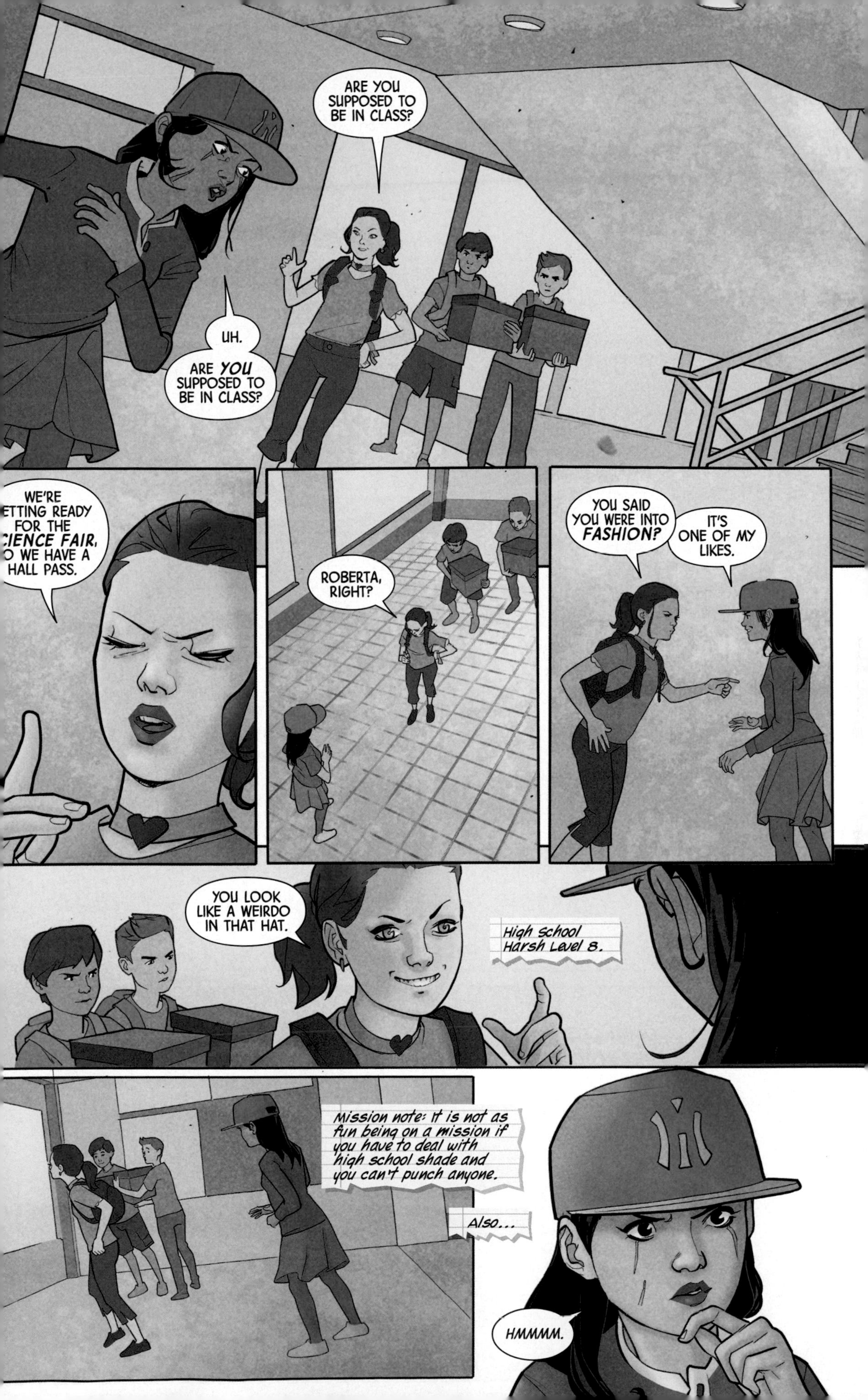
ARE YOU SUPPOSED TO BE IN CLASS?
UH.
ARE YOU SUPPOSED TO BE IN CLASS?
WE'RE ETTING READY FOR THE CIENCE FAIR, O WE HAVE A HALL PASS.
ROBERTA, RIGHT?
YOU SAID YOU WERE INTO FASHION?
IT'S ONE OF MY LIKES.
YOU LOOK LIKE A WEIRDO IN THAT HAT.
High School Harsh Level 8.
Mission note: It is not as fun being on a mission if you have to deal with high school shade and you can't punch anyone.
Also...
HMMMM.

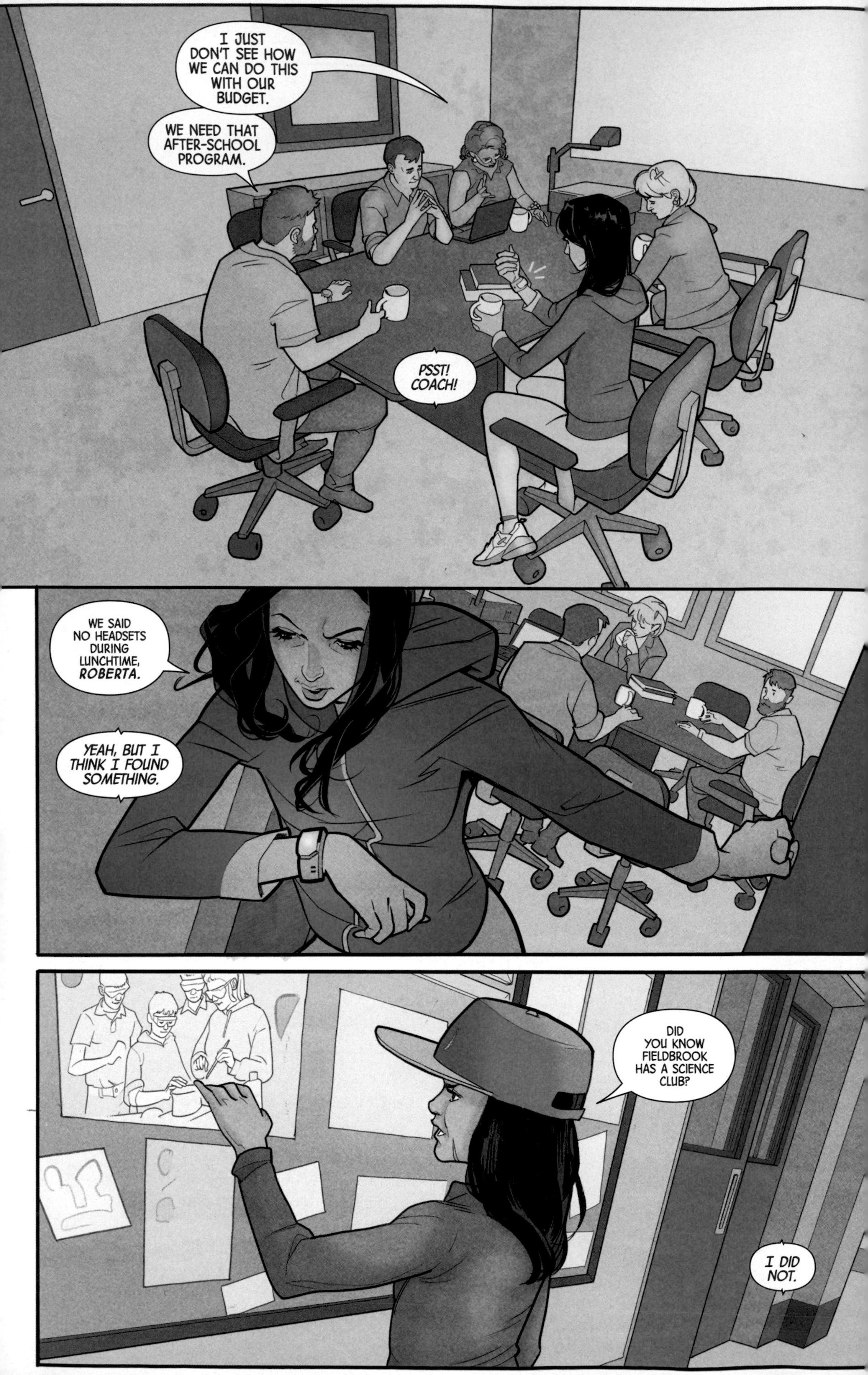
I JUST DON'T SEE HOW WE CAN DO THIS WITH OUR BUDGET.
WE NEED THAT AFTER-SCHOOL PROGRAM.
PSST! COACH!
WE SAID NO HEADSETS DURING LUNCHTIME, ROBERTA.
YEAH, BUT I THINK I FOUND SOMETHING.
DID YOU KNOW FIELDBROOK HAS A SCIENCE CLUB?
I DID NOT.

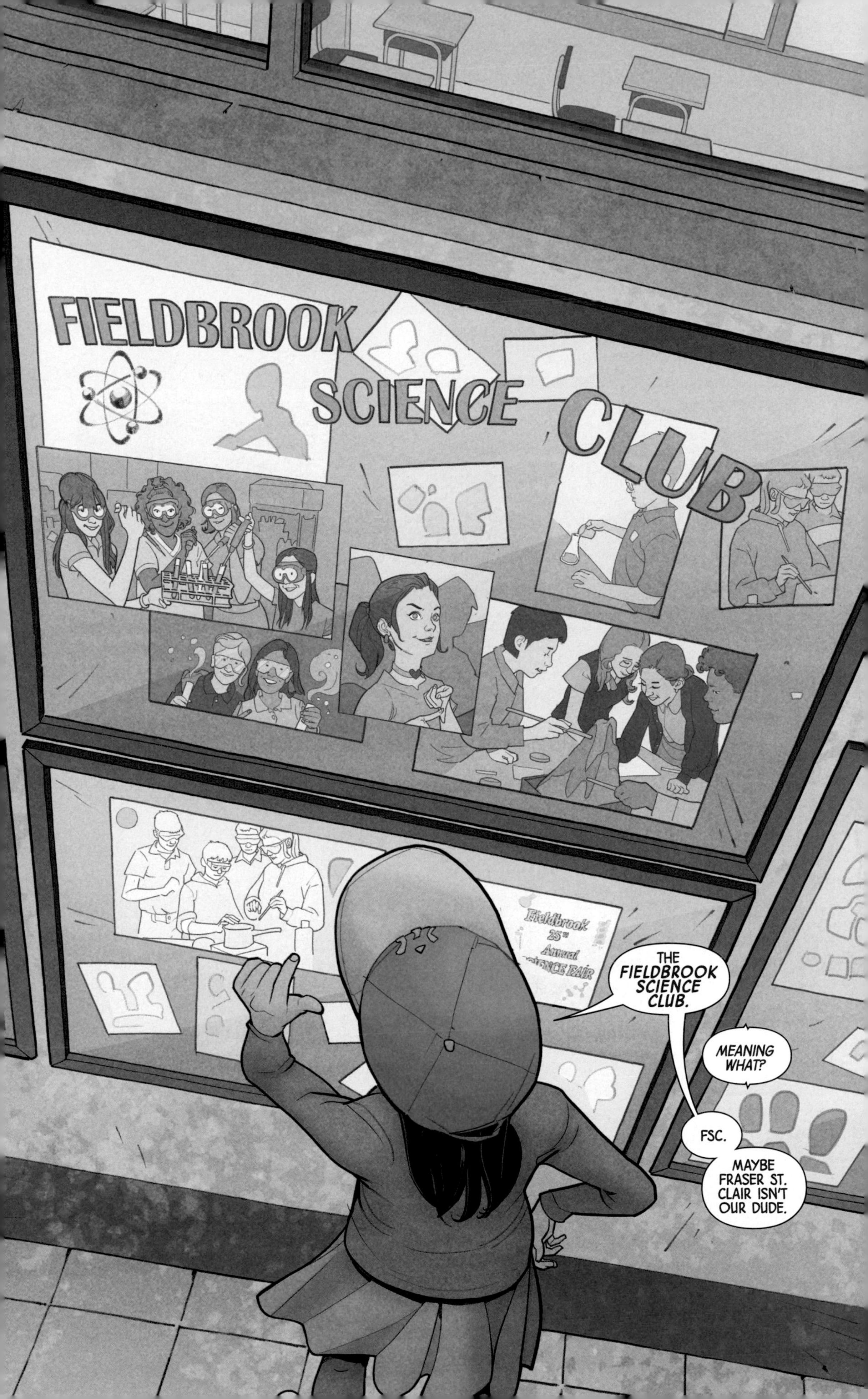
FIELDBROOK SCIENCE CLUB
Fieldbrook
25th
Annual
THE FIELDBROOK SCIENCE CLUB.
MEANING WHAT?
FSC.
MAYBE FRASER ST. CLAIR ISN'T OUR DUDE.

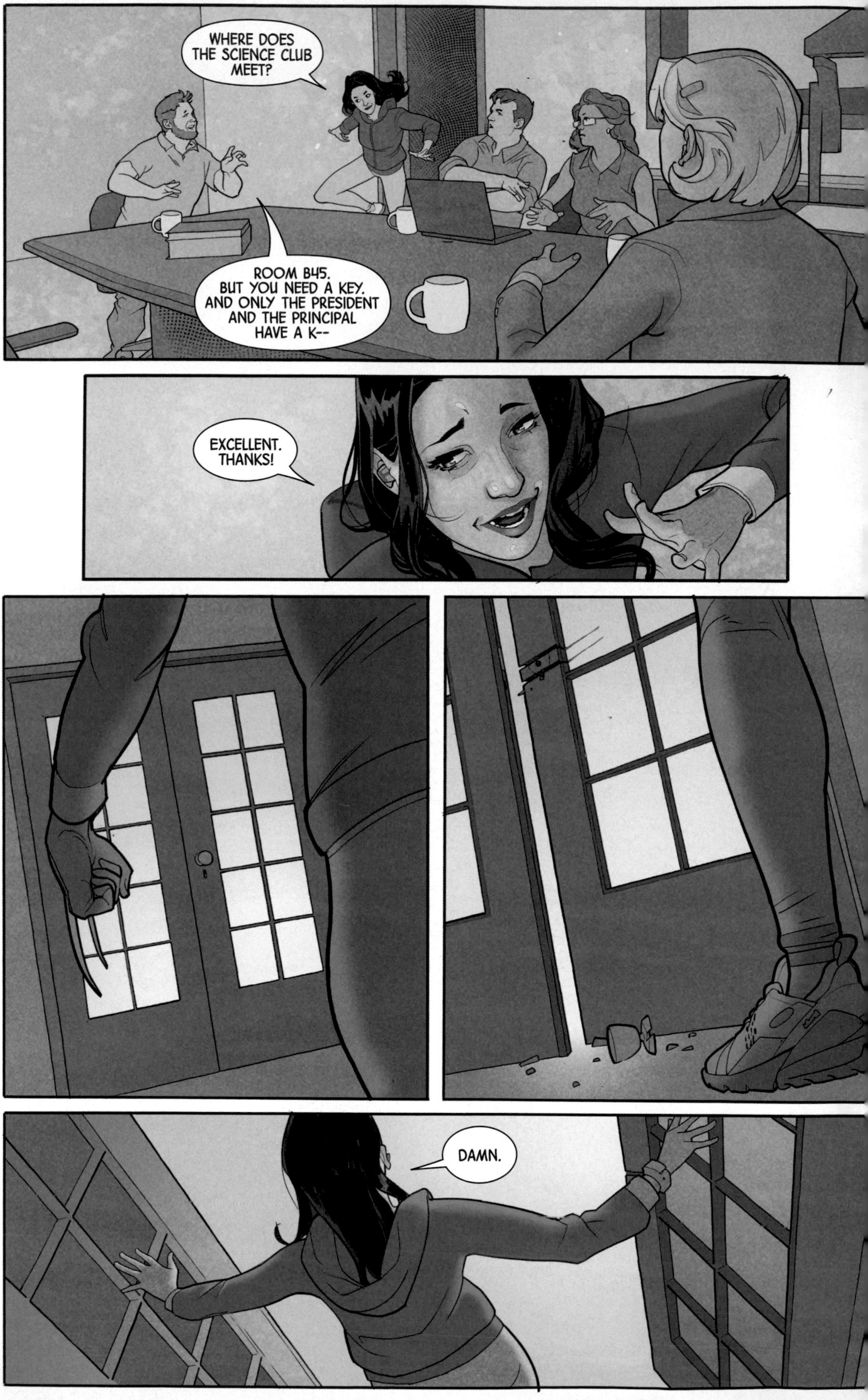
WHERE DOES THE SCIENCE CLUB MEET?
ROOM B45. BUT YOU NEED A KEY. AND ONLY THE PRESIDENT AND THE PRINCIPAL HAVE A K--
EXCELLENT. THANKS!
DAMN.

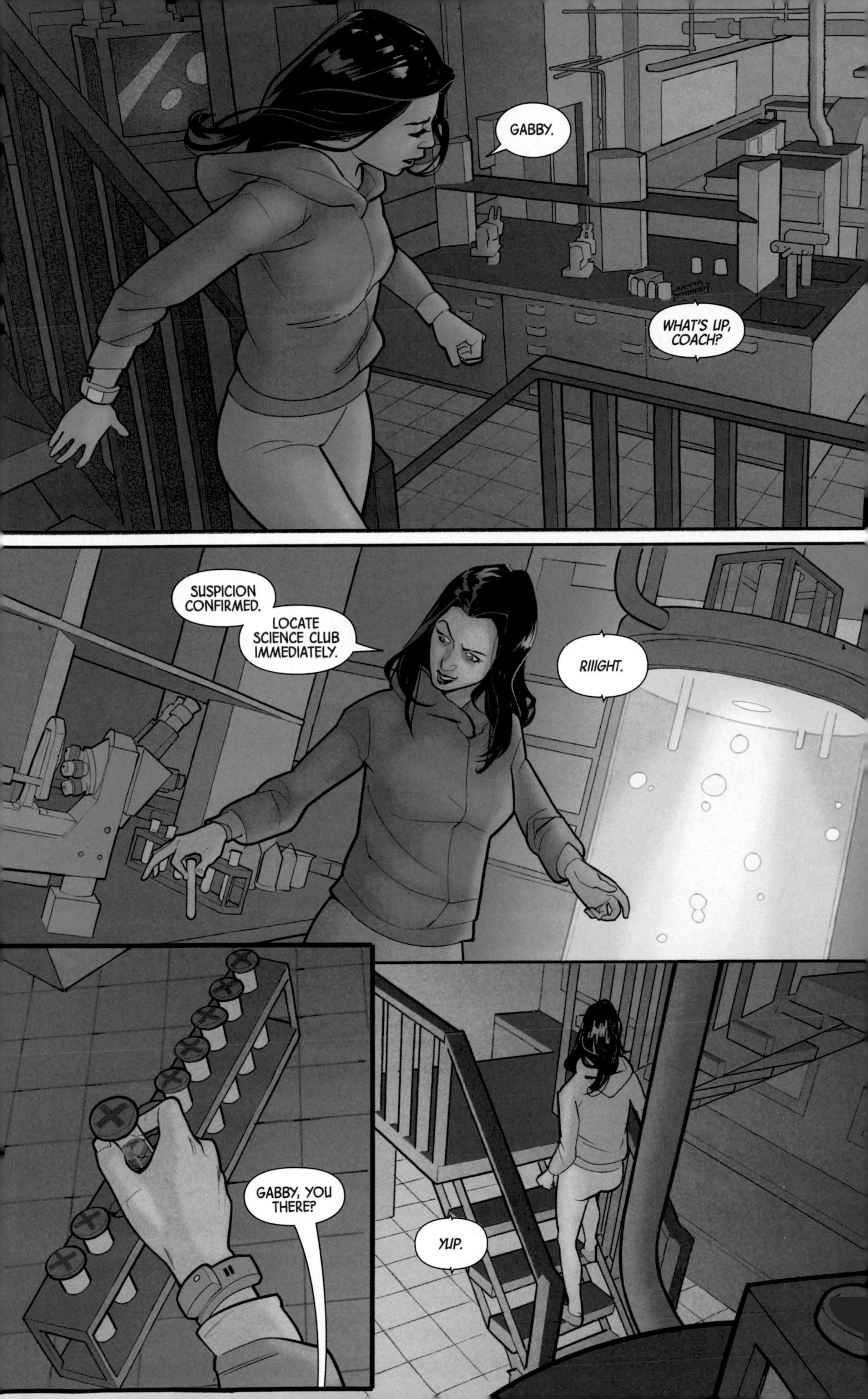
GABBY.
WHAT'S UP, COACH?
SUSPICION CONFIRMED.
LOCATE SCIENCE CLUB IMMEDIATELY.
RIIIGHT.
GABBY, YOU THERE?
YUP.

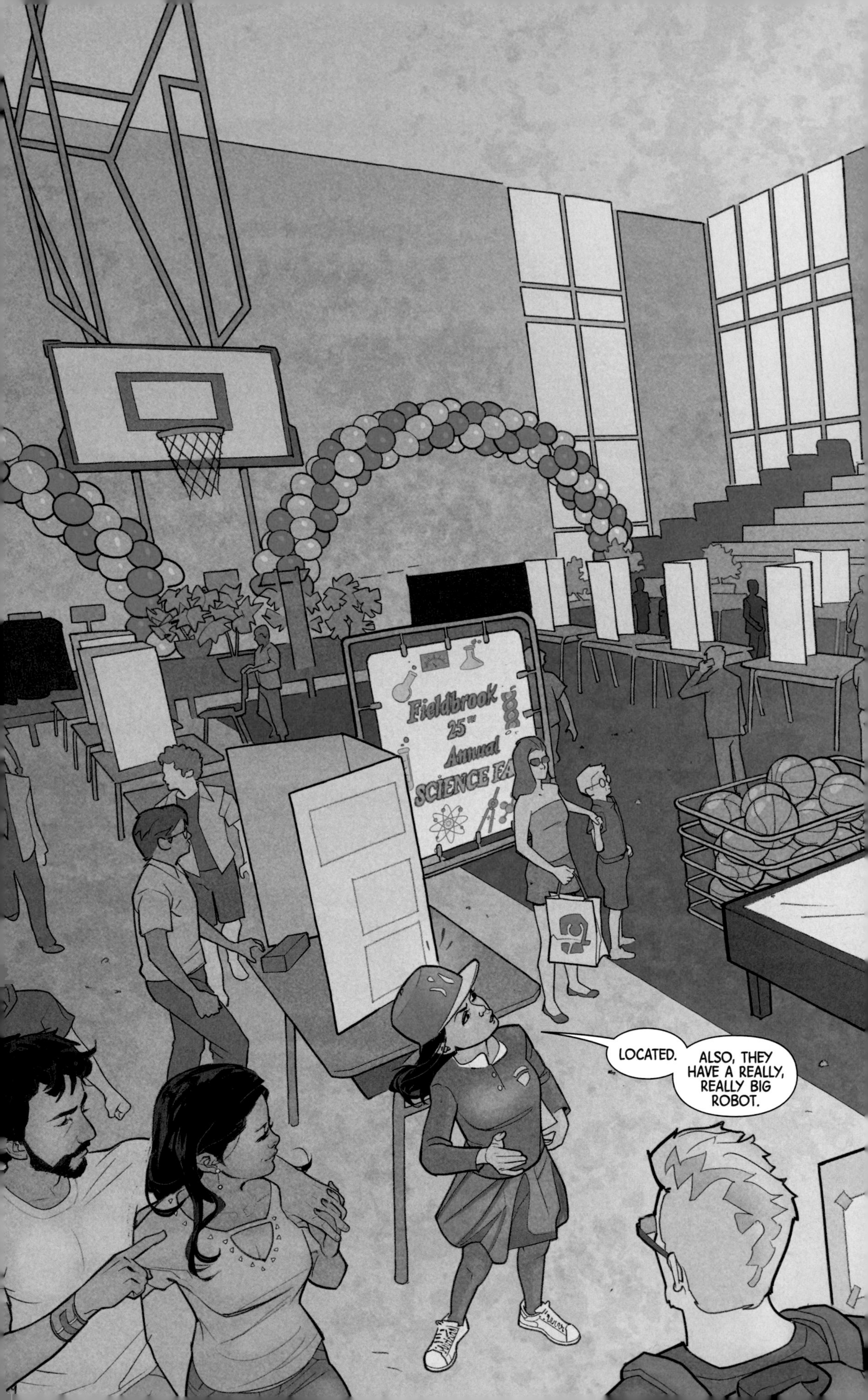
Fieldbrook 25TH Annual SCIENCE FA
LOCATED.
ALSO, THEY HAVE A REALLY, REALLY BIG ROBOT.

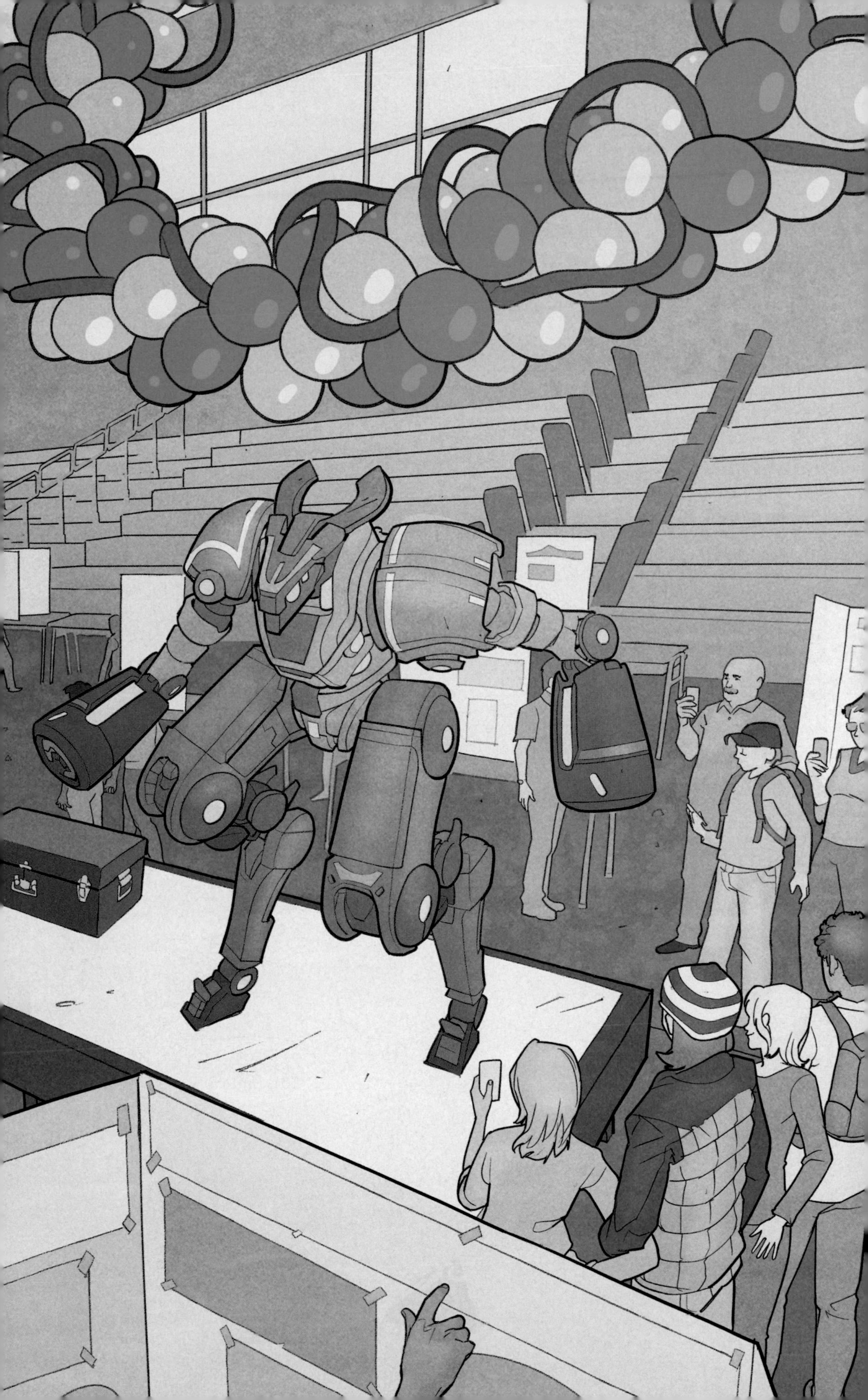

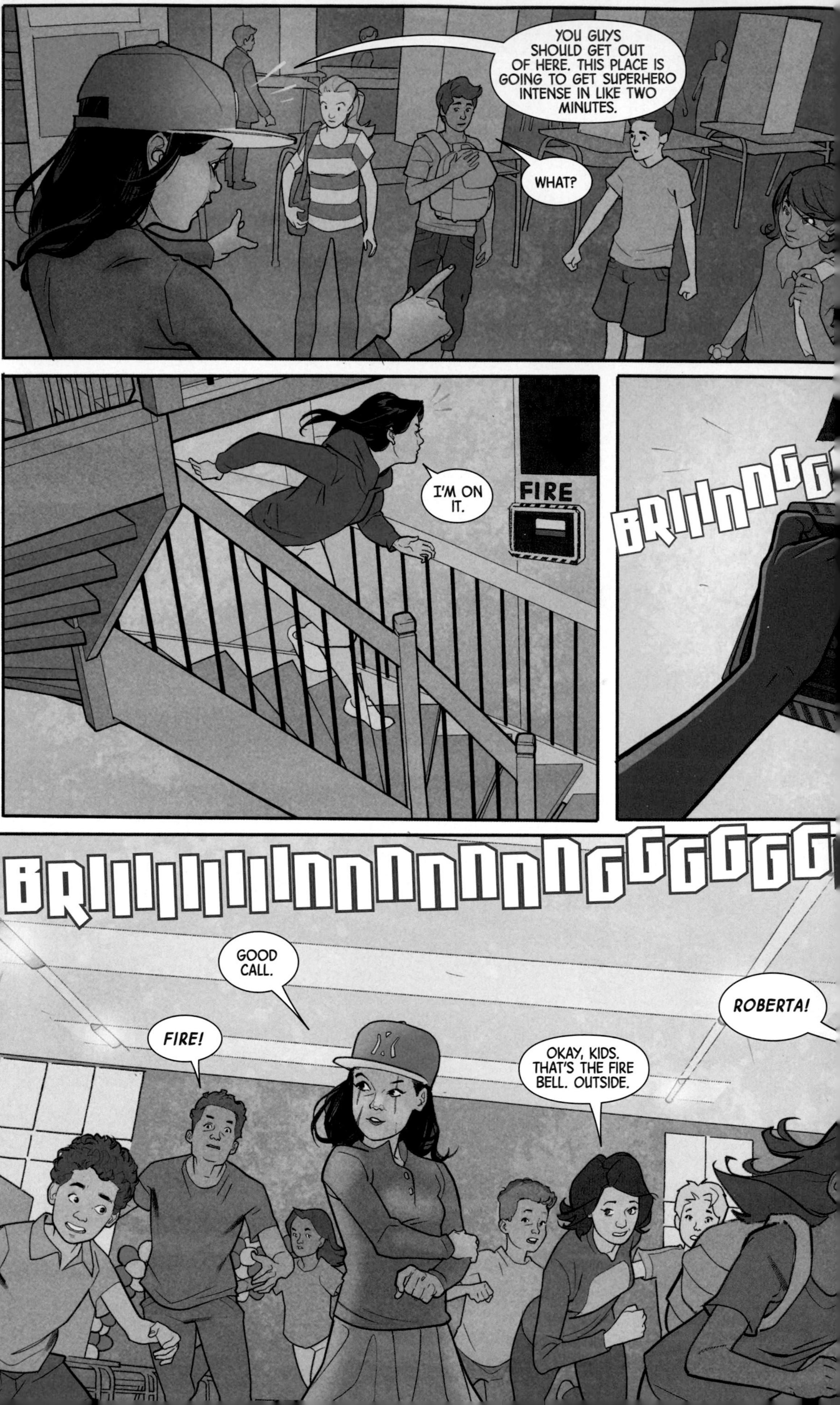
YOU GUYS SHOULD GET OUT OF HERE. THIS PLACE IS GOING TO GET SUPERHERO INTENSE IN LIKE TWO MINUTES.
WHAT?
I'M ON IT.
FIRE
BRIIINNGG
BRIIIIIIINNNNNNNGGGGG
GOOD CALL.
FIRE!
OKAY, KIDS. THAT'S THE FIRE BELL. OUTSIDE.
ROBERTA!

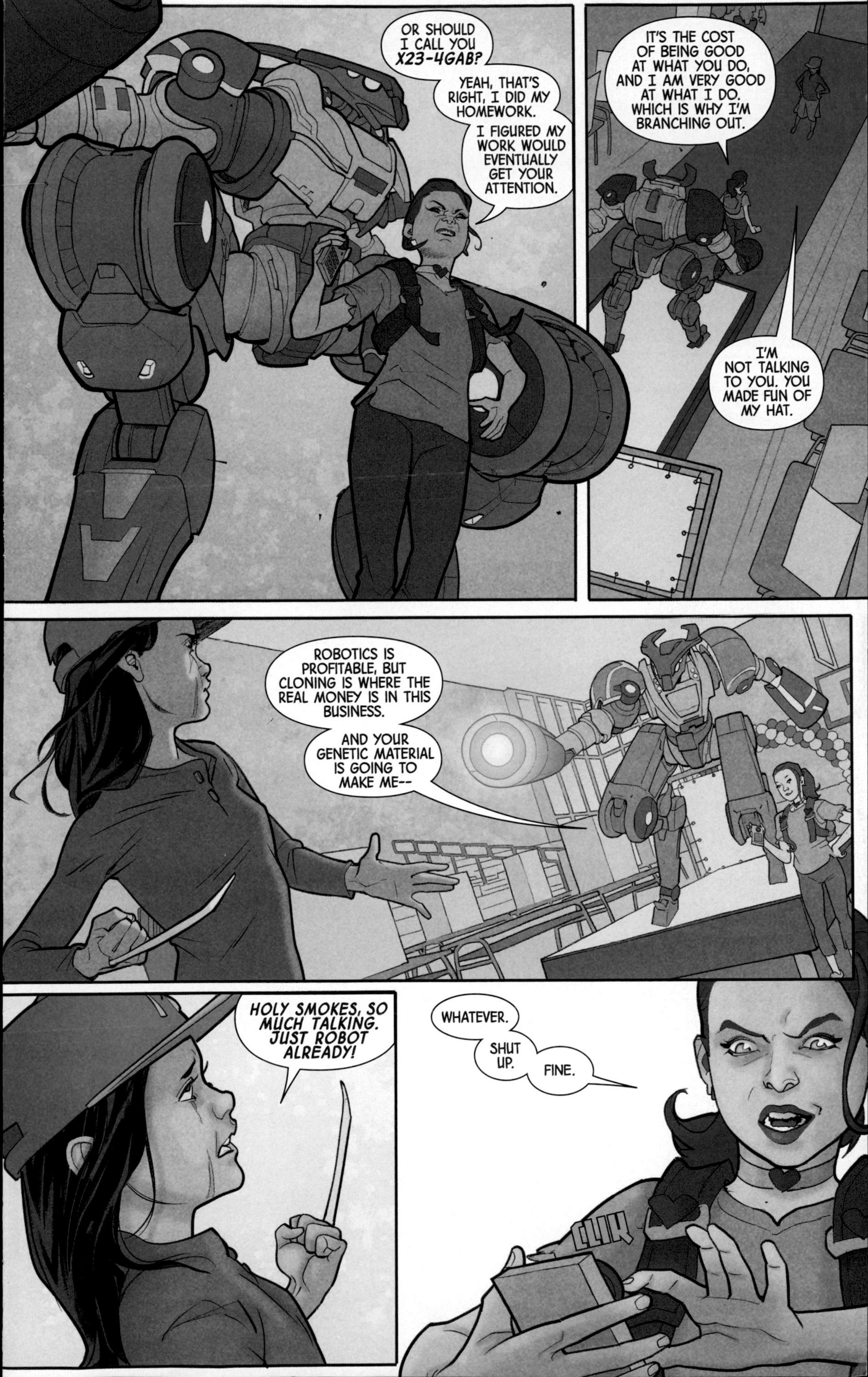

OR SHOULD I CALL YOU X23-4GAB?
YEAH, THAT'S RIGHT, I DID MY HOMEWORK.
I FIGURED MY WORK WOULD EVENTUALLY GET YOUR ATTENTION.
IT'S THE COST OF BEING GOOD AT WHAT YOU DO, AND I AM VERY GOOD AT WHAT I DO. WHICH IS WHY I'M BRANCHING OUT.
I'M NOT TALKING TO YOU. YOU MADE FUN OF MY HAT.
ROBOTICS IS PROFITABLE, BUT CLONING IS WHERE THE REAL MONEY IS IN THIS BUSINESS.
AND YOUR GENETIC MATERIAL IS GOING TO MAKE ME--
HOLY SMOKES, SO MUCH TALKING. JUST ROBOT ALREADY!
WHATEVER.
SHUT UP.
FINE.

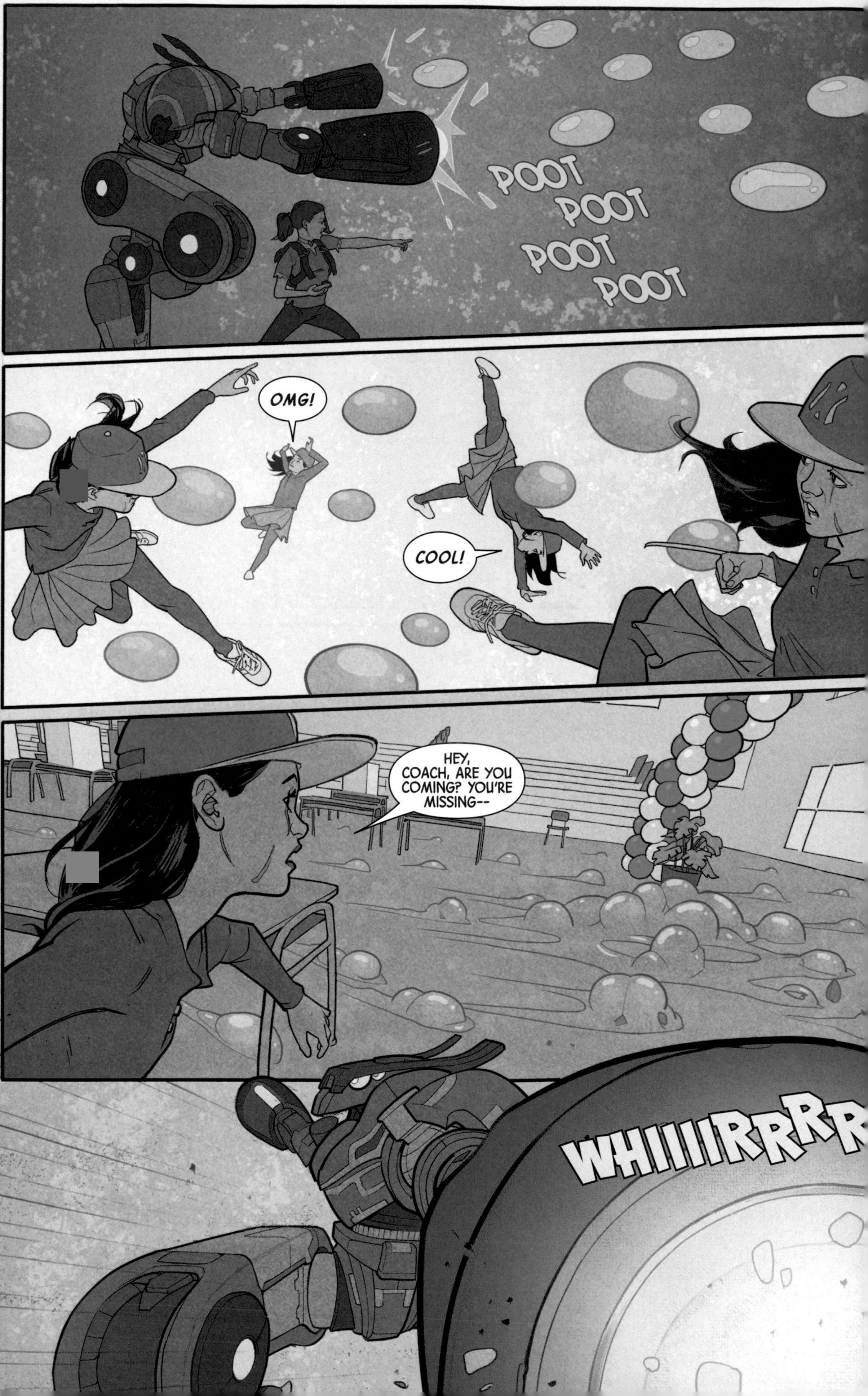
POOT
POOT
POOT
POOT
OMG!
COOL!
HEY, COACH, ARE YOU COMING? YOU'RE MISSING--
WHIIIIRRRR

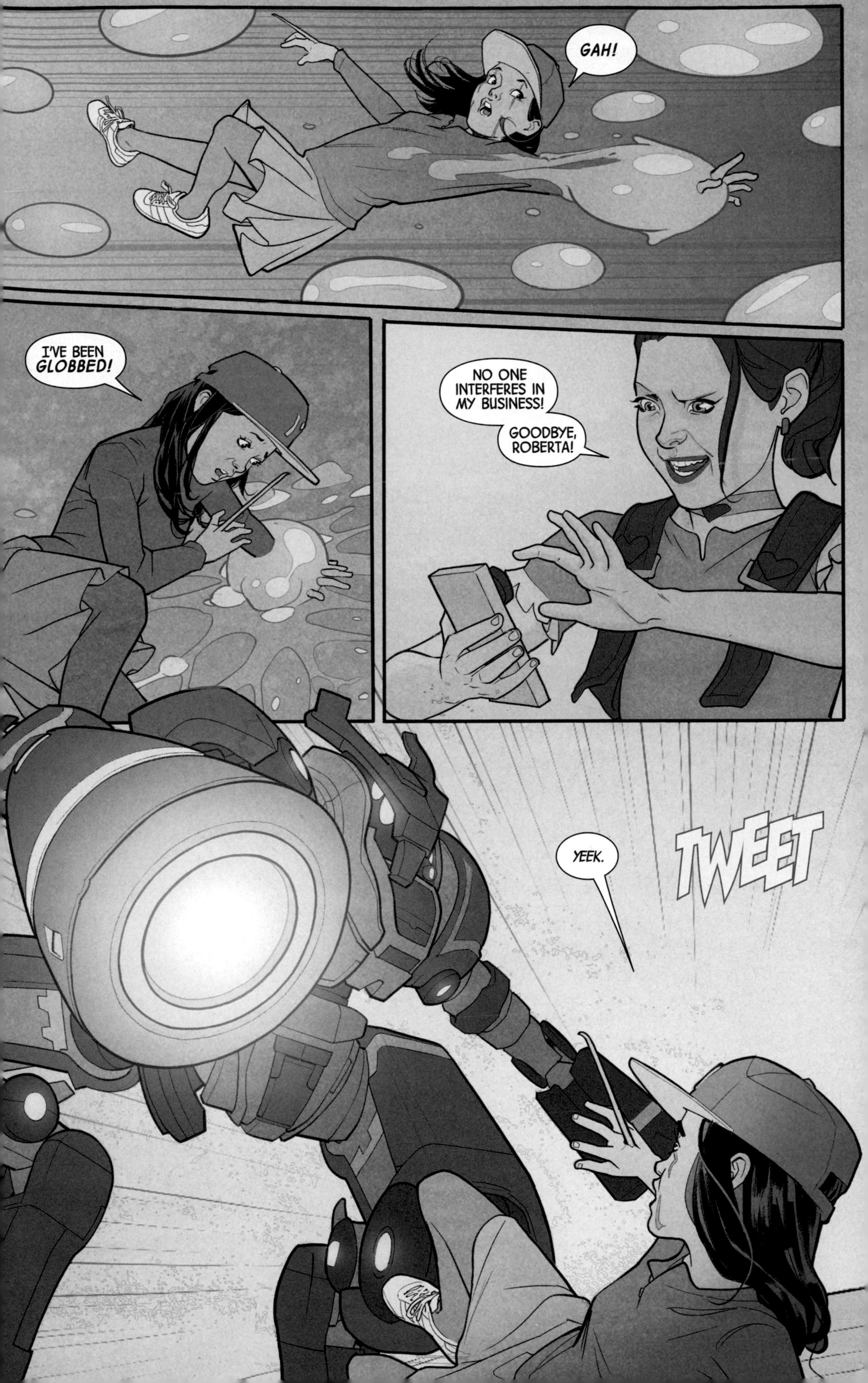
GAH!
I'VE BEEN GLOBBED!
NO ONE INTERFERES IN MY BUSINESS!
GOODBYE, ROBERTA!
TWEET
YEEK.

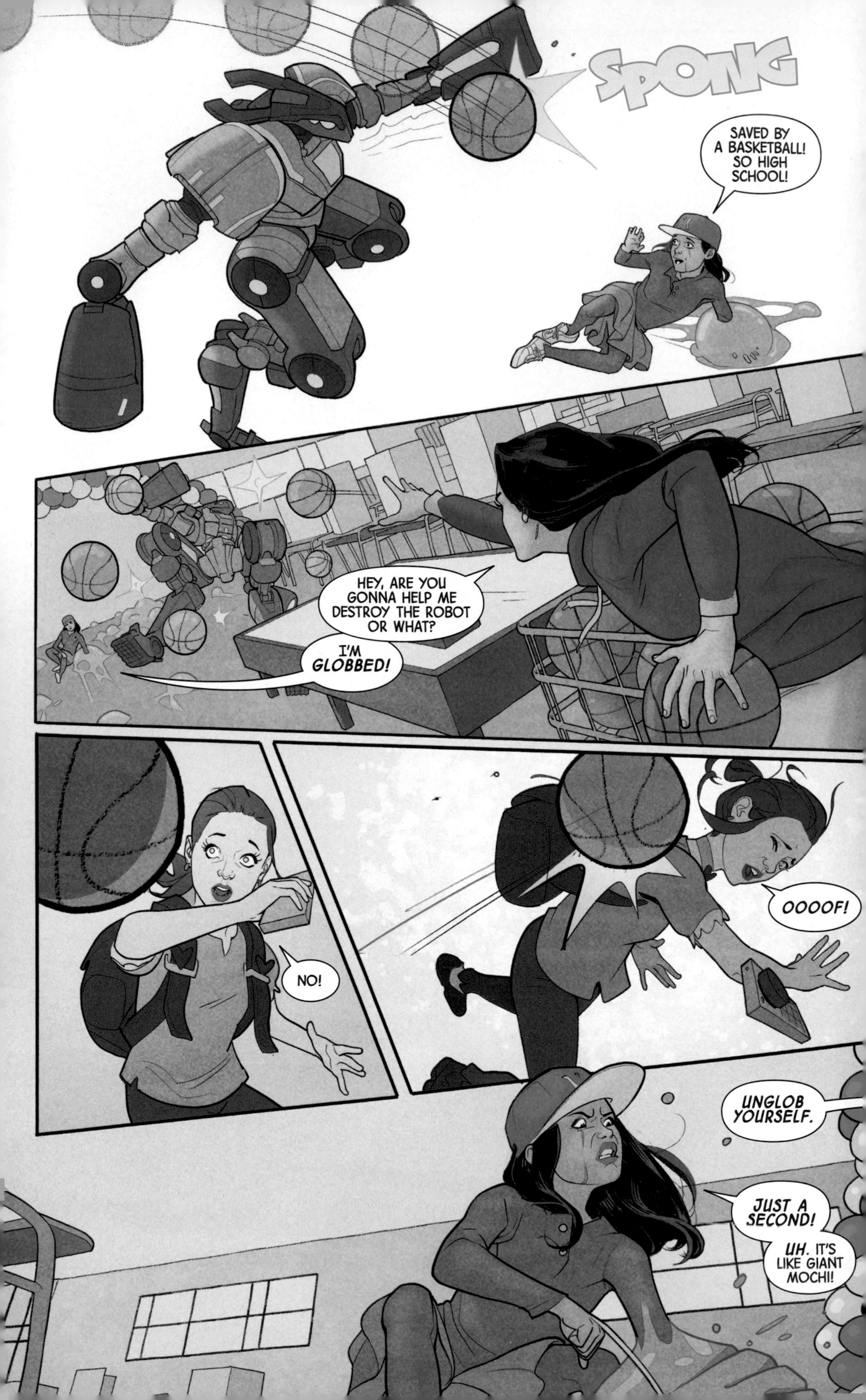
SPONG
SAVED BY A BASKETBALL! SO HIGH SCHOOL!
HEY, ARE YOU GONNA HELP ME DESTROY THE ROBOT OR WHAT?
I'M GLOBBED!
NO!
OOOOF!
UNGLOB YOURSELF.
JUST A SECOND!
UH. IT'S LIKE GIANT MOCHI!

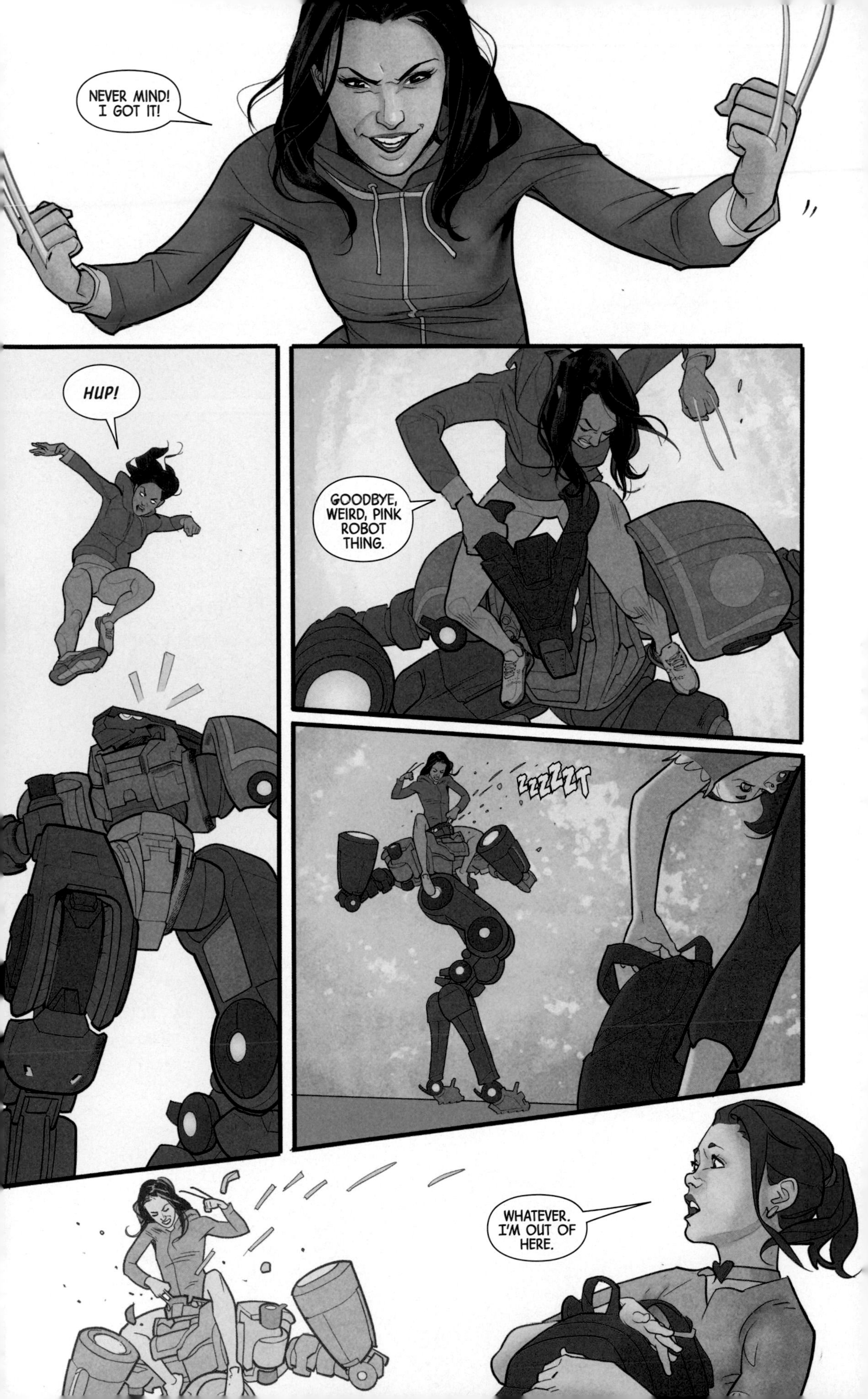
NEVER MIND! I GOT IT!
HUP!
GOODBYE, WEIRD, PINK ROBOT THING.
ZZZZZT
WHATEVER. I'M OUT OF HERE.

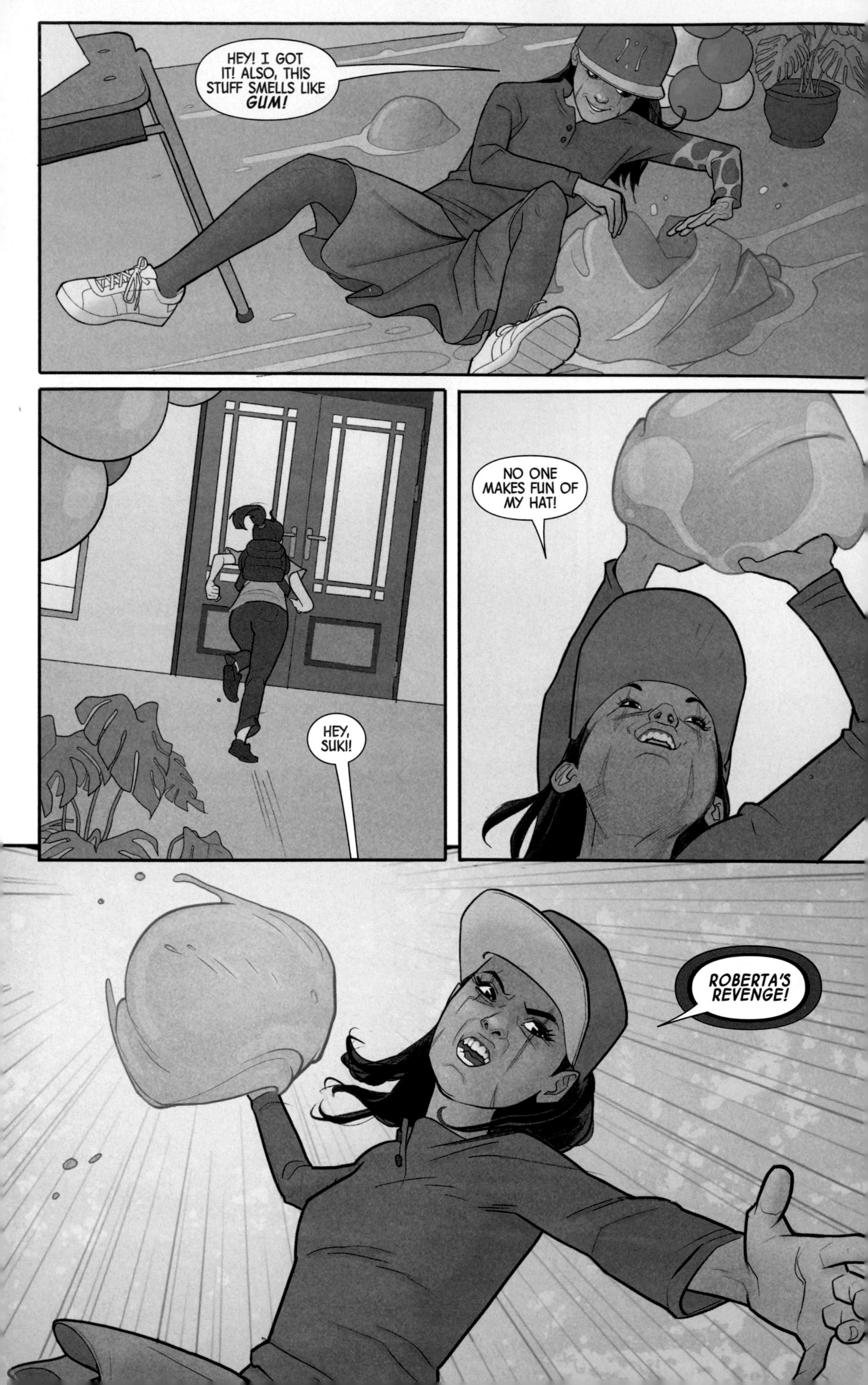
HEY! I GOT IT! ALSO, THIS STUFF SMELLS LIKE GUM!
HEY, SUKI!
NO ONE MAKES FUN OF MY HAT!
ROBERTA'S REVENGE!

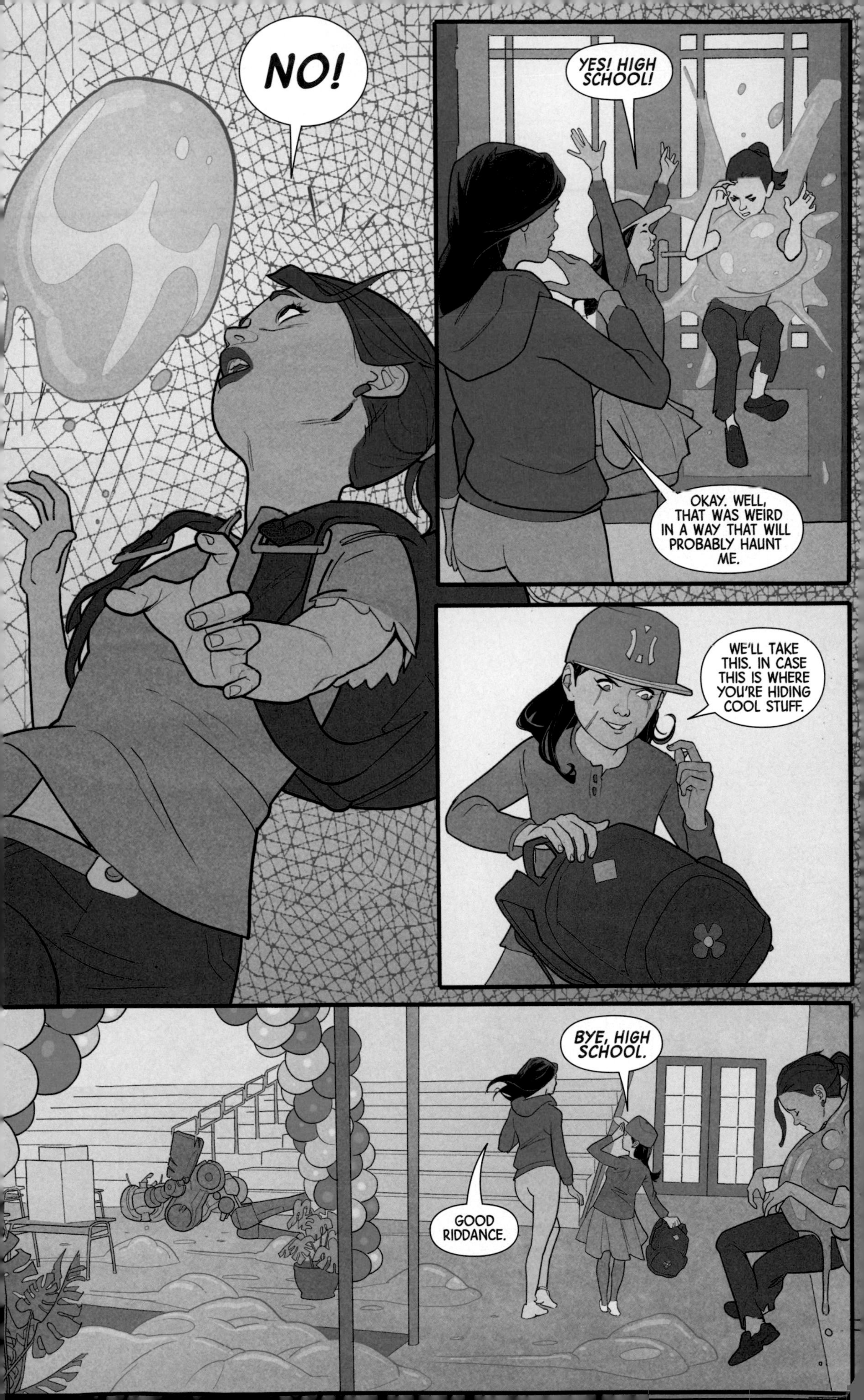
NO!
YES! HIGH SCHOOL!
OKAY. WELL, THAT WAS WEIRD IN A WAY THAT WILL PROBABLY HAUNT ME.
WE'LL TAKE THIS. IN CASE THIS IS WHERE YOU'RE HIDING COOL STUFF.
BYE, HIGH SCHOOL.
GOOD RIDDANCE.

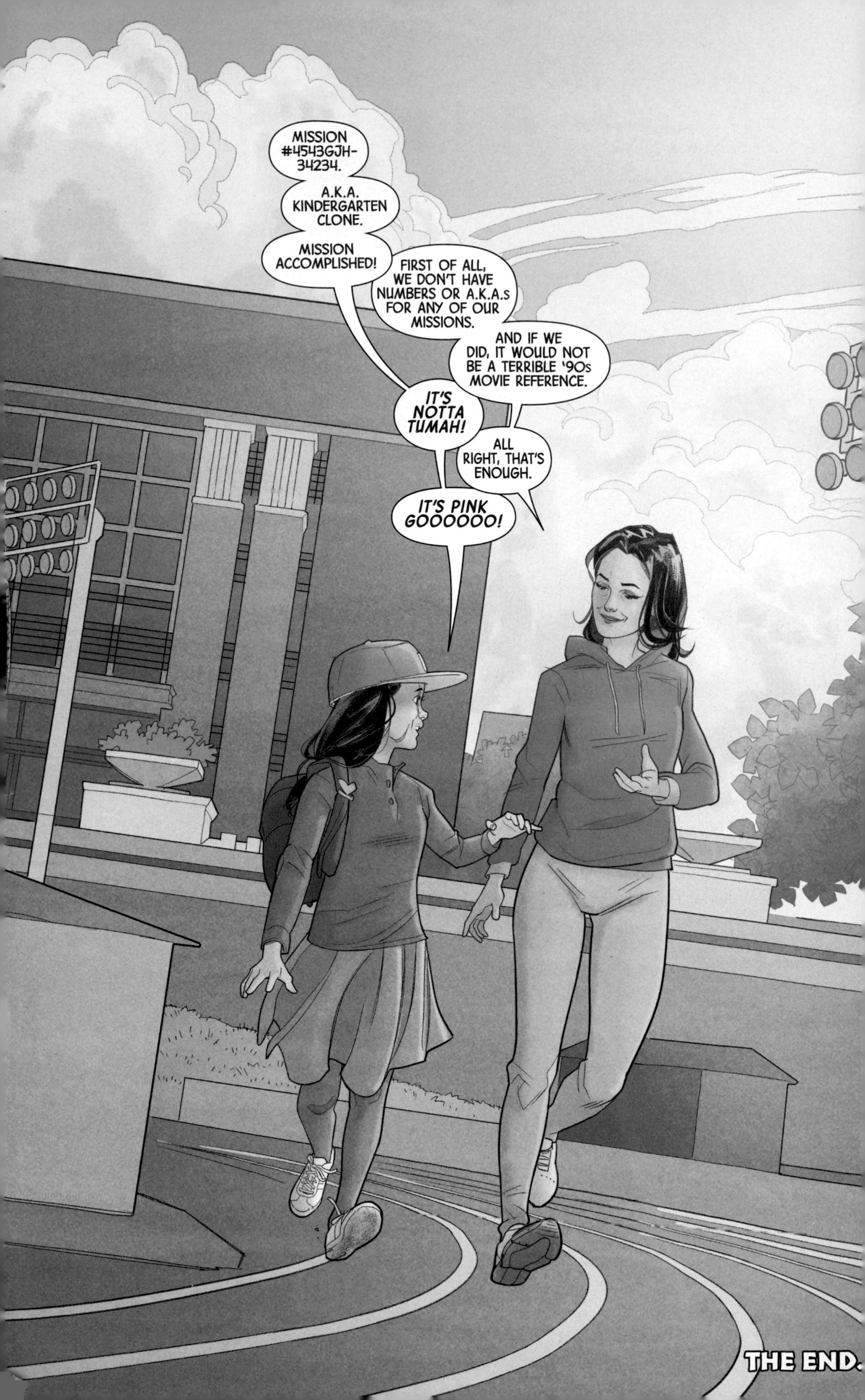
MISSION #4543GJH-34234.
A.K.A. KINDERGARTEN CLONE.
MISSION ACCOMPLISHED!
FIRST OF ALL, WE DON'T HAVE NUMBERS OR A.K.A.s FOR ANY OF OUR MISSIONS.
AND IF WE DID, IT WOULD NOT BE A TERRIBLE '90s MOVIE REFERENCE.
IT'S NOTTA TUMAH!
ALL RIGHT, THAT'S ENOUGH.
IT'S PINK GOOOOOO!
THE END.